Service-Oriented Architecture Governance for the Services Driven Enterprise

Service-Oriented Architecture Governance for the Services Driven Enterprise

ERIC A. MARKS

John Wiley & Sons, Inc.

Published by John Wiley & Sons, Inc., Hoboken, New Jersey.

Published simultaneously in Canada.

For general information on our other products and services, or technical support,
please contact our Customer Care Department within the United States at 800-762-
2974, outside the United States at 317-572-3993, or fax 317-572-4002.

Wiley also publishes its books in a variety of electronic formats. Some content that
appears in print may not be available in electronic books.

For more information about Wiley products, visit our Web site at
http://www.wiley.com.

Library of Congress Cataloging-in-Publication Data:
Marks, Eric A.
  Service-oriented architecture governance for the services driven enterprise/
Eric A. Marks.
     p. cm.
  Includes index.
  ISBN 978-0-470-17125-7 (cloth)
  1. Business enterprises–Computer networks–Management. 2. Information
technology–Management. I. Title.
  HD30.2.M374 2008
  658–dc22
                                    2008017691

Printed in the United States of America
10 9 8 7 6 5 4 3 2 1

Dedication

This book is dedicated to two special Fathers in my life: Nicholas Dardeno and Lyle Thomas Marks.

Contents

Preface

I began this book with a lofty goal: to clarify and simplify the concepts of Service-Oriented Architecture (SOA) governance such that organizations could understand the breadth, richness, and scope of SOA governance in the context of their entire enterprise. As SOA interest and adoption has accelerated rapidly despite still being in its infancy as a discipline, the challenges of governance have risen to the fore across the entire industry. Absent a governance model, SOA adoption will be stilted and hampered by a lack of engagement with key enterprise stakeholders in the important decisions and management processes that will help ensure business value through SOA. This exposes one of the Catch 22s of SOA—SOA governance is critical to SOA success, yet SOA governance is very challenging in and of itself, so much so that, to their peril, organizations may choose to avoid confronting the governance issue. This possibility would represent a major lost opportunity for any organization. After all, could it be that the ultimate value of implementing SOA in your enterprise is that you implement an appropriate enterprise governance model as a result? *Imagine, we started out doing SOA and ended up fixing our enterprise governance along the way.*

I will also confess that this has been the most challenging book project I have undertaken. Governance is a complex topic, fraught with organizational impacts far and wide depending on what you are governing and how you want to govern. And now, add to this volatile mixture the nuances of behavior and corporate culture, sociopolitical issues, incentive and reward dynamics, and funding and budgeting issues, and you can see how governance becomes a very difficult concept to wrap your arms around. For this book, I have explored a variety of governance approaches and concepts from our own federal government, from the community models of the open source community to the self-governance approaches that exemplifies the early days of the Internet. I have researched command and control structures and market-based models of resource allocation, where the dynamics of organizations evolve around the relative scarcity of resources. And I have, of course, explored the rise of IT governance and corporate governance as these disciplines assumed critical roles in the decision-making processes of both public and private corporate enterprises.

Whenever a major challenge such as governance arises, the software and tool vendors are always first responders with claims that their particular tool is the answer, the silver bullet for that particular challenge. However, with all due respect to my colleagues and friends who work for the many excellent software companies out there, the domain of enterprise SOA governance, or any form of governance for that matter, is more of a social sciences discipline—cultural anthropology, sociology, psychology, and social engineering—than it is of software tools and automation. This is most certainly the case, to be sure, in the early phases of governance in most organizations.

SOA governance has been co-opted by technologists to some extent, and this has been a disservice, leading to an over-focus on tools and technology standards and not enough emphasis on the processes and organizational models of governance. This technical emphasis has also falsely led to an overemphasis on either the design-side processes of an SOA and Services Development Lifecycle, or on the runtime aspects of the lifecycle, focusing on management of services once they are operational in a production setting. Of course, this leads to tools and technologies, which are more tangible than the social and behavioral aspects of governance, which play a much more profound and dramatic role in the success of governance.

This SDLC-focused perspective leads to underemphasis on the precursors to the delivery processes of an organization, such as portfolio management disciplines, enterprise architecture, funding and budgeting, and more. Of course, then you must consider the federated enterprise model that is very typical of large enterprises today, and the allocation of corporate roles and responsibilities aligned to and supportive of business unit-specific roles and responsibilities.

This book is also imperfect. There is no way to adequately address the nuances of governance at an operational level that would satisfy all the various approaches and perspectives on governance. While I recognize the stakeholder model for this book is broad, and I have tried to adequately represent them, there are probably another ten chapters I could have written to address all governance perspectives and stakeholders. Governance is a broad subject no matter how you focus it on a particular domain. Data governance has many of the same challenges as IT governance: Who is accountable, who "owns" the resources, who "owns" the data, and Who are the participants—the data providers and data consumers—who are stakeholders? These are fundamentally social and cultural questions, not technical questions. Enterprise governance is indeed a social science. SOA governance adds technology challenges to the social sciences, which forms a simmering brew indeed. SOA adds many technical governance challenges to an already complex task, which is why IT governance approaches are too lightweight and board-centric to address the technical, architectural and interoperability requirements of enterprise SOA governance.

As I delved into the concepts of governance, I developed a greater appreciation of why many organizations either reduce to governance boards at one extreme, or implement governance tools at the other extreme. As I dug deeper, I realized that an integrated approach to governance must find a model to enable the integration of all three governance enforcement mechanisms—boards and tools, integrated with governance processes. An overemphasis on governance boards, which is a common mistake for SOA governance, reduces the effort to an organizational design effort, which often creates overhead, generates more meetings on busy calendars, and usually does not solve the core governance needs of the enterprise. However, reducing governance to a tool, such as a repository or a service registry, or any other governance tool (or tool claiming some partial governance functionality), does a similar disservice to your enterprise. The tool-centric approach falls short because it does not accommodate the broad view of policy models, and enforcement as a combination of boards, processes and of course supporting tools. The key word is "supporting." Tools cannot do the job in and of themselves.

With this backdrop, I began this project with the following high-level objectives:

- **Develop a general model for enterprise governance.** In this book, we develop a governance assessment and model design framework that will work for any enterprise governance challenge—corporate governance, IT governance, enterprise architecture governance, portfolio management, or program and project governance across your SDLC. Our definition of SOA governance can be simplified to encompass any form of governance. After all, all forms of governance have at their core ensuring appropriate stakeholder representation in critical decisions around the best use of resources to accomplish organizational goals.

- **Address SOA governance from an enterprise governance perspective.** Our premise is that SOA governance can only be adequately implemented in the context of other enterprise governance processes and activities. Thus, we use the Four Tiers of Enterprise Governance to establish appropriate enterprise context for your SOA governance model. If you begin SOA governance without having appropriate enterprise context, it will end up as a limited scope, bottom-up governance model without executive support and lacking enterprise alignment.

- **Develop a unified approach to enterprise policies.** This book explores the lack of unified industry standards for enterprise policies, and offers a conceptual policy framework for developing a unified policy model.

Such a unified policy model will integrate technical policy approaches of the WS-Policy genre with corporate policies that are often codified in documents and enforced by oversight boards. Our view of governance and integrated policy enforcement requires a unified policy model.

■ **Develop a framework for integrated policy enforcement.** Another important goal of this book is to debunk the notion that SOA governance can be accomplished using technology alone. As we discuss in Chapters 3 and 4, implementing and enforcing enterprise policies requires a multi-pronged fabric of policy enforcement. SOA governance demands an integrated policy enforcement "fabric" comprised of three types of policy enforcement mechanisms: governance boards, governance processes, and governance technology and tools. None of these is sufficient to realize an effective SOA Governance model based on definition, provisioning, and enforcement of policies. The reality is that enterprise SOA governance requires policy enforcement using governance boards, integrated with governance processes and supported by governance technology and tools.

■ **Build upon the Weill and Ross foundation.** This book explores the complexities and nuances of IT and SOA governance that go far deeper than Peter Weill and Jeanne Ross in their excellent book *IT Governance: How Top Performers Manage IT Decision Rights for Superior Results* (Harvard Business School Press, 2004). I give tremendous credit to Weill and Ross for their work in establishing the foundation for much of today's emphasis on IT governance. However, SOA governance and policy-driven governance demand and require the details and moving parts of a complete governance model to be understood. We build on Weill and Ross, and in many respects establish an operational governance model framework that will implement right-sized, tangible governance at all levels of your enterprise.

■ **Evolve governance from "art" to "science":** In many respects, governance seems like more of an art than a science. I believe that the artistic side of governance derives from its tendency to be viewed as a collection of boards and committees, which are constructed to provide the stakeholder representation and also to assuage political concerns in the enterprise. Often, a governance model is required to overcome inherent weaknesses in the organizational structure of an enterprise and the subsequent sociopolitical structure that evolves from the physical structure. Thus the art of governance is to create governance boards, name them, charter them, and staff them with the "right" members to create the desired sociopolitical alignment and outcomes. The science of governance we attempt to establish is through an enterprise policy model that is deployed to and enforced by an integrated enforcement model comprised of boards, processes, and tools with appropriate feedback. This science explicitly recognizes the merits of blending resource allocation models such as command hierarchies, market economies, and community models into a cohesive framework that provides maximal engagement with the entire enterprise of stakeholders, not just those who have power and authority for decisions in the enterprise.

■ **Establish a new conversation and language of governance.** We felt that we needed to address governance from a holistic and far-reaching perspective, and address some of the industry challenges that have inhibited the progress of governance to date. These include the lack of industry standards for enterprise policies, the lack of integration of various tools and technologies, and the failure to address the concept of integrated policy enforcement using boards, processes, and tools. We hope that this book will create a new generation of thinking around enterprise governance much as Weill and Ross did with their seminal book in IT governance.

These goals are clearly aggressive and far reaching. We clearly viewed the subject of enterprise governance from a perspective that is well beyond current perspectives, and well beyond today's technologies, tools, and industry standards. However, we feel we have pushed the discipline of governance ahead in ways that are within the grasp of organizations and within the grasp of a new generation of tools and industry standards as well. As you read the book, focus on the chapters or sections that make sense for you. The chapters are sequential in nature, so this is not necessarily a book you can jump around in. We establish the foundation concepts in Chapters 1, 2, and 3, we establish a governance modeling framework in Chapters 4, 5, and 6, and we facilitate implementation in Chapters 8 and 9. Chapter 10 serves as a future-focused chapter on gaps and challenges that need to be addressed. Below are summaries of each of the chapters.

Chapter 1 presents the landscape of governance and some of the common mistakes organizations make as they focus their efforts on governance. This chapter sets the stage by establishing a definition of enterprise SOA governance that is adaptable and applicable to any kind of governance. Remove "SOA" from the definition and you can apply our governance definition to any form of governance. The chapter finishes with common mistakes and best practices to be cognizant of with respect to SOA governance.

Chapter 2 develops an SOA Governance Reference Model to help decompose the concept of governance into bite-sized chunks that are easier to digest. In this SOA Governance Reference Model, we explore various "layers" of governance, explaining what the "moving parts" within each of the layers are. In addition, we establish the foundation for funding and budgeting as a governance activity, and we also develop the concept of "Governance Performance Management," or the discipline of sustained enterprise governance over time.

In Chapter 3, we transform the SOA Governance Reference Model into the Four Tiers of Enterprise Governance. These tiers are then broken down into more detailed tiers to show the interplay of enterprise governance processes with SOA governance process, all of which impact enterprise architecture and SDLC delivery processes of an enterprise. This chapter also details the many processes that comprise enterprise governance by these various tiers. This enterprise governance process catalog serves as a baseline from which you can develop your own processes for governance.

Chapters 4 and 5 present a governance model assessment and design framework that is based on years of accumulated experience from the trenches of enterprise SOA governance. Chapter 4 develops the SOA governance tools and assessment framework to baseline your current enterprise SOA governance model and capabilities. Chapter 5 develops the elements of a complete enterprise SOA governance model and establishes a process for building your own enterprise SOA governance model.

Chapter 6 is a pioneering chapter focused on establishing a unified view of policies for an enterprise. This chapter exposes some of the challenges with enterprise policy enforcement, especially if you want to establish an enterprise governance framework that incorporates SOA into it. The concept of "policy" is imperfect, and we suggest a policy metamodel to help unify the concept of policies from an enterprise perspective and from an integrated policy enforcement perspective.

Chapter 7 focuses on various governance organizational models for consideration as your governance model adapts and evolves in concert with coevolving your SOA maturity. We establish a range of governance organizational models and concepts, including one we call an SOA Center of Gravity, which we think is a superior governance construct for the early phases of governance and SOA adoption.

Chapter 8 presents some concepts and discussion of SDLC governance. This chapter was contributed by Brent Carlson, a clear industry thought leader on design time and SDLC governance. This chapter develops the provider—and consumer—side aspects of services lifecycle governance, and offers some best practices for refining SDLC governance.

Chapter 9 covers the governance enabling technology and tools landscape as developed by the SOA governance reference model, and as suggested by the policy enforcement model concepts developed in Chapter 6. This chapter was spearheaded by Dennis Nadler, a colleague with tremendous experience with the broad range of SOA tools, technologies, and standards.

Chapter 10 concludes with some concepts and ideas for how we believe governance should evolve going forward. We believe that governance is an enterprise core competency that must continue to be adapted and refined through time. Governance should thus be an organization, headed by an executive position reporting to the chief executive officer or managing director of an organization.

I would like to thank the many friends and colleagues who have helped make this book a reality. I also want to thank you, the reader, in advance. I hope we have created an opportunity to advance the industry and the field of enterprise governance, as well as the discipline of SOA governance in particular. For feedback on this book, I encourage you to email me anytime at emarks@agile-path.com. No book is possible without the ideas and thinking of those before us. This book owes much to many, yet I happened to hold the proverbial pen. I hope I have done the industry a service with a book focused entirely on governance, not only on SOA governance, but a book focused on enterprise governance. Enjoy. I know I have.

Acknowledgments

This book would not have been possible without the contributions and support of many colleagues, friends, and supporters. I would like to acknowledge those who have helped make many of the concepts of this book possible. First, to my contributors, whose support for a few key chapters and reviews has been critical to this book's completion: Brent Carlson, Dennis Nadler, and Vince Snyder.

Next, there have been a few thought leaders in the SOA community who have been critical to moving this industry forward and helping develop some of the concepts contained in this book. Thanks to the following people in alphabetical order: Alan Belisle, Bill Clarke, David Cohn, Ben Morland, Jim Schultz, Mark Stender, Umesh Vemuri, Steve Verba, Adam Vincent, and Rob Vietmeyer. These people have been on the front lines of governance innovation along with me.

Of course, I have to acknowledge Peter Weill and Jeanne Ross, whose book *IT Governance: How Top Performers Manage IT Decision Rights for Superior Results* established the current foundation for IT governance in the industry such that we could advance our own concepts of Enterprise SOA Governance in this book.

Finally, I have to thank my family for their support and patience as I have gone through yet another writing project. Diane, Jonathan, Jessica, your unyielding support has been my strength!

CHAPTER 1

The SOA Governance Imperative

Since my last Service-Oriented Architecture (SOA) book, in which I dedicated an entire chapter to the topic of SOA governance, industry interest in governance has exploded. The challenges of enterprise SOA governance have moved to the foreground across the IT industry as interest in SOA has increased, and as the many SOA practitioners out there have reached the same conclusion: SOA governance is mandatory for any measure of SOA success. Understanding and implementing effective SOA governance has become a corporate imperative, and thus the topic requires the depth of coverage that this book provides. Yet, despite all the interest in the topic, governance is one of the most misunderstood, emotionally charged, and enigmatic concepts in the industry. We will attempt to address these challenges in the chapters of this book.

THE INEVITABLE SOA TREND

SOA is one of the most important trends in Information Technology today. SOA is now a top priority in most organizations. SOA is receiving all this attention because of the great potential value it offers to those who pursue it. If an organization achieves a mere fraction of the total potential value of SOA, it will be significant to that organization's bottom line, competitive posture, and overall operational effectiveness. That is why SOA is such an important strategic initiative to pursue. SOA makes too much sense technically and financially *not* to implement.

I like to define SOA as a combination of a Business Model, an IT strategy, an architectural approach, and an implementation pattern, all predicated on the concept of "Services."

In the SOA business model sense, an organization is essentially an economic engine assembled from a combination of internal and external processes and capabilities, all of which in combination enable the end-to-end execution of business processes that achieve the organization's objectives. A for-profit corporation is created to make money for its shareholders. Thus, maximum profits are achieved by optimizing execution of business

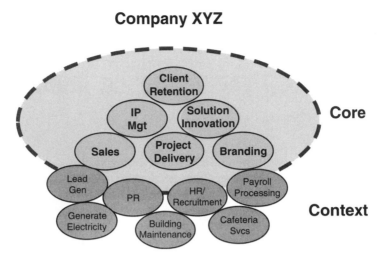

Company XYZ

Exhibit 1.1   Core vs. Context (Make vs. Buy vs. Rent)

transactions. If an organization can accomplish business transactions more efficiently and at a lower cost by performing them internally, it will do so. If, however, overall efficiency and cost optimization is achieved by others outside of the organization performing those transactions, the best model is outsourcing of those functions. These ideas are derived from the work of Ronald Coase, whose work on transaction theory provides a perfect foundation for SOA as a business model.[1] (See Marks and Bell 2006 for a discussion of Ronald Coase and transaction theory applied to SOA and services.)[2] Exhibit 1.1 illustrates the concepts of core and context, and as an extension, the combination of internal and external services to optimize the overall transactional cost and efficiency of an organization.

Per our set-up discussion above, a corporation continually evaluates the relative cost of performing business transactions internally versus externally to best optimize its overall profitability. In fact, Ronald Coase would argue that the relative size of a company, and its interactions with the marketplace, are ultimately based on relative costs of business transactions. Combining the transaction theory of Ronald Coase with the core and context concepts of Geoffrey Moore give us a tremendous foundation to apply SOA concepts to.

Many small businesses outsource human resources, payroll processing, and even their Information Technology (IT) in their early startup days, instead focusing on the innovations that will help the company grow.

However, as those functions become more critical to the enterprise, and as the cost of performing them is lower than in an internally-provided service, the organization may eventually insource those functions. In this manner, the service-oriented business model is one of optimizing core and context processes (per Geoffrey Moore's book *Living on the Fault Line*[3]), and leveraging service providers as necessary to achieve the overall optimal structure of internally- and externally-provided transactions in support of the business model. This is SOA as a business model.

SOA as an IT strategy is an extension of the SOA business model. An SOA-enabled IT strategy explicitly embraces concepts of service providers and service consumers, and seeks to optimize IT services provided to the business by leveraging SOA concepts. Thus, the combination of IT services will be optimized through a combination of internally- and externally-provided services, which helps realize the profitability goals of the enterprise. The SOA IT strategy perspective also means that there is an SOA strategy, that the SOA strategy enables the SOA business model, and that it is expressed technically through a clearly defined and articulated enterprise architecture and the resulting portfolio of services that, when exposed and implemented, enable the optimal end-to-end execution of business transactions for maximizing profit. Again, this is from the perspective of a for profit enterprise.

SOA is also an architecture approach or paradigm, along with a supporting implementation pattern that realizes that architectural approach in support of the IT strategy and the SOA business model. SOA extends an organization's enterprise architecture to include concepts of services, both logical and physical descriptions of services, as well as the required SOA infrastructure and tools, and the SOA platform for service design, quality assurance and testing, and service runtime operations.

The SOA implementation pattern includes the implementation of the SOA platform and enabling technology as well as the SOA-enabled services/software development lifecycle (SDLC) that accommodates both service provider processes and service consumer processes of the enterprise. The SOA implementation pattern enables business applications or capabilities to be assembled through the consumption of services provided through the SOA architecture and SOA implementation patterns. The assembly of business applications from reusable services is how an organization realizes SOA value through services reuse, integration avoidance, agility through application assembly and rapid time to market, and the many other benefits of SOA.

Although the definition is technically accurate, SOA is far more than an "architecture" comprised of "services." SOA is an architectural approach and operating model predicated on the concept of reusable "services," or chunks of business logic or business processes that are shared by enterprise consumers. Services are message-invoked modules of business logic, process activities, chunks of data that offer value to the enterprise through the sharing and reuse of these modular services. In an SOA, services are exposed using a standards-based interface that abstracts or "hides" its technical implementation from the service consumers. When consumers access the functionality of a service, they do so via its exposed interface using message-based communications. The service interface, by virtue of its standards-based construction, offers a simple mechanism for service consumers to find or discover a service, develop a client or access mechanism to the service, and then begin consuming the service in support of a desired business outcome. The technical complexity of the implementation is hidden behind the service interface, which enables a more simplified model for building service-based applications.

SOA offers many business and IT benefits to an organization. From a business perspective, the following SOA benefits are typically expected:

- Business agility
- Reduced time to market
- Easier to do business with
- Reduced technology costs
- Right-sized business model based on core and context—can add or subtract service providers easily

From an IT perspective, the following SOA benefits are often targeted:

- Reduced software development costs
- Reduced software maintenance costs
- Reuse of services accelerates application delivery
- Reuse of services increases software quality
- Allows easier procurement of application software as services
- Allows faster IT response to business change
- Provides for graceful evolution of IT architecture, which leads to lower operating costs and total cost of ownership

SOA as a business or IT initiative presents several challenges with which organizations must contend before they can begin to realize the benefits of SOA. An SOA strategy is a critical requirement. An SOA business case should be established. An SOA reference model and SOA enterprise architecture should be created.

First and foremost of these is an actionable SOA strategy. An SOA strategy is essential to help focus and galvanize organizational efforts, identify the appropriate uses of SOA for business benefits, and to explicitly identify the business or mission outcomes desired from investing in an SOA initiative. SOA governance is mission critical to guide and manage all the "moving parts" of an SOA strategy. An enterprise SOA governance model must be informed by an actionable SOA strategy, since SOA governance helps enable the realization of your SOA strategy.

In our experience, most organizations have skipped the definition of a reasonable SOA strategy, and until recently the same organizations have bypassed developing an enterprise approach to SOA governance. However, as interest in governance intensifies, this should spur a concomitant interest in SOA strategy development as well. To set the stage for the remainder of the book, let's explore the rise of governance as a discipline, the industry and business drivers for governance, and then translate that into the SOA-specific instantiations of governance.

INTRODUCTION TO GOVERNANCE

SOA governance, information technology (IT) governance, and corporate governance are currently hot industry buzzwords. But what is SOA governance really? What is governance in the general sense? Governance is a simple concept to understand, yet it is made complex by vendors, management consultants, and opportunists who see the increasing emphasis on governance as a chance to augment or enhance their power base in an organization. However, governance, be it IT, SOA, or corporate, does not have to be that complicated.

Governance is the process of making correct and appropriate decisions on behalf of the stakeholders of those decisions or choices. In its corporate application, governance is the process of ensuring the best interests of a company's or organization's stakeholders are met through all corporate decisions, from strategy through execution. In its IT application, governance focuses on appropriate oversight and stakeholder representation for IT spending and overall IT management.

Corporate governance has become critically important as a result of corporate accounting scandals, stock option backdating and related corporate mismanagement episodes. Corporate governance is essential to apply oversight and balanced stakeholder representation for all corporate decisions relating to hiring and retaining key executives, executive compensation, strategic direction and execution. Corporate governance in publicly traded companies is the process by which firms are managed to ensure stakeholder interests are met by corporate decisions. Stakeholders include shareholders, employees, management, and even customers. The corporate governance process is normally achieved by a board of directors, who are either appointed or elected to provide objective, balanced oversight on such key issues as executive compensation and performance and corporate strategy and decision making. The board of directors normally is comprised of inside and outside directors to ensure all stakeholder interests are represented in a balanced fashion. When corporate governance fails, it is usually because of a lack of objectivity (e.g., board members appointed by the Chief Executive Officer [CEO] of the organization, or board membership weighted too heavily toward inside interests versus external shareholder interests). Most recently, corporate governance has been in the news due to the stock option backdating scandal. Corporate governance failed in this case due to a lack of decision transparency, which enabled a few executives to unilaterally or multilaterally enrich themselves by backdating stock option agreements. In the general sense, any governance will fail if stakeholders of critical decisions are not engaged in the processes of governance. This is why governance is first and foremost about engagement of critical stakeholders in key decisions of an organization.

INTRODUCTION TO ENTERPRISE SOA GOVERNANCE

What is enterprise SOA governance? SOA governance is the process of ensuring all business and IT stakeholders' interests are served by the planning, funding, and execution of an enterprise SOA initiative. One of the early pioneers of SOA governance is the company WebLayers, located in Cambridge, Massachusetts. WebLayers defines SOA governance as follows:[4]

> *SOA governance is the ability to ensure that all of the independent (SOA) efforts (whether in the design, development, deployment, or operations of a service) come together to meet enterprise requirements.*

WebLayers developed the concept of a policy-driven SOA governance approach where in effect SOA governance is predicated on developing, formalizing, and enforcing a body of SOA policies that ensure conformance to enterprise SOA business and technology goals. In my opinion, this whitepaper paved the way for the industry to understand the scope, breadth, and criticality of policies in a SOA governance framework.

However, SOA governance must be approached from an enterprise perspective and from a comprehensive and holistic viewpoint. An enterprise approach to SOA governance offers a more robust model than focusing narrowly on SOA governance. While explicitly defined SOA policies are essential to formalize and encode the enterprise requirements for SOA governance, SOA governance must also address the convergence of other forces such as organizational structure, IT and governance processes, organizational culture, behavior and political dynamics, and metrics that help measure governance. Thus, to better address the holistic nature of SOA governance, I defined SOA governance as follows:[5]

> *SOA governance refers to the organization, processes, policies, and metrics required to manage an SOA successfully. A successful SOA is one that meets defined business objectives over time. In addition, an SOA governance model establishes the behavioral rules and guidelines of the organization and participants in the SOA, from architects and developers to service consumers, service providers, and even applications and the services themselves. These behavioral rules and guidelines are established via a body of defined SOA policies. SOA policies are specific and cover business, organizational, compliance, security, and technology facets of services operating within an SOA.*
>
> *SOA governance consists of the organization and processes required to guide the business success of an SOA and Web services. SOA governance defines and enforces the Web services policies that are needed to manage a SOA for business success.*

While this definition is sound, I realized that a simpler definition would help clarify governance and SOA governance in particular. Therefore, we will augment the complex and detailed SOA governance definition above with a more simple and elegant definition:

> *SOA governance is doing the right SOA things the right way for the SOA stakeholders.*

Let us break this definition down a bit more. There are three fundamental elements to this definition of SOA governance: (1) Do the right SOA things; (2) Do the right SOA things the right way; and (3) Do the right SOA things the right way for the SOA stakeholders. This definition can thus be expanded as follows:

> *SOA governance is the definition, implementation and ongoing execution of an SOA stakeholder decision model and accountability framework that ensures an organization is pursing an appropriate SOA strategy aligned with business goals, and is executing that strategy in accordance with guidelines and constraints defined by a body of SOA principles and policies. SOA policies are enforced via*

a policy enforcement model, which is realized in the form of various policy enforcement mechanisms such as governance boards and committees; governance processes, checkpoints, and reviews; and governance enabling technology and tools.

This SOA governance definition will be used for the remainder of this book.

Weill and Ross emphasize the allocation of decision rights in their book on IT governance, which is really the process of deciding what to do, how to do it, and who has a vote. Relating our definition to theirs, SOA governance is focused on setting priorities and applying SOA to the appropriate universe of business challenges; SOA governance involves implementing SOA according to company processes, architecture, and technology standards, and in alignment with business priorities; and finally, SOA governance explicitly involves the business and IT stakeholders in the decision-making process for input, review, and approval, and enforcement of key decisions relating to SOA.

The challenge is, with SOA, there are many more "right things" to perform the "right way." SOA governance adds many more architectural and technology dimensions to the governance equation, as well as the horizontal processes of a services/software development lifecycle (SDLC) that span design time activities, quality assurance and testing, and runtime governance and operations. Thus, SOA governance includes fundamental elements of IT governance, while adding many technical issues that require integration into the governance calculus as well. As for the stakeholders, they are the same by and large as the IT stakeholders except for two fundamental differences: First, SOA done right offers a more direct business engagement model via process modeling and analysis than previous IT architecture and development paradigms offered; second, SOA requires more internal coordination across more moving parts in order to for it to deliver on its business and IT promises.

GOVERNANCE AND RESOURCE MANAGEMENT AND ALLOCATION

Many people equate governance with management and allocation of resources and assets, such as financial and budgeting decisions, human resources, and physical assets. Weill and Ross discuss governance of key categories of assets, such as:[6]

- Human resources and personnel
- Financial assets

- Physical assets, such as buildings, property, equipment, and similar fixed assets
- Intellectual property, such as patents, trademarks, copyrights, trademarks, brands
- Information, data, and IT assets
- Relationship assets, such as customer, supplier, and regulatory relationships

In this sense, then, governance is essential where the allocation and management of critical corporate resources impacts corporate performance. Decisions relating to the management of human resources have a direct bearing on organizational performance, as well as legal and financial implications; and thus human resources can fall under a governance process. Certainly, key executive hiring and firing decisions are made by subcommittees comprised of members of the board of directors, and those decisions often fall under the Securities and Exchange Commission (SEC) reporting requirements for public companies. The same can be said for financial management, physical assets, intellectual property, IT assets, and others.

The irony is that IT governance became important after the Internet hubris of the mid- to late-1990s and the Y2K hype when IT spending seemed to spin out of control without clear accountability to the business and without a direct connection to business performance. In other words, the rise of IT governance is a backlash against the unchecked and seemingly "reckless" IT spending of the go-go 1990s. IT governance was necessary to get control of "those IT guys" and ensure they would not be able so spend corporate funds on IT toys without appropriate checks and balances. Governance was about proper oversight, transparency, and stakeholder involvement in critical decisions, ultimately the appropriate use of IT funds on behalf of the business stakeholders.

Now, with the rise of SOA and enterprise SOA governance, the meaning and emphasis of governance varies dramatically depending on what your interests are. SOA in and of itself can mean the strategic aspects of SOA, such as strategy development, program and initiative selection, and funding and budgeting. Of course, SOA governance also entails the architectural dimensions of SOA, the services aspects of SOA, the software delivery and service development dimensions of SOA, and the operational management dimensions of services in the SOA. The following are major forms of enterprise governance that are common across industry:

- **Corporate Governance.** Transparency, oversight, and conformance to corporate policies and support for key corporate decisions by the board of directors.

- **IT Governance.** Transparency and oversight for IT funding, actual IT spending, and input into key IT decisions.
- **Architecture Governance.** Oversight and conformance to the enterprise architecture (EA) standards and policies of the organization, as well as input into key enterprise architecture (EA) decisions.
- **SOA Governance.** Definition, execution, and oversight of an SOA business and technology strategy, along with ensuring technical oversight, interoperability, and enforcement of technical policies for the architecture and services that comprise the SOA.
- **Services/Software Development Lifecycle (SDLC) Governance.** Governance of services from concept to requirements, design, construction, quality assurance and testing, publishing/registration, consumption, composition, orchestration, provisioning, management, maintenance, deprecation, and retirement. Lifecycle governance often is broken into design-time governance and runtime governance, separated by quality assurance and testing, service registration and publishing.
- **Program Governance.** Oversight of major programs, projects, and initiatives from a cost, schedule, and performance perspective, often performed by a program management office (PMO) process.

We could add data governance, portfolio management, and many other dimensions into this list. What should become clear is that "governance" means slightly different things for each of these areas. While they all generically still mean "doing the right things the right way for the stakeholders," the right things, right ways and stakeholders are all different for these governance focal points.

However, when does the transition from "management" to "governance" occur, and for what kinds of assets or decisions? Governance is not the same as management, yet they are intrinsically related to one another as we will see below.

DO NOT CONFUSE GOVERNANCE WITH MANAGEMENT

Our definition of governance is critical to bear in mind as you begin developing your SOA governance model. Governance is often confused with management. In one sense, both are management activities. Governance provides management and oversight for critical activities or decisions where stakeholder representation is an imperative. Management is about execution of all business or organizational activities once the decision is made. Management activities usually do not require external stakeholder involvement or representation, whereas governance activities nearly always have stakeholder interests across multiple domains or constituencies involved. Both are related, and both are necessary in an SOA governance model. However, governance is essential where critical decisions require stakeholder involvement, and where those decisions have strategic or serious impact on business, IT or process performance. Do not confuse management processes with governance processes.

Governance is also focused on more critical aspects of the business, where management is focused on all aspects of the business, some of which may be the focus of governance oversight. One of the real challenges in SOA governance is determining what must be governed, and how, versus what must be managed as parts of normal IT or business management. In this book, we will separate out the domain of management from the domain of governance. When in doubt, ask if something is being governed versus managed. Good management processes can reduce the need for governance, but good governance requires good management.

GOVERNANCE IS ABOUT RESULTS AND APPROPRIATE USE OF RESOURCES

Without governance, there will be no results. Governance is focused on ensuring appropriate use of resources in an organization to drive the organizational actions that will bring about the desired results. Resources in a for-profit organization include funding, personnel, organizations, capital assets, and even intellectual property.

Often, a discussion of governance finishes with a statement roughly equivalent to the following: "Funding is the ultimate governance mechanism." What most practitioners would agree with is that funding is a primary governance enforcement and incentive mechanism, and judicious use of funding models can facilitate the realization of an effective and transparent governance model for your organization. Governance ensures that organizational resources are allocated to important initiatives, and that they are consumed and leveraged wisely. Therefore, governance must focus on critical aspects of the business where allocation of resources, and oversight of the use of those resources, is possible. SOA governance should follow the same approach.

INFORMATION TECHNOLOGY GOVERNANCE

But how did IT governance become so popular? IT governance is not that different from corporate governance. IT governance is the process of ensuring all IT stakeholders' best interests are being met in the planning, funding, and execution of IT for a given organization. IT governance became important when IT spending ballooned out of control in the late 1990s with the combined hype of Year 2000 and the rise of the Internet.[7] As IT spending got more and more out of control with little return on the investment, business leaders realized little to no impact on their business operations. In fact, in many cases, business leaders did not have much say on how IT spending was managed or how IT dollars were allocated to various initiatives. This lack of input and transparency led to an IT backlash, where many CIOs were reined in, fired, or placed under the oversight of the finance functions. The major change resulting from all of this was the establishment of an IT governance process, where the roles, responsibilities, and decision-making processes of IT planning, funding, and execution were managed by joint business and IT leaders, many times with business leaders having much more influence over IT decisions. Much like the rise of corporate governance, IT governance helped make IT spending and decision-making processes more aligned with the business and corporate stakeholders of the organization.

IT PROCESS FRAMEWORKS: ITIL, COBIT, CMMI, AND OTHERS

Several IT governance frameworks and models have blossomed over the years, particularly to facilitate better governance, process definition, and controls for IT. Major IT governance, process, and architecture frameworks are available for implementation, such as Control Objectives for Information and related Technology (COBIT), Information Technology Infrastructure Library (ITIL), Capability Maturity Model Integration (CMMI), and The Open Group Architecture Framework (TOGAF). These are all major process definition and standardization efforts for IT best practices, governance and audit/financial controls. These frameworks all substantially overlap, are inconsistent, approach IT from differing perspectives, and require "substantial interpretation before implementation."[8] Furthermore, the United States lags in adoption of these frameworks, which is a paradox because the Unites States leads in technology innovation, and especially in the context of SOA and its related technologies and disciplines.

The adoption of ITIL best practices, CMMI certification, and other processes seem to be sub-optimized, lacking overarching governance models to manage these processes. In fact, our experience is that IT governance competencies are wide and varied, with no single organization representing enterprise-wide IT governance for all the necessary decisions required. Most often, high-performing governance models at least demonstrate control over a few key governance dimensions, such as enterprise architecture, planning and budgeting oversight, configuration management, and IT operations readiness. Organizations with baseline competencies in some form of governance will have a far easier time adopting or extending these to SOA governance, while those without a basic governance foundation will suffer mightily to add SOA governance disciplines to their enterprise.

IT GOVERNANCE APPROACHES

IT governance is still an immature discipline for the most part, despite the IT management frameworks mentioned above. One of the more insightful IT governance approaches was developed by Peter Weill and Jeanne Ross in their book *IT Governance*.[9] Weill and Ross provide an excellent, high-level perspective of IT governance by simplifying IT governance down to five key decisions and six IT governance constructs. Weill and Ross define IT governance as follows:

> *IT governance: Specifying the decision rights and accountability framework to encourage desirable behavior in the use of IT.*[10]

Weill and Ross essentially focus IT governance on five key decisions:

1. **IT Principles.** Codifying the role of IT in supporting the business through fundamental IT principles that help with alignment and decision making.
2. **IT Architecture.** Defining enterprise integration and technology standardization requirements. (We prefer to treat this category of governance as EA, and expand the definition to include the business architecture, application architecture, technology/infrastructure architecture, and the information architecture.)
3. **Infrastructure Requirements.** Determining shared and enabling technology services, such as data centers, networks, telecommunications, desktops, and computing capacity, that are required by the enterprise.
4. **Business Application Needs.** Specifying the business need for commercial off-the-shelf or internally developed IT applications, as well as the ownership, support, and maintenance for these business applications.
5. **IT Investment and Prioritization.** Determining what initiatives, programs, and projects to fund and how much to spend. These decisions are made during the annual strategic planning processes, as well as during the execution year. This process also includes adding and cancelling

planned IT investments based on business performance as well as emergent business needs.

In addition to focusing on key IT decisions, they also described various "archetypes" for making these decisions, which include business organizations, IT-only organizations, cross-functional organizations, and more. They list the archetypes as follows:[11]

- **Business Monarchies.** A group of business executives or individual executives (CxOs) make key IT decisions. This construct includes senior business executive committees that may or may not include the Chief Information Officer (CIO). This does not include individual IT executives making decisions independently.
- **IT Monarchies.** Individuals or groups of IT executives make key decisions.
- **Feudal.** Business unit executives, key process owners, or their delegates make key IT decisions at the business unit, regional, or process level. There is no shared IT decision making with a corporate headquarters or centralized IT function.
- **Federal.** A governance structure where decisions are coordinated between a centralized corporate IT organization and individual business units, strategic business units (SBUs), or geographic or regional structures.
- **IT Duopoly.** A governance structure that involves two parties—the IT leadership and one other organization, for example, business executives.

Weill and Ross provide a compelling and simplified overview of IT governance and some of the fundamental decisions that must be made, by whom, in order to drive better IT and business performance. However, IT governance requires a deeper level of analysis than Weill and Ross provide, and SOA governance goes far deeper, as we will see.

Weill and Ross provide an excellent basis for the key IT decisions that must be made, and describe various organizational models to help allocate IT decision rights to the enterprise stakeholders. However, they fall short in providing details of how IT policies and decisions are enforced across various processes (e.g., software development lifecycles, architecture governance processes, strategic planning, and execution processes, etc.). Furthermore, they do not develop the concept of policy or a corresponding policy enforcement model for complete IT governance coverage vertically and horizontally in an enterprise that integrates enabling technology, governance processes, and organizational constructs as a comprehensive governance policy enforcement model. Their emphasis is placed on the organizational model dimension of governance, not on the total policy enforcement context for IT policies. As such, it is an incomplete governance framework.

We will explore the many facets of SOA governance in the chapters that follow so that you will not only understand what must be governed in order to capitalize on a SOA initiative, but how to begin designing and implementing SOA governance to ensure you realize the value of SOA. The rise of SOA can be considered to be an inevitable evolution of IT based on the industry adoption of key technology standards and the continued persistence of IT integration and business agility challenges. Below we discuss the SOA governance trend and how to enable SOA governance to be successful.

WHO ARE THE SOA STAKEHOLDERS?

One of the reasons SOA governance is more complex than IT governance is that SOA governance adds many more governance requirements and processes, and therefore more governance stakeholders, into the equation. In addition, as we have emphasized, the fundamental difference between management and governance is that governance requires stakeholder representation. Governance is an oversight process that ensures appropriate stakeholder representation for key enterprise decisions. Who are the stakeholders in an SOA initiative? There are a multitude of SOA stakeholders, as Exhibit 1.2 illustrates.

There are business stakeholders, which includes business unit executives who are concerned with driving revenue, sales, and profit by servicing customers with great products and services. These stakeholders are consumers of IT resources and thus will also be consumers of SOA and services. Their interests include the desire to increase market responsiveness and customer service, while driving IT costs out of their business.

IT stakeholders include IT executives, enterprise architects, project managers, business analysts, developers, and outsourcing partners. These stakeholders represent the service provider roles in an SOA initiative. Their interests include supporting business goals, increasing effectiveness of information exploitation, increasing IT efficiency and reusing of architecture and services, and speeding delivery of products and services to customers.

Service consumers are also stakeholders in an SOA initiative, as are service providers. These two groups of stakeholders are joined by the SOA/ services development lifecycle process, which receives services requirements and demand from consumers and then produces services that can be consumed and composed into business processes and applications for end users and customers. In fact, these stakeholders are best joined by re-engineering the systems development lifecycle to accommodate SOA and services. In our

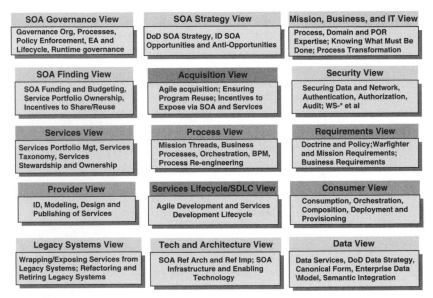

SOA Governance View	SOA Strategy View	Mission, Business, and IT View
Governance Org, Processes, Policy Enforcement, EA and Lifecycle, Runtime governance	DoD SOA Strategy, ID SOA Opportunities and Anti-Opportunities	Process, Domain and POR Expertise; Knowing What Must Be Done; Process Transformation

SOA Finding View	Acquisition View	Security View
SOA Funding and Budgeting, Service Portfolio Ownership, Incentives to Share/Reuse	Agile acquisition; Ensuring Program Reuse; Incentives to Expose via SOA and Services	Securing Data and Network, Authentication, Authorization, Audit; WS-* et al

Services View	Process View	Requirements View
Services Portfolio Mgt, Services Taxonomy, Services Stewardship and Ownership	Mission Threads, Business Processes, Orchestration, BPM, Process Re-engineering	Doctrine and Policy;Warfighter and Mission Requirements; Business Requirements

Provider View	Services Lifecycle/SDLC View	Consumer View
ID, Modeling, Design and Publishing of Services	Agile Development and Services Development Lifecycle	Consumption, Orchestration, Composition, Deployment and Provisioning

Legacy Systems View	Tech and Architecture View	Data View
Wrapping/Exposing Services from Legacy Systems; Refactoring and Retiring Legacy Systems	SOA Ref Arch and Ref Imp; SOA Infrastructure and Enabling Technology	Data Services, DoD Data Strategy, Canonical Form, Enterprise Data \Model, Semantic Integration

Exhibit 1.2   SOA Governance Stakeholder Landscape

experience, most SDLC processes are not well-suited to SOA or services, even in their most agile instances. Agile development does not directly translate into an SOA/Services SDLC, although an SOA/Services SDLC process will be far more agile than its precursor. It has to be.

Because the nuances of SOA demand a holistic approach to governance, there are more stakeholder requirements and perspectives to consider in an SOA initiative than the usual IT application delivery view. The bottom line is that all of these interests are valid in an SOA initiative, and all of these roles are stakeholders in an SOA. The real challenge of SOA governance is defining the critical stakeholders and ensuring their interests are served by the SOA strategy, planning, and execution through effective SOA governance. The following questions will help frame the high-level requirements of enterprise SOA governance:

- What are the goals of your SOA initiative? What must be governed to help ensure these goals are realized?
- Who are the primary stakeholders of your SOA initiative? Is your SOA business-driven or IT-driven?
- What key decisions, assets, or resources must be governed today? What are the key governance concerns and challenges you must overcome to realize the targeted benefits of SOA?
- Who owns the processes, assets, and resources that must be governed?

▪ What outcomes do we seek from SOA governance? How will we measure performance of governance?

SOA governance is confusing to many organizations for a variety of reasons. In many cases, SOA governance is approached from too narrow of a perspective, such as services governance, technical design governance, or SOA platform governance. These SOA governance perspectives represent the technical stakeholders of the SOA initiative very well, but do not articulate the requirements of other business and IT stakeholders.

Another common tendency is to focus on higher-level governance activities, such as the service portfolio management or funding and budgeting processes, too early, when most organizations do not even have a "portfolio" of services available to manage nor enough governance maturity to successfully address these challenges. Oftentimes, focusing on governance basics will go a long ways toward enabling success with more challenging dimensions of governance. We address this later.

Of course, accompanying these are two other very interesting forces: Too many stakeholders may be vying for control of governance, or there may be complete apathy toward governance of any kind. This dichotomy is very real depending on the culture and relative governance maturity of the organization, as well as the political dynamics that may surround and affect all other factors. We have seen both, and the governance model implementation roadmap must be structured to take into consideration both perspectives.

ADDRESSING SOA STAKEHOLDER BIASES

Governance is essential to represent the needs of your stakeholders. However, you must realize that while all stakeholder perspectives are valid, they must be balanced with the needs and requirements of the enterprise. There are some natural SOA stakeholder biases to watch for as you begin formulating your SOA governance model:

▪ **Services Governance.** Focus is too narrow in scope: Many SOA governance enthusiasts mistakenly restrict SOA governance focus to governing services from a technical design- or runtime perspective. In this mode, the focus tends to be technical service design, service interface design, and service implementation.

▪ **SOA Security Emphasis.** While critical, security often focuses only on technology issues and not business or process issues, and does not encompass organizational requirements or business decisions.

- **Partial SDLC Governance.** Design-time bias or run-time/operations bias: Another common stakeholder bias derives from focusing on either design-time governance of services, which emphasizes compliance to architecture and technical design standards, or on run-time governance, which emphasizes operational requirements for performance, quality of service (QoS), service-level agreements (SLA), and security. IT Bias: SOA governance focused on optimizing IT goals, which often are concentrated on service reuse, design-time governance, and architecture and technical compliance. These biases tend to emphasize provider-side goals of SOA, which center on reuse and provider-side optimization.
- **Business Bias.** SOA governance focused on how SOA and services drive business goals for speed to market, business value, and process optimization, as opposed to IT biases toward reuse and technical or architecture compliance. In my opinion, there is not enough focus on the business stakeholders yet, as organizations are still very immature with their SOA initiatives and the supporting SOA governance that supports those SOA strategies. You must understand the natural biases and tendencies that accompany these various stakeholder perspectives, and incorporate them into your governance model. These will become more apparent as we decompose the requirements of enterprise governance in subsequent chapters.

SOA GOVERNANCE IMPACTS IT GOVERNANCE AND ENTERPRISE ARCHITECTURE

A key consideration when planning SOA governance is that it will have a rather profound impact on your current IT governance processes as well as your current enterprise architecture process. Oftentimes SOA governance efforts will expose weaknesses in both governance processes. Exhibit 1.3 depicts how an SOA initiative will impact IT and enterprise architecture governance.

For example, SOA initiatives will always stress IT strategic planning processes, project submission and approval, project management processes, funding and budgeting decisions, asset ownership issues, and portfolio management processes (if they exist). Many of these IT governance processes are not very robust, and thus SOA exposes the absence or fragility of these processes very quickly.

Enterprise architecture (EA) governance processes will similarly be challenged by the inception of an SOA initiative. Depending on the

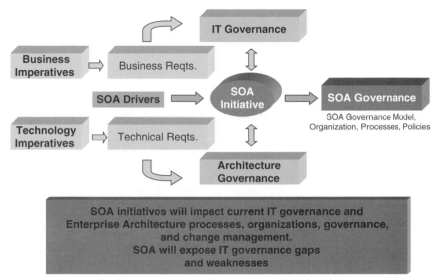

Exhibit 1.3 SOA Governance Impacts Existing Governance Organizations and Processes

robustness of current enterprise architecture disciplines, organizations will have a relatively easier time introducing SOA governance into their EA governance model, especially if they have already formalized architecture governance processes, policies, and oversight of projects as they are managed through the project delivery process in that organization.

SOA governance will place greater demands on those IT organizations whose EA discipline is lacking or whose architecture governance is weak to nonexistent. In these scenarios, many times the EA organization, process, and capabilities must be upgraded in order to successfully accommodate a SOA approach. If there is not an EA organization or discipline, one must be established with executive sponsorship in order to support fundamental SOA.

Our experience from the field suggests that when an enterprise has implemented a rock-solid EA process as well as appropriate architecture governance processes and mechanisms, SOA governance is easier to implement. Adding SOA governance to an existing and successful governance paradigm is easier than starting from scratch. However, transitioning from a poor governance paradigm to a more effective, policy-driven governance framework can be equally challenging.

SOA GOVERNANCE REQUIREMENTS VARY BY SOA MATURITY

Another SOA governance misconception is that once you implement an SOA governance initiative, you will not have to revisit it again. This is patently false. SOA governance is fluid, evolving, and dynamic. SOA governance is a sustained and ongoing capability for your enterprise. The requirements for ongoing SOA governance will vary based on the organization and the relative maturity of SOA in that organization. Exhibit 1.4 depicts an SOA adoption lifecycle model that illustrates the fundamental phases of SOA that an organization will proceed through on its journey to some SOA steady state.

These SOA adoption phases in Exhibit 1.4 are described in detail below:

- **SOA Inception.** Initial SOA and Web services pilots and proof of concepts (POC) occur here, where early learning and gaining SOA experience for a core team of practitioners are the project goals.
- **SOA Strategy and Planning.** This phase often follows the SOA Inception phase and attempts to align all SOA activities under a coherent strategy and roadmap for execution under the sponsorship and leadership of a corporate executive. Our field experience shows that many organizations proceed directly to the next phase, SOA Governance Model Development, *prior* to developing an SOA strategy. We advise doing them in parallel, starting with the SOA strategy and beginning the SOA governance model development shortly thereafter.

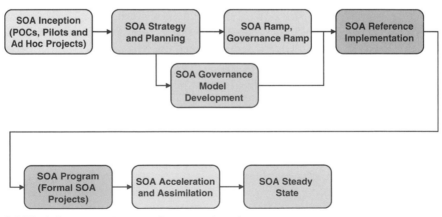

Exhibit 1.4 SOA Adoption Phases (Preferred)

- **SOA Governance Model Development.** This phase involves development and implementation of an SOA governance model that aligns to and supports the realization of an organization's SOA goals and objectives. As mentioned above, often the SOA governance phase is started before an organization has defined its SOA strategy. Thus, the first gap to close in order to implement effective SOA governance is the development of an SOA strategy.
- **SOA Ramp and Governance Ramp.** This SOA adoption phase is focused on preparing for the formal, programmatic execution of an SOA initiative in an organization. SOA ramp activities include training for the core team, developing reference architecture artifacts, service design and interoperability standards, specifying and acquiring the SOA development, testing and run-time platforms, defining the SOA development lifecycle, implementing SOA governance processes, and organizations and artifacts. The ramp activities will prepare the organization for SOA execution according to the defined SOA strategy and under the oversight of the SOA governance model.
- **SOA Reference Implementation.** The SOA reference implementation phase is a milestone phase. Once the organization has done its preparation and ramp activities, it can begin to implement its first true SOA project. This project should be carefully selected, planned, and executed such that it represents, on a small, controlled scale, your SOA end state. This is what we mean by a SOA reference implementation. It represents your end-state SOA implementation from a business, process, governance, and technology perspective, and includes or implements most or all of the many facets of SOA that you will require to realize the benefits of SOA according to your SOA strategy and SOA governance model. The SOA reference implementation phase represents a major milestone and a major organizational win if it is performed well, and will serve as the nucleus around which your team will iterate and expand its SOA capabilities, processes, governance and implementations.
- **SOA Program.** The SOA program phase is where your organization is beginning the formal execution of SOA projects in accordance with your SOA strategy and SOA governance model, and leverages your SOA Reference Implementation as the platform for execution. Programmatic execution of SOA in this phase will begin slowly, with a few programs or projects, and will accelerate as your maturity evolves. In our experience, many organizations attempt to transition directly from the SOA Inception phase to the SOA program phase by skipping SOA strategy and planning, SOA governance model development, and SOA ramp and governance ramp. These organizations often will stall under

this scenario, or will end up with a very limited bottom-up SOA implementation with limited business value.

- **SOA Acceleration and Assimilation.** The acceleration and assimilation phase of SOA adoption is where the organization leverages the reference implementation to add new SOA capabilities, add new processes, expand the consumption and development of new services, and accelerate the adoption of SOA by its IT and business consumers. The SOA acceleration and assimilation phase is where SOA becomes internalized by the organization as the primary means by which business capabilities will be enabled by the IT organization, and the primary means by which the IT organization will operate. This phase involves rapid iterations around the SOA reference implementation core, expansion of SOA governance, and achievement of a repeatable SOA realization model.

- **SOA Programmatic Execution.** In the SOA programmatic execution phase, SOA has become a standardized and repeatable model for the delivery of business capabilities and solutions via services. This phase represents the point at which the SOA strategy is being executed crisply and steadily as a formalized program. SOA governance is robust and guides all SOA activities from strategic planning through sunsetting and retirement of services. This phase represents when an organization should be delivering SOA value through rapid delivery of service-enabled capabilities, where reuse of services is accelerating, and where desired organizational benefits can be measured and demonstrated.

- **SOA Steady State.** By the time an organization reaches the SOA steady state adoption phase, the phrase "Service-Oriented Architecture" and the "SOA" acronym will probably not be in use anymore. SOA will have become the fundamental model by which IT services are delivered. These will be no other model except for services. This phase of SOA adoption is a long way off, but it represents some point at which SOA is the clear and assumed model for business and IT. It will have become so ingrained in the organizational culture that services are just a natural way of architecting and delivering business solutions. At SOA steady state, SOA governance will be natural and infused throughout the organization. The SOA strategy will become just another aspect of both the business and IT strategies, and will not necessarily be documented separately anymore. At SOA steady state, the next big IT trend will probably be well on the way, and we'll be exploiting the opportunities that the SOA wave created for us.

As you might surmise, the activities, processes, capabilities, and SOA governance requirements are all different for the various SOA adoption lifecycle phases. We will detail some of these SOA governance differences in Chapter 8. In the meantime, review the SOA Adoption Model and determine where your organization is in its SOA maturity. After you have done this, write down the SOA governance processes, boards, policies and enforcement mechanisms you have in place now. Then examine the next two stages of SOA maturity and consider what additional SOA governance requirements you may have to consider as you add more services and expand SOA to more projects or to an enterprise level. What you will realize from this exercise is that SOA governance is an evolving, changing, and sustained activity, and your organizational requirements for SOA governance will vary based on internal organizational factors as well as relative SOA maturity.

SOA BILL OF RIGHTS

As our definition of SOA governance states, enterprise SOA governance can be summarized as doing the right SOA things the right way for the SOA stakeholders. The author (2006) captured many of these "rights" in a whitepaper entitled "AgilePath's SOA Bill of Rights," which is excerpted below:[12]

> *Service-Oriented Architecture (SOA) is being vigorously pursued by most organizations today. That said, SOA is still a very new discipline. There are many aspects of SOA that must be carefully planned and executed to avoid common pitfalls such as wasted effort, misspent funding, and inappropriate application of SOA concepts. So, while we applaud these early SOA adoption efforts, we are compelled to offer our "SOA Bill of Rights." These are the essential SOA elements and capabilities that you* must *get right in order to ensure your SOA success. AgilePath's SOA Bill of "Rights" are listed below and explained in detail:*
>
> - *Pursue the* Right *SOA Strategy*
> - *Apply SOA to the* Right *Challenges*
> - *Identify and Build the* Right *Services*
> - *Build Your Services the* Right *Way*
> - *Get your SOA platform* Right
> - *Establish the* Right *SOA Governance Model and Policies*
> - *Encourage the* Right *Organizational and Cultural Behavior*
> - *Achieve the* Right *SOA Results*

PURSUE THE "RIGHT" SOA STRATEGY

A SOA strategy is critical to establishing the appropriate business and mission context for your SOA initiative. But what constitutes the "right" SOA strategy? While there are recurring themes in our clients' SOA goals and objectives, the exact SOA strategies pursued are very much customized to the specific requirements of a given organization. Agility. Faster time to market. Reduced software maintenance costs. Faster application development. Reduced application development costs. Reduced integration costs. Be easier to do business with. Software reuse. We believe the SOA strategy must be business aligned and mapped to urgent "fix-it-or-else" imperatives in your organization. The following statements summarize what makes an SOA strategy "right" for your organization.

- Business aligned—maps to business and IT imperatives, supports business or mission goals
- Focuses on clear business or mission needs—addresses desired business outcomes and has business sponsorship
- Targets appropriate SOA opportunities within a realistic time horizon using a SOA Opportunity Roadmap
- Leverages SOA where services add value, make sense, solve business problems or create new opportunities; SOA is not the solution for every challenge you face.
- Has a business case associated with it, but more importantly achieves clear business value

SOA GOVERNANCE IMPLICATIONS

A well-conceived SOA strategy is essential so that SOA governance is aligned with, and leads to the successful execution of, the SOA strategy. The SOA strategy defines the "right SOA things" to focus on, targeted at key enterprise imperatives, and sponsored at the executive level.

An SOA strategy and roadmap is essential. You must have clear business goals and alignment identified up front, and you must have business support for SOA to maximize SOA value.

APPLY SOA TO THE "RIGHT" CHALLENGES

SOA is not a solution for every challenge in your organization. SOA offers tremendous business value when applied to the right areas. However, if you apply SOA to the wrong challenges, you may end up creating more problems. Where are services, Web services and non-WSDL-described services beneficial to your organization and what's the difference between them? When can an organization benefit from sharing an enterprise assets as opposed to building and maintaining their own silos of assets? How can your enterprise benefit from sharing consistent information across business processes? How can real-time event services eliminate inaccurate data and data latencies which can result in bad decisions and dissatisfied customers? The point is to seek SOA opportunities where the fit of reusable interoperable services returns the most value to the business, as dictated by the SOA strategy being pursued. We recommend creating an SOA *Opportunity Roadmap*[TM], or a short list of the high-value areas of your enterprise where SOA and services solve immediate problems and offer great potential value. This will become an ongoing aspect of your SOA maturation process, continually identifying and applying SOA concepts to new opportunities over time.

SOA GOVERNANCE IMPLICATIONS

SOA governance provides the overall decision-making framework and processes for determining how best to allocate and focus resources on SOA initiatives. SOA governance should define the SOA principles that align with strategic goals and imperatives, and that will ensure effective application of SOA to appropriate problems or opportunities. The SOA Opportunity Roadmap is one device to help identify, evaluate, prioritize and execute SOA-centric projects to support the SOA strategy under the guidance of SOA governance.

IDENTIFY AND BUILD THE "RIGHT" SERVICES

Without services, you cannot have an SOA. Furthermore, an SOA comprised of services with no business or organizational value is well nigh worthless. Therefore, getting your services right is essential. What are the right services? The right services support business and mission objectives.

The right services are derived from your SOA strategy and align with your future direction. The right services support your SOA goals. The right services offer a balance between immediate value and long term investment. The right services should be reusable and shared to ensure rapid return on investment, short payback periods and cost avoidances.

The right services can be quickly identified by examining the SOA opportunities that are documented in your SOA strategy. By performing a process decomposition operation on each of the opportunities in your SOA Opportunity Roadmap, you can quickly identify processes, applications, and candidate services that meet the criteria for being the right services. Of course, to really ensure these are the right services, you must perform service modeling and design activities on the candidate services to achieve appropriate functional scope, encapsulated functionality, granularity, and reusability as well as assessing risk and business fit. Getting the right services is a function of focusing on the right SOA opportunities using an SOA Opportunity Roadmap that supports your SOA strategy.

SOA GOVERNANCE IMPLICATIONS

Building the right services is an extension of "doing the right SOA things." Identifying and building the right services is based on targeting the right SOA opportunities and processes for SOA enablement. These, naturally, are selected based on the SOA strategy and SOA governance framework.

BUILD YOUR SERVICES THE "RIGHT" WAY (DESIGN-TIME GOVERNANCE)

Once you have identified the right services, whether they are existing services or candidate services mapped to your SOA strategy, you must still build them such that they enable the business value you desire. That means building your services right so they are reusable, composable, atomic, stateless, extensible, and agile. In other words, build them the right way. For example, there is a lot of debate about SOAP/WSDL Web services versus RESTful services in the industry today, which in our opinion is the wrong debate. The debate should not be about which technical services paradigm is better than the other, but about when and how to match the appropriate technical implementations of services to the needs and demands of your enterprise. This is why an SOA strategy is so important. Any services that do not support the SOA strategy must be postponed. Any technical service implementation approaches that do not support your SOA strategy or enable services interoperability and reuse must be avoided. There may well be a use for both SOAP/WSDL and RESTful services in your SOA, but you must understand the business and technology issues that support this decision and plan accordingly. This must be an explicit choice rather than one you discover after the fact. We suggest mapping your SOA services taxonomy to the various service technologies and implementation models available, and then making the right choices based on your SOA strategy and Opportunity Roadmaps.

If your SOA strategy calls for orchestration of processes using BPEL, then you should invest in a portfolio of SOAP/WSDL Web services that lend themselves to composition. If your SOA strategy is based on leveraging infrastructure and technical services, be sure you invest in robust SOA enabling technology that exposes security and authentication services, logging and audit services, and related technical components across all application development activities. If you need to expose legacy mainframe functionality as XML Web services, these may impose a different set of Web services design conventions on your organization.

Bottom line: Building your services the right way is subjective to your organization's requirements, its SOA strategy and goals, and what services add value to its business and customers. However, in all cases, we urge you to leverage industry standards to build your services the right way, which will ultimately help you solve integration challenges, increase agility, improve data accuracy, increase customer service, and more. Building services the right way is essential once you've identified the right services.

SOA GOVERNANCE IMPLICATIONS

Building services the right way refers to the design-time SOA governance processes for applying industry standards, internal design principles and patterns, ensuring conformance to EA and SOA enterprise architecture extensions. In addition, building services the right way relates to ensuring appropriate governance oversight as SOA projects proceed through your project delivery process, or SOA/Services Software Development Lifecycle (SDLC), with appropriate quality assurance and testing processes.

GET YOUR SOA TOOLS PLATFORM "RIGHT"

This SOA "right" is essential to the realization of your SOA strategy, yet our field experience shows that many organizations implement their SOA technology platforms before they understand their services requirements. When we say get your SOA platform right, we mean making sure your SOA run-time technical platform supports your planned and current services and your target state architecture. Ensure that your SOA platform does not place dependencies or limitations on your services. Understand the trade-offs of investing in various SOA platform elements such as service registries, enterprise service buses (ESBs), Web services management tools, and SOA security solutions.

Many organizations invested prematurely in UDDI service registries before they had any services available, or even an SOA strategy and roadmap to guide their investment decisions. Similarly, before buying an enterprise service bus, make sure you really need one. Perhaps your organization's messaging and integration requirements can be addressed by Web services management (WSM) solutions or other alternatives. Most likely, you will end up with both solutions anyway, but if you are budget-challenged and can only implement one or the other, understand what you are buying with your SOA platform investments. Below are a few guidelines to consider as you try to get your SOA platform right:

- **Services-Driven Platform Selection.** Select your SOA platform based on the requirements of your services. This is what we mean by services-driven. If you pick your SOA platform before you understand what services you will be building, you may end up with a mismatch of SOA enabling technology and services requirements.
- **SOA Strategy–Enabling.** Be sure your SOA platform supports your SOA strategy and enables the right services that support your SOA strategy. Your SOA platform should not limit the realization of your SOA goals and objectives.
- **Provides the SOA Platform Core Functions.** Be sure your SOA platform will eventually include coverage for the four core SOA platform requirements: Web Services Management (WSM), Reliable Messaging/Transport (ESB, WSM or other messaging solutions), Service Registry (UDDI), and SOA Security. Start with these core functions before you get distracted by orchestration tools, BPEL engines, and other ancillary tooling.
- **Separate Your Services from Your Platform.** Make sure your platform supports your services, but do not let your platform constrain your services. Decouple your services from your SOA platform.

SOA GOVERNANCE IMPLICATIONS

SOA governance provides the decision-making framework for specifying, selecting, and implementing your SOA platform, tools, and technologies. However, your SOA platform will also provide the means to automate certain design and run-time aspects of services as well, such as service registries and metadata repositories, Web services management tools, and messaging infrastructure, among others. Thus care must be taken to govern the selection of SOA platforms and tools, since these will support your technical SOA governance processes for design and run-time policy enforcement.

CREATE THE "RIGHT" ORGANIZATIONAL, CULTURAL, AND BEHAVIORAL MODEL

Along with SOA governance comes the essential yet softer side of SOA: organizational challenges, cultural issues, and the behavioral reinforcement of governance and policies. These are aspects of SOA that are underemphasized because they are difficult to manage, and because it is much easier to buy a vendor software solution than focus on the processes, culture, and behavior that actually make SOA take hold. We will discuss Conway's Law and the implications of organizational structure on enterprise governance and IT/SOA governance.

Consider the following suggestions to help you get your organization and culture right for SOA:

- Understand how your corporate structure inhibits or supports your SOA governance model and enforcement of policies
- Determine how your corporate culture can assist the migration toward SOA or, conversely, how it may not support it
- Latch onto corporate mantras where possible with your SOA initiative
- Determine how to weave SOA goals into organizational and personal incentives
- Use reviews, incentives, rewards, and penalties to achieve a culture of SOA
- Be sure your SOA metrics and scorecards include organizational and individual metrics for success.

Many organizations ignore corporate culture and behavior. SOA, however, demands attention be paid to incentives for appropriate behavior and conformance to the architecture. Be creative, and be bold. Your current IT architecture is a behavioral artifact. If you want to achieve SOA, you must change behavior first and then architect forward.

SOA GOVERNANCE IMPLICATIONS

SOA governance provides the key frameworks, principles, and policies for making appropriate decisions in an enterprise. In order to achieve SOA success, SOA governance must transition from a body of explicitly enforced policies to a fabric of culture, norms, and behaviors implicitly understood by the collective makeup of the organization. The outcome of good SOA governance is appropriate SOA behavior as defined by the SOA strategy and SOA governance model goals.

ACHIEVE THE "RIGHT" SOA RESULTS

What are the right SOA results? They are the goals and objectives you identified in your SOA strategy. The right results are those that support your business and mission objectives. Use metrics and SOA scorecards to track SOA value and results. Demonstrate how SOA is helping your business consumers achieve their goals, and also ensure you are improving IT delivery as well. Caution though: Do not let your SOA be reduced to a reuse project or get hijacked as a technology initiative. Explicitly align your SOA initiative to support your business and mission objectives. Consider the following suggestions to help you achieve the right SOA results:

- Consider establishing a SOA Value Hypothesis to test the value you can achieve via a SOA in a number of controlled experiments. Do not bet on a big bang model. Implement SOA incrementally based on your desired end state.
- Work backward from your desired business end state and set clear, intermediate goals for your SOA projects and initiatives. Use a hypothesis-based approach to test assumptions and expected SOA results. Estimate expected value and benefits from controlled SOA implementations, and then adjust strategies and initiatives according to the results.

■ Assiduously track your progress through clear metrics that prove SOA value and business value.

■ Use Big Hairy Audacious Value (BHAV) as the gauge of SOA success. Be bold yet realistic with your SOA goals. Do not settle for reuse as the end state and ultimate objective of your initiative. There is much more enterprise value to be realized. You just have to plan for it.

■ Stay the course and work through difficult challenges. Anything worthwhile takes sustained effort. SOA takes work, and SOA is worthwhile.

SOA GOVERNANCE IMPLICATIONS

Achievement of the "right" SOA results brings us back full circle to our SOA strategy, goals and objectives. SOA governance, as we have maintained, must be tightly aligned with the SOA strategy and explicitly linked to the SOA goals. The right results will follow from SOA governance, which again ensures we are doing the right SOA things the right SOA way for our SOA stakeholders.

ESTABLISH THE "RIGHT" SOA GOVERNANCE MODEL AND POLICIES

SOA governance is essential for managing the decisions and policies of your SOA. You must get your SOA governance model right to achieve your SOA goals, period. SOA governance establishes alignment of your SOA strategy to your business, as well as defining the enterprise architecture policies and interoperability standards for the services in your SOA. SOA governance is a must! SOA governance is more than the technical policies and design standards for building reusable interoperable services. SOA governance also establishes the decision framework for funding SOA efforts and initiatives, for assigning ownership of various classes of services, as well as ensuring appropriate development lifecycle processes support SOA. Below are a few SOA governance considerations to get your governance model right:

■ **SOA governance is more than technology and tools.** Many vendors are on the SOA governance bandwagon with service registries, repositories, distributed enforcement tools, and more. However, before you can successfully implement the tools, you must establish the SOA processes, policies, and enforcement mechanisms that support and enable SOA success. Separate the process of governing SOA from the supporting technology and tools. *Do not buy any SOA technology or tools and expect to solve your SOA governance needs.* This simply is not possible.

- **Govern the "right" things.** SOA governance means establishing roles and responsibilities for many things, such as funding and budgeting, services ownership and portfolio management, and software development lifecycle governance. However, as you begin to establish SOA governance, focus on two or three critical areas that you must get control of first. Some areas to consider first include EA processes, service design standards, service interoperability standards, and establishing clear accountability for various types of services. Focus on areas where you are weak and need to assert SOA governance and policy enforcement.

- **Expect changes to your current governance processes.** SOA governance impacts your current business and IT governance processes, as well as your current enterprise architecture processes. In our experience, implementing SOA governance properly almost always involves slight to major organizational changes. You can implement SOA governance in phases to more gradually adjust to the governance demands of SOA. However, get your processes, organizational model, and policy enforcement model right first, then consider implementing SOA governance tools.

- **Do not mistake governance with implementing governance boards.** This is the first and most common mistake we see in the field— mistaking the implementation of governance boards for effective governance. While some boards are going to be necessary to implement your SOA governance model, the boards are just one of many governance mechanisms you have available in your SOA governance toolkit. But, if you begin with boards first, before you know what you are trying to govern, you will waste time and end up starting over. Implement boards for the right reasons, but only after you have a clear understanding of why you need them. Boards do not equal governance.

- **Do not go "overboard" with boards.** Boards and committees are perfectly appropriate governance mechanisms, but they are not the only ones. Do not implement too many additional boards, whether they are standing, virtual, or event-triggered. Attendance on boards requires a time commitment, and too many boards, virtual or otherwise, will chew up a lot of preparation and participation time.

- **Any governance will feel like over-governance initially.** When you first implement SOA governance, it may feel like it is heavy-handed to your organization. It may feel as if the SOA police are here to stay. This feeling is a natural result of transitioning from lack of governance or informal governance to explicit, policy-driven governance. When you begin enforcing policies using clear, transparent, and enforceable policies, it will seem like you are over-governing. You *are*, and you *must*, in order to assert control over key SOA activities. You must remember to temper this by focusing on critical SOA governance concerns (e.g., SOA Reference Architecture, services design standards, implementation patterns). Over time, SOA governance policies and expectations will not be new, and thus you will be able to remove some governance processes as SOA governance becomes part of the fabric and culture of your enterprise. This will take a few years. In the meantime, be prepared to over-govern.

- **Staff boards with rising stars.** One way to gain support for SOA governance is to send a clear message that it is crucial for the organization. The importance of SOA governance can be demonstrated by appointing senior executives to the initial governance boards, and by selecting corporate rising stars to participate as well. The worst thing your organization can do is staff governance boards with marginal performers who do not have anything better to do.

SOA governance is an essential aspect of SOA to get right. Do not cut corners on establishing clear policies that align with business and IT goals and your SOA strategy. Think of this as your SOA operating system—you must get it right.

COMMON SOA GOVERNANCE MISTAKES

SOA governance is immature. This relative immaturity of SOA leads naturally to many mistakes in how organizations implement SOA governance. These mistakes come in a variety of shapes and sizes, depending on the approach to SOA governance. As with any new technology trend, software vendors rush their "new" tools to market to solve the problem, usually ahead of an organization's ability to take full advantage of the tool. The normal progression then is that the tool replaces the more appropriate focus on processes and outcomes.

Another SOA governance trend is the opportunistic repositioning of software tools as "SOA governance" solutions. Web services management (WSM) tools are now "runtime governance tools." Metadata repositories are now "design-time SOA governance platforms." And network routers and security appliances are now runtime governance policy enforcement solutions. Regardless, the overarching message here is simple: Do not reduce SOA governance to a software tool, and do not confuse opportunistic product repositioning as a true SOA governance solution.

The following is a partial yet representative overview of common SOA governance mistakes we have seen in the short time SOA governance has been top of mind for IT executives. See if your organization is guilty of any of these approaches.

- **Buying a Tool versus Implementing Robust Processes.** As described above, this SOA governance mistake is very common. Many organizations believe that they address SOA governance by implementing software tools before defining processes, policies, and organizational models to support their SOA governance requirements. Many organizations, for example, have acquired service registries, metadata repositories, and other related software tools in anticipation of meeting all of their SOA governance challenges. However, very quickly these organizations realize that they are only able to govern a small segment of their SOA policies—the technical policies for services design and run-time governance for security for example. The point is that many of these policies can be automated using tools and technologies. However, the large preponderance of SOA policies are business and process policies for conformance to architecture, reuse, and other decision-making processes. In other words, many business, process, and conformance policies cannot be automated very easily, and these are the critical aspects of SOA governance that must be managed for success. Tooling can of course facilitate these SOA governance processes, but tooling cannot replace them. This SOA governance mistake results from entrusting software vendors too much, or from engaging opportunistic consulting firms for SOA governance when they do not have the insights or credentials to implement SOA governance.

- **Mistaking Governance Boards for SOA Governance.** Another common mistake we see is mistaking the implementation of governance boards for the implementation of SOA governance. Certainly governance boards will most likely be necessary to provide a means for stakeholder participation in SOA governance key decision-making processes, but do not assume that governance boards are effective in their governance. SOA governance is more than an organizational model. SOA governance requires policies, processes, alignment to strategy and goals, and metrics to help monitor progress and performance. Governance boards, then, are one of multiple governance mechanisms that will be used to implement SOA governance. They are one of the tools in your SOA governance tool box, but not the only one and perhaps in some ways not the most critical. This mistake is also a common result of entrusting your SOA governance model to consulting firms that do not have the skills or experience to develop and implement SOA governance.

■ **Overcomplicating the Model—Too Many Boards.** In many cases, we see organizations attempting to implement holistic enterprise governance processes when in fact they need focused SOA governance. There are many ways in which one may overcomplicate SOA governance: In one scenario, the organization implements too much governance complexity by implementing too many boards and committees. This heavy organizational footprint often fails because it requires too much organizational overhead and friction too early in the SOA adoption process, and normally before most firms have proven to themselves that SOA can deliver on its potential. In another scenario, there is a mismatch of SOA governance processes and policies to the current demands for SOA governance. For instance, many times we see inexperienced consulting firms pushing sophisticated portfolio management models of governance upon their clients when basic SOA governance gaps have not been closed yet. Why would you need service portfolio managers for a complex collection of service portfolios when you have not even defined basic services design patterns and implementation standards, and do not have an SOA run-time platform specified and implemented yet? You see the challenge. Normally, service portfolio management is a more mature SOA undertaking, usually unnecessary until the organization has enough services to merit a portfolio management approach.

■ **Oversimplify the Governance Model—Lack of Process Coverage.** Another common mistake is oversimplifying SOA governance by omitting key processes or by implementing software tools on the assumption that they provide that process for you. We addressed the software tool issue above. The lack of governance process coverage derives from the absence of an overarching perspective and reference model for SOA governance. This oversimplification normally occurs when governance novices attempt to derive an appropriate SOA governance model from the bottom-up, or from a partial or incomplete frame of reference. For example, if my experience is metadata repositories, my governance process will center on design-time service governance. If my experience and interest is EA, my SOA governance processes will emphasize enterprise architecture governance over other processes. In most cases, organizations have not devised a solid Services Development Lifecycle for the robust and repeatable development, testing, and implementation of services in the context of a SOA strategy. The solution for this mistake is leveraging an SOA governance reference model to help identify and map key governance processes, identify gaps, and then implement robust governance processes supported by appropriate tools and technologies.

■ **Reduce Governance to an Event or Milestone versus a Sustaining Process.** A very common, almost universal, SOA governance mistake is the assumption that SOA governance is an event or a milestone. "Once we implement SOA governance, we're all set." SOA governance is not an event, a "one and done" kind of activity. Rather, it is an ongoing, sustained process of reviewing SOA and services on an ongoing basis. SOA governance must be managed, evolved, measured, and tuned based on the relative maturity and progress of SOA adoption. You must evolve and manage your SOA governance model, processes, principles and policies, all as you maintain alignment to the business and IT strategies as well as business and IT goals. SOA governance is a process, to be sustained and managed over time. Your initial SOA governance model will not be your end-state SOA governance model.

- **Overly Technical Governance—Focus too Narrowly on Technical Policies.** One of the most common mistakes we see is focusing too narrowly on technical service policies and run-time governance. This is a mistake only if the other aspects of SOA governance are ignored. The technical governance issues must be addressed; however, they must be addressed from an overall SOA governance perspective, working top-down from the SOA strategy and goals, and then determining what SOA governance will help ensure realization of the SOA strategy and goals, using metrics to track progress. The most interesting aspect of the technical governance focus is that most of these SOA policies can be enforced using automation and software tools. However, the most challenging SOA policies to define and enforce are business and processes policies, which are difficult to automate and normally require manual enforcement via governance boards, reviews, and manual process checkpoints. These are the policies that drive behavioral and cultural changes, and thus demand the most attention and offer the most value. The body of SOA business and process policies most directly affect the value of SOA and an organization's ability to capitalize on their SOA investments.

- **Substitute Governance Processes and Policies with Faith-Based Governance.** The last SOA governance mistake we will discuss here is substituting a formally defined SOA governance model, processes, and policies with *kumbaya* governance or what I call "faith-based governance." Kumbaya governance is where an organization entrusts its SOA governance to informal processes and personal empowerment rather than an explicit, policy-driven, formally defined governance model and clear, unambiguous processes. Under kumbaya SOA governance, we hold hands, believe in each other, and trust that something good will happen. Voila!!! SOA governance happens. But optimally effective SOA governance does not and cannot happen this way. SOA governance requires an explicit governance model with clear policies, well-defined processes, clearly-defined roles and responsibilities, and alignment to the organization's SOA strategy and goals. Only under these conditions can SOA be governed and the value proposition of SOA, achieved. Kumbaya governance does not work, period.

RIGHT-SIZED SOA GOVERNANCE: HOW MUCH GOVERNANCE DO WE NEED?

Many organizations are anxious about governance, especially when it is construed as adding layers of overhead and interfering in decision making processes that are not broken. Weill and Ross observe that all organizations have some form of governance or IT governance. Whether the current governance is explicit or effective is a completely separate inquiry. While SOA governance does have many moving parts and requires integrating many perspectives and stakeholders in SOA decisions, SOA governance does not have to add tremendous complexity. Yet SOA governance will add new processes, extend current IT governance processes, and require more attention be paid to SOA-centric activities.

In order to keep things in perspective, we break out Henry David Thoreau's famous quote: *"That government is best which governs least."* SOA governance is best implemented a little at a time, as much as is needed to control key processes and decisions, and by implementing as much as necessary to ensure SOA success. Any amount of SOA governance is more than most organizations want, regardless of the nature of it. That said, SOA governance is essential and therefore you must get it right. Enough to govern critical SOA governance requirements, and yet not so much that innovation and progress is stifled. A better SOA governance quote might be as follows:

That governance is best that governs best with the least.

You must always ask yourself if your SOA governance model is right-sized for your organization, culture, and current SOA objectives.

SUMMARY

SOA governance does not have to be complicated, but it often can be, owing to the many valid stakeholder viewpoints in a SOA initiative. In order to make sense of SOA governance, there are a few dynamics to keep in mind.

- All the stakeholders' views are valid, yet all are not as critical early on as they will be later.

- Representing all SOA stakeholders is difficult. Assuaging them with SOA governance is more challenging.
- Governance will not be fun or easy.
- You will have to over-govern in the short term. This will be uncomfortable.
- You will inevitably take decision rights away from some individuals and organizations, while assigning them to others. This transfer of authority and control will anger people. Deal with it.

IT governance is also extremely important based on the structure of the IT function in an organization. The structure and organization of IT similarly has a dramatic and direct effect on how SOA governance must be structured.

Notes

1. Ronald H. Coase, "The Nature of the Firm", *Economica* 4, 1937, pp. 386–405.
2. Eric Marks and Michael Bell, *Service-Oriented Architecture: A Planning and Implementation Guide for Business and Technology*, John Wiley & Sons, 2006.
3. Geoffrey Moore, *Living on the Fault Line, Revised Edition: Managing for Shareholder Value in Any Economy*, HarperCollins, 2002.
4. WebLayers Whitepaper: *SOA Governance*, 2005, p. 9.
5. Eric Marks and Michael Bell, *Service-Oriented Architecture: A Planning and Implementation Guide for Business and Technology*, John Wiley & Sons, 2006, p. 248.
6. Peter Weill and Jeanne Ross, *IT Governance: How Top Performers Manage IT Decisions for Superior Results*, Harvard Business School Press, 2004, pp. 6–7.
7. See Eric Marks, *Business Darwinism—Evolve or Dissolve: Adaptive Strategies for the Information Age*, John Wiley & Sons, 2002.
8. Charles T. Betz, *Architecture and Patterns for IT Services Management, Resource Planning, and Governance: Making Shoes for the Cobbler's Children*, Morgan Kaufmann, 2007, p. xxii.
9. Peter Weill and Jeanne Ross, *IT Governance: How Top Performers Manage IT Decisions for Superior Results*, Harvard Business School Press, 2004.
10. Ibid., p. 8.
11. Ibid., p. 59
12. Eric A. Marks, "AgilePath's SOA Bill of Rights: Aspects of SOA You Must Get Right" AgilePath Corporation, 2006.

CHAPTER 2

SOA Governance Reference Model

$\mathbf{S}$ervice-oriented architecture (SOA) governance, Information Technology (IT) governance, and corporate governance in general are complex and misunderstood topics. With the industry focus on SOA and SOA governance, it is no surprise that the concept of governance has become so nebulous. The objective of this chapter is to clarify what SOA governance is and is not. We will do this by describing SOA governance using an SOA Governance Reference Model. The SOA Governance Reference Model will focus on enterprise SOA governance as a unique discipline relative to other governance disciplines, but with clear linkages and relationships to these other governance disciplines.

Governance does not have to be complex, but it must be effective. Ensuring SOA governance effectiveness revolves around a few simple questions:

- What must be governed right now and in the future to meet our goals?
- What policies are necessary to govern effectively?
- How will those policies be enforced?
- When and by what and by whom?
- How will exceptions be managed?
- How will we monitor the effectiveness of governance?

That is it. Answer these questions, and you can get to the heart of SOA governance. Remember the SOA governance definition from Chapter 1:

SOA governance is the definition, implementation and ongoing execution of an SOA stakeholder decision model and accountability framework that ensures an organization is pursing an appropriate SOA strategy aligned with business goals, and is executing that strategy in accordance with guidelines and constraints defined by a body of SOA principles and policies. SOA policies are enforced via a policy enforcement model, which is realized in the form of various policy enforcement mechanisms such as governance boards and committees, governance processes, checkpoints and reviews, and governance enabling technology and tools.

Of course, SOA governance is more complex than that, which is why we have created the SOA *Governance Reference Model*[TM].[1] The SOA Governance Reference Model establishes a framework for identifying enterprise SOA governance requirements and creating an appropriate governance model that works for your organization.

WHY AN SOA GOVERNANCE REFERENCE MODEL?

An SOA Governance Reference Model services multiple purposes. First, it creates an abstracted view of SOA governance such that the model can be customized to the specific governance requirements and needs of an organization. This abstracted view begins and ends with business goals and SOA strategic goals, which help align the governance model to desired SOA outcomes. Governance is performed for a reason, and it is not because organizations love governance processes and oversight boards. SOA governance is performed to help ensure business outcomes will be realized through allocation of resources to SOA initiatives, programs, and activities, as agreed to and governed by appropriate stakeholders.

Second, the SOA Governance Reference Model creates a view of governance that explicitly balances the role of technology and tools with the organization, processes, and roles and responsibilities of governance. Tools and technologies will be essential ingredients in your SOA governance model, but you should not start with tools and then determine what governance challenges you must address. Furthermore, the SOA Governance Reference Model is completely technology- and vendor-neutral. A technology agnostic reference model provides opportunities for all tools that support governance to potentially fit into the governance implementation, but the SOA Governance Reference Model does not begin with tools, does not mention categories of tools, and does not even mention technology standards. We feel that an SOA Governance Reference Model will help organizations select better and more appropriate SOA tools and platforms once the organizations have performed the appropriate analyses of SOA governance goals, requirements, and processes.

Third, the SOA Governance Reference Model establishes an organic framework for enterprise governance based on an SOA strategy, goals, and objectives. This approach enables a more comprehensive and pre-aligned view of governance, as opposed to trying to scale a very narrowly defined view of technical services governance into a model that governs processes, portfolios, and the alignment of SOA activities to business and mission goals. Many organizations start with a very technical and narrow scope for their governance activities. For example, services design governance, while critical to services construction and run-time fidelity, is a very technical subset of SOA governance that the developer and enterprise architecture community will naturally gravitate to. However, there are business and process governance considerations that directly impact service design and run-time governance, and those precursors must be defined and understood prior to building services and deploying them to an SOA runtime platform, especially if those services are to help in realizing some targeted business need.

ELEMENTS OF THE SOA GOVERNANCE REFERENCE MODEL

The SOA Governance Reference Model is a layered model that we will explore working top-down, beginning with SOA governance strategy and goals. The SOA Governance Reference Model is depicted in Exhibit 2.1.

The SOA Governance Reference Model consists of layers that describe governance considerations that are essential to successful enterprise SOA governance. These layers can be grouped into four primary classes, which

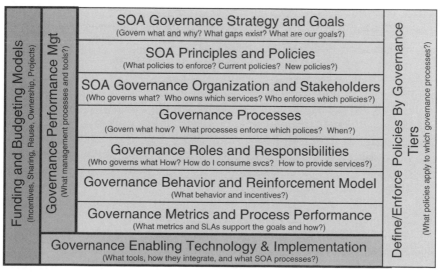

Exhibit 2.1 SOA Governance Reference Model

SOA Governance Strategy and Goals
(Govern What and Why? What Must Be Governed? To What End?)
SOA Principles and Policies
(What SOA principles and policies are needed? How will they be enforced?)

- Govern **What** and **Why?**
- **What** must be Governed **now?**
- **To What End?** (Goals alignment and realization)
- **SOA Goals, Principles, and Policies**

Exhibit 2.2   SOA Governance Reference Model

help in tailoring this Governance Reference Model to your organization's specific governance requirements:

1. **Governance Strategy and Policy Dimensions.** What SOA strategy provides the backdrop and direction for SOA governance? What strategies and objectives are we governing to ensure that we achieve them? What resources, decisions or processes must be governed to support this strategy? What business, process, and technology policies are necessary based on the stated SOA strategy and governance philosophy? Exhibit 2.2 depicts these layers of the SOA Governance Reference Model and key concerns.

2. **Organization, Process, and Roles/Responsibility Dimensions.** What organizational models and processes support the SOA governance model and enforce the desired policies? How will governance boards and committees integrate with governance processes, checkpoints, and reviews? What roles and responsibilities are necessary to achieve SOA governance? Who governs what and how? Exhibit 2.3 depicts these layers of the SOA Governance Reference Model and key concerns.

3. **Behavior and Metrics Dimensions.** What behaviors and reinforcement processes are needed to institutionalize governance in the organizational fabric? How do metrics and governance performance management support the behavioral model? How do we achieve the results we are targeting? Exhibit 2.4 depicts these layers of the SOA Governance Reference Model and key concerns.

4. **SOA Governance Management Dimensions.** This category includes SOA funding and budgeting, governance performance management, and principle and policy management processes. In the SOA Governance Reference Model, these dimensions are the two vertical bars on

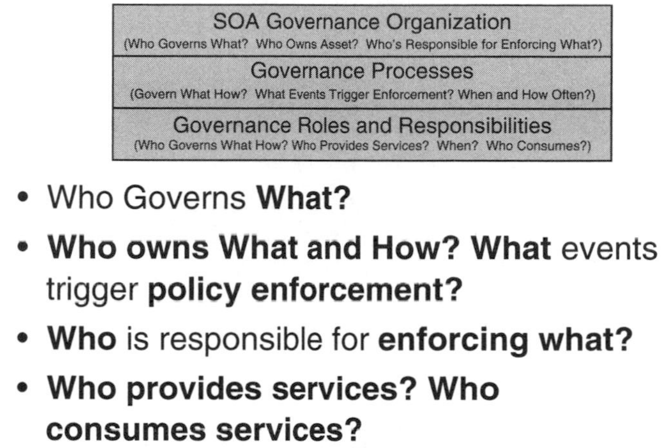

SOA Governance Organization
(Who Governs What? Who Owns Asset? Who's Responsible for Enforcing What?)
Governance Processes
(Govern What How? What Events Trigger Enforcement? When and How Often?)
Governance Roles and Responsibilities
(Who Governs What How? Who Provides Services? When? Who Consumes?)
• Who Governs What?
• Who owns What and How? What events trigger policy enforcement?
• Who is responsible for enforcing what?
• Who provides services? Who consumes services?

Exhibit 2.3 SOA Governance Reference Model

left-hand side of the model. SOA funding and budgeting is critical because of its direct impact on shaping the alignment of business unit strategy and goals to the enterprise, as well as on shaping the selection and implementation of key programs and projects that implement corporate strategy. Funding and budgeting are the ultimate governance levers.

At the same time, we believe the role of governance in most enterprises is becoming so important that it merits a more scientific model than in the past. We call the ongoing discipline and process of governance "Governance Performance Management." This dimension is the ongoing management and execution of governance in an enterprise.

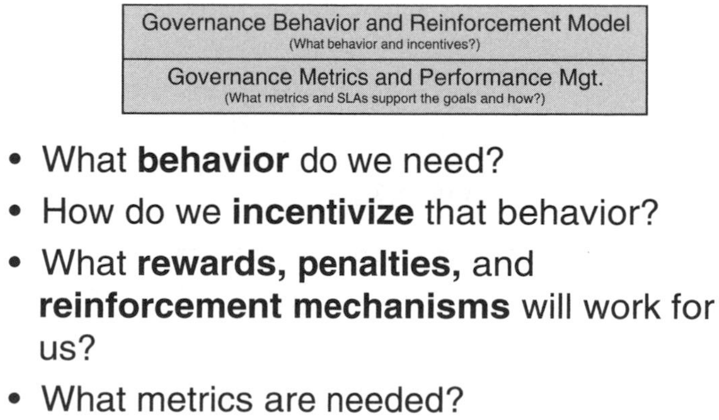

Governance Behavior and Reinforcement Model
(What behavior and incentives?)
Governance Metrics and Performance Mgt.
(What metrics and SLAs support the goals and how?)
• What behavior do we need?
• How do we incentivize that behavior?
• What rewards, penalties, and reinforcement mechanisms will work for us?
• What metrics are needed?

Exhibit 2.4 SOA Governance Reference Model

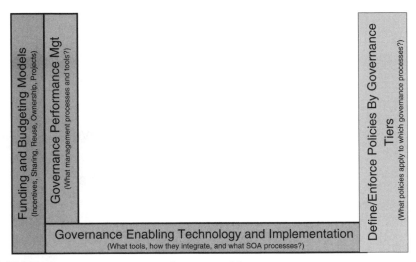

Exhibit 2.5   SOA Governance Reference Model

Taken together, these two dimensions establish the overarching environment for SOA governance in an enterprise. Exhibit 2.5 depicts these layers of the SOA governance reference model and key concerns.

The SOA Governance Reference Model forces you to examine the reasons why you need governance, as well as the organization and process considerations of governance, prior to considering technology and tools. These five major categories of SOA governance are broken into their respective dimensions in the sections that follow. As you will see, when taken as a whole, the SOA Governance Reference Model helps place critical SOA governance focus on strategy and goals, organizational, and process considerations, and policies as they span the enterprise, all supported by key management processes.

DECOMPOSING THE SOA GOVERNANCE REFERENCE MODEL

In this section, we will break down the SOA Governance Reference Model into its components. This exercise will provide an understanding of the many aspects of SOA governance and how they interrelate. Once the components of the reference model are understood, you will be able to apply it to your organization.

SOA Governance Strategy and Goals

The first elements of the SOA governance reference model are the SOA governance strategy and goals layer. This aspect of SOA governance answers a very simple and compelling set of questions:

- What must be governed and why?
- What must be governed now?
- To what end? What end result do we seek from SOA?
- What SOA policies are necessary based on the governance goals

These are the most fundamental questions to help focus your governance efforts where they address key business challenges and ensure that appropriate activities are conducted by the business, and that appropriate oversight and business controls are in place.

The strategic context for SOA governance is essential to determining what must be governed, why governance is important for the organization, and what goals will be realized from governing (as opposed to not governing). These decisions will set the stage for defining goals, principles, and policies of your governance model, and establish the enforcement mechanisms that will ensure conformance or compliance to those policies.

Many organizations embark on defining an SOA governance model without knowing what SOA strategy they are supporting. Just as the absence of an SOA strategy renders SOA governance somewhat meaningless, so, too, does an ill-defined strategy. Your SOA strategy should be defined, stipulating its goals and target outcomes, so that the SOA governance model can help ensure all activities lead to and support those defined SOA goals and outcomes. Governance ensures that the "right" things are being pursued in support of the SOA strategy.

Governance essentially means ensuring conformance to something, such as a standard, a body of laws, rules, and norms, or a defined reference architecture. Governance is behavior, or more accurately, governance is ensuring that behavior conforms to norms, expectations and guidelines set forth by the community or elected leadership of a community. So, in this example, SOA governance essentially aligns all SOA activities to the SOA strategy to ensure that the desired goals are achieved. For example, if a major element of the SOA strategy is focused on retiring legacy asset retirement, services reuse, and cost reductions, then SOA governance must ensure that appropriate policies and processes are established that lead to those goals. Below are some "typical" reuse goals we might expect to see in an SOA strategy:

Reuse Goals

- Achieve overall reuse of 30% of business and mission services
- Reduce application development costs by 25% through reuse of infrastructure, technical and business services
- Improve time to market for software development by 20% through reuse

In order to achieve reuse as a component of an SOA strategy, the following kinds of governance processes must be in place:

- Requirements and demand management process to identify, aggregate, and prioritize requirements to identify reuse
- Portfolio management processes ensure that existing projects, platforms, applications, and services are leveraged before anything new is acquired or built
- Funding and budgeting processes support creation and maintenance of reusable assets, as well as subsidize cost deltas for making services reusable for multiple consumers
- Services lifecycle processes deliver services that do meet the requirements of multiple constituents
- SOA infrastructure and runtime platforms support discovery and reuse of services, infrastructure, and technical services such as authentication, authorization, audit, logging, single sign-on, and so on.

As you can see, answering the fundamental questions, "Govern what and why," will guide the remaining steps in establishing SOA governance for your organization. Once these questions are answered, we must next establish the body of SOA policies that will operationalize SOA governance as a body of enforceable tenets that constrain behavior and lead to SOA governance goals.

SOA Policies

SOA policies are the means by which SOA governance becomes enforced through various enforcement processes and governance mechanisms. Policies define specific rules, guidelines, and standards that will be enforced in order to "govern" something (e.g., enterprise architecture conformance, services design standards compliance, security policy conformance, or runtime quality of service and service level agreements). In an SOA context, policy examples include such things as security policies, reuse policies, service design policies, and interoperability policies. As such, policies can become an intimidating topic because of the number of polices that require enforcement in an SOA governance model.

Based on the SOA governance goals and strategy, what kinds of policies will you need in order to govern effectively? What governance challenges that you face demand more formalized and explicit policies? What high-level policy enforcement models are under consideration? SOA policies, as we will discuss in Chapter 6 are the secret sauce that allows SOA governance to transcend pithy recommendations and high-level aspirations and become an explicit reference to shape the implementation of SOA, services and capabilities that lead to defined business outcomes. Policies make SOA governance real.

In the SOA Governance Reference Model, we also place policies as a vertical bar that extends from the SOA strategy through organization, process, and roles and responsibilities, all the way through metrics and SOA governance implementation. Policies fall into all of these categories. Corporate policies and business policies shape and inform organizational and process policies, which directly impact technology policies at service design time, quality assurance and testing, and into run time. Policies therefore are placed in two locations on the SOA Governance Reference Model. Policies are a layer directly associated with the SOA strategy and goals, and then are also placed as a vertical slice as cross-cutting requirements of all other SOA governance dimensions.

However, this is one of the paradoxes of SOA policies. While a security policy may seem complex, there are multiple levels of policy granularity to consider.

While most SOA practitioners are concerned with the granularity of their services, an equally and perhaps more challenging issue is *policy granularity*. SOA policies vary depending on a variety of factors, such as the type of policy, where it is enforced, and how it is enforced. Furthermore, policies can be described as parent policies with multiple child policies, and thus enforcement can occur at the parent level, or at the individual child policy level, or both.

Policy granularity is further complicated by whether a policy is a corporate policy, a business policy, a process policy, or a technical policy.

The concept of policy granularity is an important one, and is critical to understanding the entire scope of governance in a particular organization. This is why policies in our SOA Governance Reference Model are shown in two places: as a horizontal layer associated with the SOA governance strategy and scoping element, and as a vertical slice that spans all SOA governance activities. Policies are associated with almost all dimensions of SOA governance, and thus must be considered at every level of governance, including enterprise governance and Services Development Lifecycle Governance.

Policies will be covered in great detail in Chapter 6. For now, understand that policies must derive from SOA goals and supporting principles. Policies actuate SOA governance by providing standards, rules, guidelines, and norms by which SOA will be realized in an organization.

SOA Governance Strategy and Goals

The SOA governance strategy and goals dimension of the SOA governance reference model is a critical one. Many organizations are racing forward with SOA governance initiatives before they have defined even preliminary SOA strategies. How can you govern anything without aligning to a strategic perspective or compass of some kind? This fundamental question begs the following additional questions that relate to this dimension of SOA governance:

- What SOA strategy will your governance model support?
- What goals and outcomes do you seek from your SOA initiative?
- How does SOA governance ensure those goals are realized?
- What SOA governance strategic goals are important to you?
- What business metrics will guide SOA governance performance?

The governance strategy and goals layer does not suggest that you need a SOA governance strategy. Rather, it urges that you align SOA governance to the SOA strategy and goals of the organization. SOA governance must have a strategy and goals as inputs into the governance model. SOA strategy provides the context, business and technology alignment, goals and business case for action. The SOA strategy informs the organization as to what the right SOA activities are, so that you can ensure all programs, projects, and initiatives align to the strategy and goals via the enterprise SOA governance model.

SOA Governance Organization

The SOA governance organization is the next major dimension of the SOA Governance Reference Model to be explored. The SOA governance organization refers to the organizational models, governance boards, working groups, team composition, reporting relationships, and related structural aspects of SOA governance.

The SOA governance organizational model, governance processes, and governance roles and responsibilities must be explicitly described, modeled, and implemented in order to realize effective SOA governance. Structural and organizational considerations play a crucial role in shaping the SOA governance model, organizational model, and process models necessary to implement effective SOA governance.

What kind of SOA governance organizational model will you consider? Virtual? Standing teams? Working groups? How will SOA governance map to and align to corporate business structures? How is the IT organization structured? How are current governance activities structured? Is there explicit alignment of corporate and IT governance to business structures? When is a governance board necessary for your governance model? Does it need to be a standing board, or a virtual board that is triggered to meet by a governance event?

Remember: The structure of an organization strongly influences the performance of the organization. Be mindful of how your organization is structured at the corporate and operational levels, and then understand how the IT organization is structured. The interplay of these organizational models will have a direct impact on how you structure the governance organizational model and what kind of performance you can expect.

Many of the organizational aspects of SOA governance can be determined by the as-is structure of the enterprise as a whole, and then by how the IT organization is structured. Once you understand the structure of the IT organization, you can determine how IT is governed, and what if any governance gaps exist. This simple exercise will accelerate your ability to understand the as-is governance model and processes, as well as identify changes necessary to accommodate a SOA initiative.

- **Functional.** A functional organizational construct is organized by major business functions, such as finance, manufacturing, sales, marketing, service, procurement, and distribution/logistics. A functional organization attempts to optimize by major functional activities, but the structure tends to work best for smaller to midsize organizations that are geographically concentrated, and offer relatively few products or services.
- **Divisional.** Divisional structure is formed when an organization is split up into a number of self-contained business units, each of which operates as a profit center. Such a division may occur on the basis of product or market, or a combination of the two, with each unit tending to operate along functional or product lines, but with certain key functions (e.g., finance, personnel, corporate planning) provided centrally, usually at company headquarters.
- **Geographic.** Organized by major geographic segments, with each segment having autonomy to make decisions that optimize for its respective region. A geographic structure will usually report to a corporate entity.

- **Product Lines.** Organized by major product families (e.g., HP Printers versus HP consumer products).
- **Markets/Customer Segments.** The organization is organized by major market or customer segments, such as enterprise customers, consumer markets, mid-size corporations.
- **Matrixed.** A matrix structure combines elements of functional and divisional structures. A matrix model is a dual organization comprised of functional expertise and customer- or geographically-aligned segments. An employee will typically report to a general manager within his division, as well as to a functional manager at a central location who oversees that function across all divisions. A matrix structure can help to ensure better coordination of divisional and company-wide objectives, but it can also lead to inefficiency if the authority of both the divisional managers and centralized, functional managers is not well clarified.

IT organizations are usually mirrored to reflect corporate structures. There is a clear and direct relationship between structure and performance of your organization.

Enterprise SOA Governance will often be implemented to overcome weaknesses imposed by a chosen structure and organizational model. As you develop your governance organizational model, bear in mind the strengths and weaknesses of various organizational models, and how governance will reflect those choices, and how governance may be a tool that helps mitigate weaknesses of various structural and organizational models.

How Is Information Technology Organized?

Once the organization's enterprise structure is understood, the IT organization must also be determined. The IT organizational structure will influence SOA governance, although most times SOA governance has a more dramatic impact on IT governance. Based on the key stakeholders and the current corporate and IT organizations, an effective SOA governance organization can be implemented.

Is the IT organization centralized or distributed? Is there a federated structure? If the IT organization is federated, is it loosely or tightly federated? Beneath these coarse organizational models, how is IT organized internally? By technology or platform? By processes or projects? By customer or business unit supported?

The IT organization will in many respects reflect the corporate structure of the organization, but will also reflect aspects of governance and empowerment for key decisions as well.

SOA Governance Processes

SOA governance is clearly more complex than IT governance, despite it being an extension of IT governance. As such, there are many governance processes that must be included, linked and extended to accomplish SOA governance. We will discuss these processes in Chapter 3 in more detail. Often, organizations attempt to implement governance around key processes that require a great deal of organizational maturity to effectively govern them. For example, beginning your SOA governance efforts by focusing portfolio management processes is not necessarily your first priority, nor is it an easy governance process to implement. We would suggest that you focus on key SOA governance processes in accordance with your business, your IT and SOA strategy, and based on where your key governance gaps are. Questions to consider when determining what SOA governance process coverage you require include:

- What SOA governance processes are needed?
- What is the current state of governance in your organization?
- What governance gaps must be closed in order to realize the business goals you seek from your SOA initiative?
- How do you align all SOA activities to the SOA strategy to ensure you are taking the right actions?

Our definition of SOA governance centers on doing the right SOA things the right way for the SOA stakeholders. The list of processes below focuses on doing the right things from an enterprise and strategic governance perspective:

Key SOA Governance Concerns to Focus on (Right Things/Strategic Governance Processes)

- SOA Strategy Alignment
- SOA Requirements, Demand Management, and Specification Development
- SOA/Service Submission, Evaluation, and Prioritization
- SOA/Enterprise Architecture Review
- Service Portfolio Management Review
- Project Selection and Final Approval
- SOA Funding and Budgeting Review

Once your governance model has helped your organization determine the right things to do, you must still execute them. The following processes are mid-level and lower-level governance processes that help ensure you are doing things the right way:

Key SOA Governance Concerns to Focus on (Right Actions)

- Project Execution/Program Management Office (PMO) Process (Project Management Reviews)
- SOA/Enterprise Architecture Governance (Architecture Reviews across the Services/Software Development Lifecycle (SDLC)
  - Services Design
  - SOA Platform Utilization
  - Security Conformance
  - Data and Schema Conformance
  - Pre-Publishing Service Validation
- Service Reuse (Service Portfolio Reviews during project planning, submission, approval and early SDLC reviews)
- SOA Operations Readiness Reviews
- SOA/Services SDLC Process Reviews (ensure service delivery model, processes and resources can deliver)
- Manage Service Portfolios (in coordination with other portfolios, e.g. application portfolio, technology portfolio, process/capability portfolio, program/project portfolio)

As we have stated earlier, SOA Governance processes map to the governance strategy and goals of the organization. SOA governance processes support definition, management, and enforcement of the policies of the organization. The policies of course help close key governance gaps identified during an assessment of the organization's current state SOA governance.

Governance processes include enterprise processes that are strategically organized, as well as execution processes organized to get things done tactically. In fact, you might consider broad processes to include planning processes, ongoing management processes, and project or program execution processes.

SOA Governance Roles and Responsibilities

The roles and responsibilities of governance are critical. Stakeholders must have clarity of purpose and intent, and everyone must know how they fit into the SOA governance framework. One of the most important artifacts or outcomes from an SOA governance model is clarity of purpose, definition of roles and responsibilities, and clear accountability for decisions and action.

Governance roles and responsibilities define who does what in a governance model. In an SOA context, one of the biggest challenges is defining the consumer-provider relationships and the services delivery processes that connect them within an enterprise and across multiple enterprises. In addition to consumer-provider roles, basic aspects of asset ownership, portfolio management responsibilities, and other roles and interactions add to the SOA governance confusion in an enterprise.

SOA roles and responsibilities derive from early and basic decisions about asset ownership as well as process ownership and control.

The following questions must be considered here:

- Who owns various SOA assets and services? Who has funding and budget authority for key SOA decisions?
- What governance processes, roles, and responsibilities are necessary? Who governs what how?
- How do funding and budgeting processes define or impose constraints on service domains, process ownership, and other structural relationships?
- How do the SOA governance organizational model and enforcement processes clarify decision making for SOA?
- Are roles and responsibilities clearly defined? Are they publicly known and communicated? Are potential conflicts anticipated and remediations planned?

The SOA governance roles and responsibilities dimension is fraught with risk and conflict since it has direct bearing on the people and process facets of SOA governance. Clear delineation of roles and responsibilities will smooth the transition to SOA governance. But be advised, any changes under the umbrella of governance will cause organizational conflict and organizational friction. You can define a "perfect" governance model and it still will cause conflict and friction. Anticipate it, mitigate it, and deal with it.

Governance Behavior and Reinforcement Model

This sub-dimension explores the relationship between behavior and reinforcement of norms, mores and values that contributed to SOA governance. The behavioral aspects of SOA come through a variety of hard and soft reinforcement mechanisms, including recognition and compensation as well as penalties for failing to conform to SOA governance policies, guidelines, and norms. Questions to consider here include:

- What is the corporate culture of the organization? How does it help or hinder the transition to SOA governance?

- What behaviors are currently rewarded and recognized? How do they align with the requirements of SOA governance?
- How can SOA governance be aligned with recognition and reward models?
- How are current reward and recognition models inconsistent with the requirements of SOA governance?
- What are the politics of the organization? Who are the influencers on decisions?
- Can governance metrics and performance measures be aligned and linked to influence behavior?

Ultimately, SOA governance is a behavioral reinforcement mechanism. In order to achieve SOA, your governance model must explicitly recognize that IT architecture is a behavioral artifact resulting from a pattern of decisions and choices derived from the corporate culture and leadership of the organization. If SOA is to be achieved, behavior must be changed. Addressing behavior and culture as explicit dimensions of SOA governance will help in dramatic ways. Failing to incorporate behavior and culture into your SOA governance model is a recipe for disaster.

SOA Governance Metrics and Performance Management

This sub-dimension focuses on the metrics of governance and how an organization will be able to monitor the effectiveness of its SOA governance model. The governance metrics model is purely dependent on the SOA strategy and goals. Once the business goals are defined, a set of metrics can be developed to help align all SOA activities and governance activities and ensure progress toward meeting SOA goals. The author and Bell[2] (2006) discussed the concept of a "federated metrics model," where SOA metrics are organized into a "balanced scorecard" framework. The congruence of metrics will help make sure everything is ultimately focused on the targeted business objectives. Questions to consider here include:

- What are the business goals of our SOA initiative?
- What metrics are necessary to monitor our progress toward those goals?
- What federated metrics, or SOA balanced scorecard, support realization of these business goals?
- How will data for these metrics be gathered? Can we automate any of the data collection for the SOA balanced scorecard?

Governance Dashboard and Performance Metrics Management

This sub-dimension is all about providing a single point of access to all SOA governance policies, principles, metrics, services, and overall information related to the SOA initiative of an organization. The idea of "SOA Governance Performance Management" is essentially the process of managing the performance of the SOA, SOA governance, and the federated metrics that lead to the desired SOA results. Governance performance management focuses on the following activities:

- Provides a single point of access to all SOA and SOA governance information, e.g., via a portal or a dashboard
- Provides access to the following information in a four-quadrant view:
  - Dashboard displaying such business metrics as cost savings, reuse, development benefits, return on investment (ROI) accrued from the SOA initiative, as well as overall progress toward business goals.
  - Service monitoring and alerting dashboard (feed from a Web Services Management (WSM) tool)
  - Service catalog access to track volume of services (feed from service registry)
  - Metadata catalog or repository to view SOA policies, governance information, service design standards, and so on (feed from metadata catalog)

Most organizations are not mature with their SOA metrics frameworks, nor have they considered the notion of SOA Performance Metrics Management to continually monitor SOA progress through various measures of success, e.g. # of services, reuse per service, # of clients per service, cost avoidance savings through reuse, integration cost reductions, and more. We urge the definition and management of SOA metrics as part of the SOA governance model design process.

SOA ENVIRONMENTAL DIMENSIONS

The last major category of SOA governance includes the environmental determinants of effective governance. These include SOA funding and budgeting, governance performance management, and governance enabling technology and implementation. These are environmental considerations because they in many ways shape the effectiveness of the other dimensions of the SOA Governance Reference Model. Questions to consider include the following:

What management processes are required to gauge and assess governance performance? How do we evolve our governance as we mature our SOA efforts? How can we reinforce governance with appropriate budgeting and funding practices that support sharing and reuse of services and other corporate assets? How do we manage, version, and deprecate business and technical policies that help us govern what must be governed?

SOA Funding and Budgeting

Strategic planning, program planning, and funding and budgeting processes are strategic activities that are often not managed strategically in many organizations. This is one of the ironies we find in helping organizations establish governance models. Many strategic planning exercises are not very strategic, and thus the resultant IT funding and budgeting activities are handicapped and focused on tactical versus strategic horizons.

SOA funding and budgeting is a root cause dimension of SOA and SOA Governance and one that typically is very challenging to address. Any time you make changes to funding and budgeting processes, you threaten existing power structures and political constructs within your organization. For example, one of the key benefits of SOA is the sharing and reuse of services. Sharing and reusing services has a number of funding, budgeting, and control implications:

- Sharing my service means my organization will incur increased support and infrastructure costs. How will my organization recoup the costs for increased usage of my services beyond the initial demand we originally planned for?
- Reusing another organization's service means I may lose the budget allocated to my organization for similar requirements. Budget authority is a measure of power, stature, and authority in my organization. Thus, why would I voluntarily diminish my power and stature?
- If I rely on another organization's service, how will they ensure my requirements are satisfied, and how will they ensure my service level agreements, quality of service, and performance requirements are met? How will they guarantee this performance? What is my alternative if they cannot meet my requirements? What penalties can I impose?
- What incentives (financial and otherwise) can we implement to encourage sharing and reuse of services? Can a budget be established for these scenarios?
- How can we incentivize the adoption of services through a funding pool that encourages sharing of services?

SOA funding and budgeting is fundamental to realizing many of the business benefits of SOA, and thus is intimately tied to the success of SOA governance. Adequate funding and budgeting is essential to establishing a multi-year program that will realize SOA value, as well as to supporting the incentive models for SOA, sharing, and reuse.

Governance Performance Management and Evolution

Governance Performance Management (GPM) is a new discipline in the making. Governance Performance Management is the ongoing corporate process and capability for sustaining SOA governance, evolving and adapting governance as the organization changes and matures, and establishing ongoing processes of policy definition, management, provisioning, and enforcement.

Governance Performance Management transforms the usual treatment of governance as a milestone event or a management check box into an ongoing strategic management activity with direct bearing on corporate financial performance. Activities in the process of Governance Performance Management minimally include:

- Governance process management, execution and facilitation, and communication
- Governance metrics, performance management, and reporting
- Governance change management, evolution, and sustainment
- Governance policy definition, management, enforcement, versioning, and deprecation

As a new category of business processes, GPM will increasingly become a management discipline in organizations, with its own executive leadership and accountability for all facets of governance, from corporate and regulatory oversight to IT governance and SOA governance.

SOA Policy Definition Enforcement Dimension (Vertical)

The SOA Governance Reference Model depicts SOA policy definition and enforcement in two places, one directly linked to SOA governance strategy and goals, and the second one as a vertical slice that spans all the other dimensions. This second vertical policy slice is intended to ensure that you consider SOA policies at all levels of the enterprise—from the business and enterprise levels to the process, architecture, services design, and run-time levels. The concept of multi-level SOA policies will be described later. For now, bear in mind that any discussion of policies must take into consideration what kind of policy you are enforcing, and where in the enterprise it will be enforced. This is why policies must be viewed in this vertically oriented fashion—they span the enterprise and must be considered in that context.

Governance Enabling Technology and Implementation

This category includes the enabling technologies and tools that support SOA governance. While the governance tools and technologies are essential for policy-based SOA governance, they should not be the first decision you make in implementing governance. Thus, we place the tools in this layer of the SOA Governance Reference Model so that they and the technologies that claim to implement or support SOA governance are balanced in importance relative to the strategy, goals, processes, policies, and behavioral considerations of SOA governance. We will discuss various governance tools and technologies in detail in Chapter 9.

APPLYING THE SOA GOVERNANCE REFERENCE MODEL

The purpose of the SOA Governance Reference Model is simple and powerful. The SOA Governance Reference Model must be adapted to your particular organization and governance challenges by answering a few basic questions first. In order to structure enterprise SOA governance for the most effective outcomes, we suggest the following steps:

"Work" the SOA Governance Reference Model

As a way to get started, we suggest that you follow the decomposition of the SOA Governance Reference Model as we have described it in this chapter. Following the major categories of the model, establish key questions, statements and goals for each of the broad dimensions of the SOA Governance Reference Model. The first thing you must do for your governance initiative is to establish the scope of the inquiry.

- What is the scope of the problem?
- What aspects of governance are you focused on? Do the right things? Or do right things right?
- Is it an enterprise problem or a business unit level problem?
- What governance challenges are you hoping to address?

Per Exhibit 2.6, frame your enterprise SOA governance model goals, requirements and challenges by the major categories of the model.

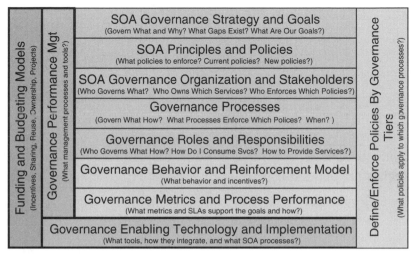

Exhibit 2.6 SOA Governance Reference Model

Develop an SOA Governance "strategy" document that is organized by the following chapters or sections:

- SOA Strategy and Goals
- SOA Principles and Policies
- SOA Governance Stakeholders and Organization
- SOA Governance Processes, Events and Reviews to Consider
- Governance Roles and Responsibilities, documented using a RASIC chart
- Governance Behavior and Reinforcement Model
- Governance Metrics and Performance
- Governance Policies and Policy Enforcement Model
- Governance Enabling Technology and Tools
- Governance Funding and Budgeting Model
- Governance Performance Management and Evolution

As you document your enterprise SOA governance objectives using the SOA Governance Reference Model, focus on the goals, challenges, obstacles, and general requirements for each of these topics. This will help you prepare for a detailed SOA governance assessment and governance model design process, which are steps covered in the following chapters.

Define Your Overarching SOA Governance Challenge

Defining the SOA governance problem domain is the next aspect of adapting the SOA Governance Reference Model to your organization. Key themes here include:

- What must be governed at this time? Why?
- What is the outcome you seek from more effective governance?
- Where do we think our current governance gaps are? Why?

Establish the SOA Governance Value Hypothesis

Another critical activity is to approach SOA governance from a deductive modeling approach, using a governance value hypothesis. What we mean here is to define precisely what will be improved based on governing your SOA better. What will better SOA governance buy you? How will you recognize the improvement? This hypothesis-based approach helps create a set of objective criteria by which you can evaluate the effectiveness of governance up front, and then adjust course as needed. The SOA governance value hypothesis must be specific enough to measure–one cannot simply state that better SOA governance will help. With a well-defined SOA governance value hypothesis focusing on more specific dimensions of SOA, we can establish a hypothesis:

If we govern X better, Y will be the result.

Identify Critical Organizational Dynamics

This is a simple exercise to immediately determine what potential organizational bottlenecks, political hurdles, contentious relationships, and overall organizational dynamics exist that can either be leveraged for SOA governance success or must be avoided or negotiated to prevent SOA governance failures. A detailed assessment will identify these relationships and organizational dynamics, but often a few direct questions to the sponsors will shed light on the current organization and its culture and relationship dynamics.

Focus on Elements of a Total Governance Model

As you frame the enterprise SOA governance challenges of your organization, consider the following elements of a complete enterprise governance model:

- **Governance Strategy, Scope, and Philosophy.** What you are governing and why? Describe your overall approach to governance? What "style" or "culture" will your governance require (e.g., command and control, collaboration, community model, market exchange?)?
- **Governance Stakeholder Model.** What groups or organizations should be represented in key IT and SOA decisions? (Stakeholders for this step should consist of organizations, groups, or roles, and not individuals.)
- **Governance Goals, Principles, and Policies (Policy Model).** What are the governance goals? Are principles and policies documented, aligned with business goals, and used to make decisions? Are policies enforced? Are they detailed enough to be enforced?
- **Policy Enforcement Model (PEM)/Policy Provisioning Model (PPM).** Provisioning and allocation or assignment of polices to various policy enforcement mechanisms, including processes and reviews, governance boards, or automated tools. Policy provisioning and policy enforcement are relatively new concepts in the industry, but are essential in migrating to a holistic model of governance based on policies rather than guidance or decree.
- **Governance Processes, Events and Reviews.** What processes help enforce policies? What are the various governance processes that actually implement policies or enforce policies? How are multiple processes linked together into a "governance thread" that enforces a policy at multiple enforcement points in an organization? What activities, events, and triggers cause policies to be enforced? How are policies enforced across various governance processes?
- **Governance Organizational Model.** How to governance boards enforce policies and manage exceptions? Do you have necessary decision boards and committees that represent stakeholders? Is the stakeholder model representative of the entire organization, or the scope of the governance decisions? Does the board provide forums for gaining stakeholder input, reviews, approval/sign-off, and ongoing policy enforcement, exception management, waivers, escalation, and appeals?
- **Governance Enabling Technology and Tools.** How can governance tools enforce policies automatically, such as at run time? How can various governance tools and enabling technology solutions be deployed to support, complement, or automate enforcement of various types of policies?
- **Governance Exception, Waiver and Escalation Process.** How will exceptions and waivers be handled? How will escalations and appeals be managed? Who has final say for key decisions that may be controversial? How will you learn from exceptions (e.g., add new policies, update old or ineffective policies)?

- **Governance Metrics and Behavioral Model.** What metrics, monitoring, and visibility mechanisms will be used to determine the effectiveness of your governance model? How will you gather data? How will you tie metrics and performance to organizational and individual behavior? How will incentives and rewards be incorporated into the governance metrics and feedback models?
- **Governance Feedback and Review Process.** How will you obtain feedback from governance stakeholders and participants on the effectiveness and value of governance? What feedback processes will be used? What management and process reviews will be used to continually assess and refine the governance model?
- **Governance Communication Model.** How will new policies and updated policies be communicated to stakeholders and affected organizations? Will there be a collaboration process for two-way interaction between policy boards and consumers of policies?
- **Governance Performance Management and Sustainment.** How will governance be established and maintained as an ongoing competency rather than as a milestone to be checked off a list? What sustaining processes will endure beyond the initial preparation, implementation, and roll-out of SOA governance? How will policies, processes, and organizational models be tuned, refined, and adapted to your gradual SOA maturation?

These SOA Governance model elements are explained in great detail in Chapters 4 and 5. As you answer the questions above using the SOA Governance Reference Model, review these key SOA Governance Model elements and think about how you will address them during your assessment and model design activities. This should help you establish an environment and governance process that is complete, enterprise scale, and enables the total fulfillment of your SOA business objectives.

SUMMARY

This chapter presented a SOA Governance Reference Model to frame the total enterprise SOA governance challenge for you. By breaking governance down into the fundamental elements of the SOA Governance Reference Model, we hope to simplify your assessment, analysis, and design of your enterprise SOA governance model. The value in this model is focusing you on the key dimensions of SOA governance, while balancing your natural impulse to buy governance tools and technologies with the absolute necessity to define your overall SOA governance requirements, organizational models, processes, and policies. The SOA Governance Reference Model may be tailored to your organization or circumstances, although we feel it represents a holistic abstracted representation of an enterprise SOA governance framework. In the chapters that follow, we will expand on the SOA Governance Reference Model to develop a repeatable framework for the assessment, analysis, and design of your target SOA governance model.

Notes

1. Developed by AgilePath Corporation.
2. Eric Marks and Michael Bell, *Service-Oriented Architecture: A Planning and Implementation Guide for Business and Technology*, John Wiley & Sons, 2006.

CHAPTER 3

Four Tiers of SOA Governance

This chapter presents a four-tier view of the Service-Oriented Architecture (SOA) *Governance Reference Model*^{TM} discussed in Chapter 2. The four-tier model is not a replacement of the SOA Governance Reference Model, but instead represents a more functional, process-driven view of an enterprise SOA governance. The four tiers are organized as (see also Exhibit 3.1):

1. Enterprise/Strategic Governance
2. SOA Operating Model Governance
3. SOA/Services Development Lifecycle Governance, and
4. SOA Governance Technology and Tools

The four tiers consist of three governance process tiers and a governance technology tier. The process tiers help place emphasis on the many processes that are related and involved in all forms of enterprise governance— corporate governance, Information Technology (IT) governance, and SOA governance. It is essential for you to understand the variety and relationships among various governance processes *prior* to acquiring SOA governance technology and tools. A thorough SOA governance assessment and gap analysis will identify governance requirements, governance gaps, and then lead to an action plan to close those critical gaps.

This four-tier view of enterprise SOA governance is also instructive because it helps break governance into an enterprise, and therefore strategic, view, as well as identifies the supporting processes that lead to the implementation of the strategic intent of the organization. The Enterprise/ Strategic view is based on strategic planning processes and/or enterprise governance activities, or determining what to do in a given strategy execution year through various strategic initiatives, programs and projects. From our SOA governance definition, these activities are focused on "doing the right things" for the SOA stakeholders. These activities set strategic direction, define the programs and initiatives that are being pursued as part of the strategic agenda of the organization, establish funding and budgets to execute these strategic programs, and provide oversight to ensure alignment

Enterprise/Strategic Governance

> **IT/SOA Strategic Planning, Funding and Budgeting, Business and Technology Alignment, Enterprise Portfolio Mgt., Enterprise Architecture, Tech Acquisition, Reqts and Demand Mgt, PMO**

SOA Operating Model Governance

> **SOA Opportunity Management, Service Portfolio Management, Service Realization and Utilization, Service Promotion/Demotion, Legacy Asset Retirement, Management and Process Reviews**

SOA and Services Lifecycle Governance

> **SOA Service ID, Modeling, Design and Development, Publishing, Discovery, Consumption, Composition, Orchestration, Operations, Maintenance, Versioning, Deprecation, Retirement**

Governance Enabling Technology

> **Design-Time, Publishing/Discovery, Runtime**
>
> Repositories, Registries, Intermediaries, Policy Engines, Distributed Enforcement Points

Exhibit 3.1   The Four Tiers of Enterprise Governance

of all organizational activities and processes toward the execution of these plans and the achievement of corporate goals.

Another view of these four tiers shows the Governance Enabling Technology tier as a vertical bar spanning the other three tiers. This modified four-tier view is depicted in Exhibit 3.2.

This is a more functionally accurate depiction of SOA governance enabling technology and tooling, as there are tools available today that span the Enterprise/Strategic Governance, SOA Operating Model Governance, and SOA/Services Development Lifecycle Governance tiers. We suggest that you place emphasis on the three process tiers first, and hold off on the governance tools until you have developed and implemented key SOA governance processes.

In the sections that follow, we will decompose the Four Tiers of SOA Governance into their respective governance processes and explain how they are related to one another. This overview will help your organization identify SOA governance gaps and determine what critical SOA governance processes are necessary to govern your SOA initiative right now. We will focus primarily on the three process tiers in this section, saving the SOA Governance Technology tier for Chapter 9.

Enterprise/Strategic Governance	Governance Enabling Technology
IT/SOA Strategic Planning, Funding and Budgeting, Business and Technology Alignment, Enterprise Portfolio Mgt., Enterprise Architecture, Tech Acquisition, Reqts and Demand Mgt, PMO	Design-Time, Publishing/Discovery, Runtime
SOA Operating Model Governance	Repositories, Registries, Intermediaries, Policy Engines, Distributed Enforcement Points
SOA Opportunity Management, Service Portfolio Management, Service Realization and Utilization, Service Promotion/Demotion, Legacy Asset Retirement, Management and Process Reviews	
SOA and Services Lifecycle Governance	
SOA Service ID, Modeling, Design and Development, Publishing, Discovery, Consumption, Composition, Orchestration, Operations, Maintenance, Versioning, Deprecation, Retirement	

Exhibit 3.2 Technology Tier Spans Other Governance Tiers

EXPANDED FOUR TIERS OF GOVERNANCE

Another view of the four-tier model is depicted in Exhibit 3.3. This expanded view breaks out SOA Enterprise Architecture activities into two "tiers"—one focused on the SOA "Architecture" governance requirements, and the other focused on SOA "Services" governance.

SOA "Architecture" governance refers to the SOA Enterprise Architecture activities and references architecture artifacts that focus on the overall SOA reference architecture, the logical and physical views of the SOA reference architecture, and the SOA platform architecture and specifications.

SOA "Services" governance focuses on the many dimensions of governing the services described by the SOA Enterprise Architecture process. Thus we would be focusing on areas such as the services reference model, the services layers of the overall SOA enterprise architecture, services design and implementation standards, interface design standards, payload design standards, service naming conventions, version management standards, and best practices for services identification, modeling and design, and implementation. While the services are integral to a service-oriented architecture, separating the services-centric governance activities from the architecture-centric aspects of SOA will help ensure better interoperability and clear separation of services from the platform.

A critical layer of the Expanded Four Tiers of Governance to focus attention to is the SOA and Services Lifecycle Governance tier. This tier

Enterprise/Strategic Governance

Strategic Planning, Funding and Budgeting, Business and Technology Alignment, Enterprise Portfolio Mgt., Enterprise Architecture, Tech Acquisition, Rqts and Demand Mgt, PMO

SOA Operating Model Governance

SOA Opportunity Management, Service Portfolio Management, SOA EA, Service Realization and Utilization, Service Promotion/Demotion, Legacy Asset Retirement, Management and Process Reviews

SOA "Architecture" Governance

SOA Reference Architecture, Services Reference Architecture, SOA Platform Architecture (the stack), SOA Logical and Physical Models

SOA "Services" Governance

Services Reference Model, Services Layers/Logical Model, Services Design Patterns, Interface Design Standards, Payload Design Standards, Runtime Standards, Versioning and Naming Conventions

SOA and Services Lifecycle Governance

Service ID, Modeling, Design and Development, QA/Testing, Publishing, Discovery, Consumption, Composition, Orchestration, Integration Testing, Operations, Maintenance, Deprecation, Retirement

Governance Enabling Technology

Design-Time, Publishing/Discovery, Runtime

Repositories, Registries, Intermediaries, Policy Engines, Distributed Enforcement Points

Exhibit 3.3   Expanded Four Tiers of Enterprise Governance

includes design-time governance, quality assurance and testing, and run-time governance for services and service-based applications. The SDLC governance process and activities is almost always an area of weakness as organizations embark on their SOA journeys. The Expanded Four-Tier Model breaks out the SDLC governance tier of processes explicitly because it is so critical to SOA governance, and because it is almost always inadequate for a SOA initiative.

TIER 1: ENTERPRISE/STRATEGIC GOVERNANCE TIER

The Enterprise/Strategic Governance tier includes activities that are typically performed at the enterprise or corporate level of an enterprise as part of the annual strategic planning processes of the organization. In addition, many of these functions are entirely or partially performed at the enterprise or business unit level in a federated or distributed organizational model. Federated governance adds additional complexities regarding the distribution and alignment of enterprise/strategic governance processes from the corporate enterprise to the operating business units. Enterprise/strategic governance is focused on enterprise-wide strategic planning, resource allocation and management, portfolio management, business and IT alignment, enterprise architecture, enterprise acquisition processes, and program execution oversight via program management office (PMO) supervision processes.

Enterprise/strategic governance processes may or may not involve IT. Enterprise governance processes may focus on compliance to regulatory requirements, such as Sarbanes-Oxley. Enterprise governance processes can focus on human resources (HR) or other personnel-related matters. Enterprise governance processes can focus on process portfolio management or other enterprise initiatives where stakeholder representation and participation is important for the success of a particular initiative. However, there are also enterprise governance processes that directly relate to IT and SOA, such as the annual strategic planning process for business and IT, and project and initiative planning, prioritization, and funding activities.

Activities that are part of the enterprise strategic planning process include business and IT strategic planning, enterprise requirements and demand management, enterprise architecture management, portfolio management (application portfolio, technology portfolio, project portfolio, process/capability portfolio, and of course in an SOA, a service portfolio), funding and budgeting processes, and project and program planning. These activities are performed annually during the strategic planning and budgeting process, and are then monitored or "governed" for compliance purposes to ensure that implementation of these strategic goals and plans follows enterprise guidance. Exhibit 3.4 depicts the governance and management processes we assign to the Enterprise/Strategic Governance Tier.

These governance processes are managed by corporate executives, performed annually with regular management oversight, and are directly related to funding and budgeting processes in most enterprises. From an SOA Governance perspective, many of the challenges of SOA governance derive from how well or poorly some of these enterprise/strategic governance processes are performed.

For example, most organizations do not have formal and robust requirements, nor a demand planning process that captures new business and technology requirements, evaluates and prioritizes these requirements,

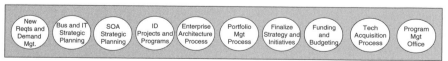

Exhibit 3.4 Enterprise/Strategic Governance Processes

aggregates this new IT demand into similar categories of needs and potential solutions, and compares these solution requirements against existing portfolios (projects, applications, technology, process/capability, services) to identify potential reuse and resource leverage for the organization. While most SOA initiatives claim to desire service reuse as an outcome, they normally do not have well-defined processes that link enterprise requirements and demand management first to portfolio management and then to an SOA and Services Development Lifecycle. How can you hope to achieve reuse of any enterprise asset without an explicit process for identifying its reuse? A process that begins with requirements and demand management, balances those requirements against existing portfolios, and then and only then, assuming no existing assets can be reused, issues a new service development request to your service provider organization?

By the same token, organizations with well-established enterprise architecture (EA) processes, in our experience, have a better innate ability to extend their EA processes, reference architectures, design and implementation patterns, and governance to the world of SOA and SOA governance. However, as with enterprise requirements and demand management, a poor EA process, or an organizationally misaligned enterprise architecture process, can spell trouble initially for implementing the SOA and services governance processes needed early in your SOA implementation.

Enterprise Requirements and Demand and Management

Enterprise requirements and demand management processes are organized to capture, evaluate, aggregate, and prioritize new business and technology requirements. This is sometimes a formal process in an enterprise, but is not a consistent governance discipline in most organizations. Enterprise requirements and demand management are often identified bottom-up through submitted projects and programs, rather than through a formal process of capturing and vetting new ideas and requirements from business units, individuals, and stakeholders.

The enterprise requirements and demand management process involves multiple activities as described below:

- Identify and catalog new business and IT requirements
- Analyze, aggregate, and prioritize requirements
- Organize requirements into programs, projects, and initiatives that support the corporate business and IT strategy
- Evaluate business and technology requirements and demand against existing resource portfolios to avoid duplication and achieve enterprise asset leverage and reuse.

- Satisfy enterprise requirements and demand through various fulfillment processes, such as new product development, new business programs, or IT projects.

Enterprise requirements and demand management processes are often informal and thus leave gaps in fulfilling various business requests for new technology, new capabilities, and new customer products. Enterprise requirements and demand management are critical for an SOA initiative because it is at this process where reuse of capabilities, processes, products and services is realized. While many executives state that service reuse is a critical driver for their SOA initiative, they often have no process of identifying and aggregating common requirements, a process which would directly reveal potential reuse opportunities. SOA and services reuse begins with requirements analysis and demand aggregation processes. In our experience, enterprise requirements and demand management processes are typically informal and weak, which limits enterprise visibility into needs and requirements, which then restricts reuse and portfolio leverage opportunities across the enterprise.

Annual Strategic Planning Processes

The annual strategic planning and budgeting process of an organization has a direct bearing on enterprise SOA governance activities, in particular because the business strategy, IT strategy, and SOA strategy all articulate and document the strategy, goals, objectives, and initiatives that will lead to desired business results for the organization. The strategic planning process defines what the right things are to focus on for the benefit of the organization, and it allocates resources—funding, personnel, technology, equipment and facilities—to programs and initiatives that are deemed necessary to execute the strategic plan.

From an SOA governance perspective, the strategic planning process defines the programs and projects that will be executed in the next operating year or fiscal year, in the context of some longer-term corporate strategy or vision. It will be through these programs and projects that SOA and services will be realized, and budgets and funding is allocated. As you ramp your SOA initiative, you must be able to position SOA as an enterprise initiative with program status, funding, and executive sponsorship. In the interim, you will have to opportunistically establish SOA and services at the project level as these programs are executed.

We will discuss the SOA strategy later in this chapter when we discuss Tier 2. The main point to be made here is that SOA must become integrated into the enterprise strategic planning process over time, but in our experience, given the immaturity of SOA in the industry, SOA is not yet positioned as an enterprise initiative. It must become so in order to realize the enterprise value of SOA.

Program and Project Identification and Selection

Related to enterprise requirements and demand management is program and project identification and selection. This process identifies all projects and programs that merit consideration for inclusion in the business and IT strategy, and thus require approval and funding. The annual planning process evaluates, prioritizes, and selects those programs and projects that will be approved, and therefore funded, for execution in the next fiscal or operating year. The salient difference between this process and enterprise requirements and demand management is the process by which requirements and projects are identified. Some organizations have neither a top-down nor a bottom-up model for gathering requirements and demand. Their programs and projects are often derived bottom-up only from profit centers or business units, and any potential synergies or reuse opportunities surface only post facto, when it usually is too late.

Another gap is project execution in a given fiscal year. Many organizations begin the fiscal year with a list of programs and projects that have been approved for funding. However, by the end of the year it is no surprise that perhaps 50% of the projects have been executed, and the other 50% were cancelled or replaced by other projects. This indicates a fundamental weakness in the linkage between enterprise requirements and demand management, strategic planning, program/project selection, and funding/budgeting processes. If a program or project is planned and approved during the strategic planning process, and subsequently is not executed during the calendar or fiscal year, then by definition there should be a negative impact on the business.

Another challenge with program/project identification and selection is the process of bottom-up budgeting. In large organizations and federated organizations, programs and projects are often originated from within business units or divisions, and then are aggregated upward into the strategic plan and an associated budget. The issue with this practice is achieving enterprise alignment to corporate vision, goals, and strategy. That alignment must have a top-down process that can identify programs and projects that align to, support, and implement the corporate strategy. Bottom-up budgeting and project selection may not lead to alignment of programs to corporate strategy.

Enterprise Architecture Governance

EA is a recent discipline, but one that has risen to the fore in recent years due to the emphasis on achieving better IT performance, return on investment, better business-IT alignment, and overall gains in business agility and IT flexibility. EA is the description of the current and/or future structure and behavior of an organization's processes, information systems, personnel, and organizational sub-units, aligned with the organization's core goals and strategic direction. Although often associated strictly with IT, it relates more broadly to the practice of business optimization in that it addresses business architecture, performance management, organizational structure and process architecture as well.[1] EA is both a management process and a documentation framework that provides an actionable, coordinated view of an enterprise's strategic direction, business services, information flow, and resource utilization.[2] The primary purpose of creating an EA is to ensure that business strategy and IT investments are aligned. As such, EA allows traceability from the business strategy down to the underlying technology.

Enterprise architecture is typically documented and managed along four major dimensions:

1. **Business Architecture.** Comprised of major business organizations and structures, business processes, and functional models of the enterprise.
2. **Application Architecture.** Comprised of the application portfolio of the enterprise, their interfaces to one another, as well as their business interfaces with other internal or external business partners.
3. **Information Architecture.** Comprised of the business domains and business objects, semantic models, logical and physical data models, and the data dictionary that documents the data architecture of the enterprise.
4. **Technology Architecture.** Comprised of the infrastructure, networks (LAN/WAN), computing infrastructure, telecommunications infrastructure, and all supporting IT infrastructure that supports and enables the other architectures.

EA governance is the process of enforcing compliance to the defined and documented EA, through reviews of projects as they are executed across the enterprise project delivery process or SDLC. These reviews occur across the SOA/Services Development Lifecycle as projects proceed from requirements definition through technical design, construction, unit testing, and eventual deployment to production. Exhibit 3.5 depicts a typical enterprise architecture process.

EA normally requires a process for development, management and change management, processes for maintaining various artifacts, reference models, policies and standards, design patterns, and more, as well as processes for communicating, governing, and supporting the implementation of the EA at the project or program level.

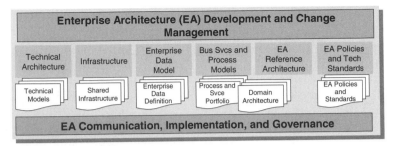

Exhibit 3.5   Enterprise Architecture Governance Process

Portfolio Management (Capability/Process, Project, Technology, Application and Service Portfolios)

Portfolio management is the process of managing a collection of assets of any kind to optimize return on investment and business benefits: physical assets, personnel assets, financial assets, and IT assets are common examples. In the context of IT and SOA governance, there are multiple portfolios that should be governed in an organization. These include the project and program portfolio, the application portfolio, and the overall IT or technology portfolio. The most common practice is application portfolio management. In reality, most organizations are not very good at portfolio management, which is interesting given the potential return on investment from portfolio management experiences.

Dennis S. Callahan, executive vice president and CIO of Guardian Insurance, and Rick Omartian, CFO of Guardian's IT group and chief of staff, claim that portfolio management has reduced their companies' overall IT applications expenditures by 20% and that, within that spending reduction, maintenance costs have gone from 30% to 18%, or a decrease of 40%. Eric Austvold, a research director at AMR Research, says companies doing portfolio management report saving 2 to 5% annually in their IT budgets.[3]

Portfolio management as a sustained enterprise discipline is not typically performed well in most organizations. In fact, most often it is not practiced at all. Portfolio management requires dedicated management staff and processes, and often, portfolio management entails reallocation of budgetary control to portfolio managers operating at an enterprise level rather than stovepiped management embedded within a business unit, a business region, or a functional silo.

In some cases, organizations attempt to implement portfolio management processes early in their SOA efforts, when in fact it requires a more sophisticated management and governance model than many organizations are prepared for. Again, to perform portfolio management properly, the organization must be able to identify the costs associated with various port-folios, and then manage those portfolios accordingly. To effectively manage those portfolios, rather than merely report on them, portfolio managers should have complete funding authority for their respective portfolios as well. Transitioning to a portfolio management model requires reallocation of personnel, budgets, and authority for those portfolios.

The following are typical portfolios that may be inventoried and managed using a portfolio management process:

- **Process and Capability Portfolio Management.** The process and capability portfolio is the total collection of business processes or capabilities that can be managed as core assets from a strategic differentiation or market competitive analysis process. By inventorying and managing corporate capabilities and processes from a portfolio management perspective, an organization can assess relative performance of key processes and capabilities and reallocate spending and funding models against that assessment.

- **Project and Program Portfolio Management.** Management of the total collection of programs and projects to provide visibility and oversight of the resources allocated to the programs. Project portfolios can be evaluated by risk, by technology areas (infrastructure, applications), by business units, or other useful views. Normally the project and program portfolio is managed by the enterprise PMO or a similar executive.

- **Application Portfolio Management.** The governance and management of all business applications of the enterprise as separate entities from the IT or technology portfolio. Depending on the enterprise, strategic business middleware applications may be included in the application portfolio. However, normally these will fall within the technology portfolio, described next.

- **Technology Portfolio Management.** Governance and management of the IT/technology portfolio, which includes all infrastructure, networks, and computing technology of the enterprise. This portfolio does not include any business applications, which are managed via the application portfolio.

- **Service Portfolio Management (see the Tier 3: SOA Operating Model Governance Tier section later in this chapter).** The governance and management of the services portfolio of the enterprise, which is essentially a services view of the enterprise. Service portfolio management requires establishing service domains for various classes of business, data and technical services across the enterprise.

Exhibit 3.6 is another view of Enterprise/Strategic Governance processes with various portfolio management processes identified by their respective "owners" in a generic enterprise.

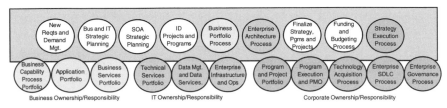

Exhibit 3.6   Enterprise Portfolio Management Processes

In this illustration, we break out business portfolios, IT portfolios, and corporate portfolios as follows:

Business Portfolios (owned or managed by business stakeholders with IT support or input):

- Business Capability and Process Portfolio
- Application Portfolio
- Business Services Portfolio

IT Portfolios (owned or managed by IT stakeholders with business stakeholder input):

- Technology Portfolio
- Technical Services Portfolio
- Information and Data Services Portfolio

Corporate Portfolio (owned or managed by enterprise or corporate stakeholders with business and IT stakeholder input):

- Enterprise Program and Project Portfolio
- Enterprise Program Execution and PMO
- Enterprise Project Delivery/SDLC Process
- Enterprise Technology Acquisition Process
- Enterprise Governance and Compliance Processes

As you consider building a portfolio management discipline and process into your enterprise, carefully study your needs and imperatives first. Portfolio management can be a complex endeavor if your organization is yet immature at supporting foundation disciplines, such as enterprise architecture.

Enterprise Funding and Budgeting Process

Enterprise funding and budgeting processes are critical for understanding the history of how things got the way they are in a given organization.

Enterprise funding processes validate in a sense the important initiatives and programs of an organization by actually allocating funding for those programs deemed worthy and reflective of the organization's business and IT strategies. There are two forces at work within the enterprise funding and budgeting process: what gets funded, and how important programs are funded.

The process of determining what gets funded relates to other enterprise/ strategic processes, including requirements and demand management, program and project evaluation and selection, enterprise portfolio management, and EA management. Based on vetting various candidate programs against these "filters," as well as evaluating the business case (or equivalent tool for submitting new projects and programs for funding consideration), candidate programs are selected for implementation during the next execution year, which may be a fiscal year or calendar year. Some initiatives, however, may be multi-year programs that require funding for two, three, or more years. Such strategic programs could include merger and acquisition (M&A) activities; multi-year IT programs such as infrastructure upgrades, data centers, or other large capital expenditures; or major business transformation efforts involving a fundamental makeover of corporate strategy, products and services, and even business models themselves, often supported by M&A activities.

The other aspect of enterprise funding and budgeting is *how* programs are funded. There are many "buckets" of funding available in most organizations, such as business operations, IT, strategic initiatives, and others. With respect to IT spending, many organizations break the IT budget into two broad categories: strategic initiatives or new initiatives, and maintenance and operations. Some call these categories "grow the business" and "run the business." Of course, there are very complex charts of accounts for the IT budgets and business budgets, and thus these are generalities. However, the funding decision often begins with "Who will pay for this?" and "Where will that money come from?" and "Who will benefit?" In most IT organizations, for example, 70 to 80% of the budgets are allocated to maintenance and operations, while 20 to 30% of the IT spend is eligible for strategic investments or new programs. Thus the competition for scarce strategic investment funds is fierce, and the accountability for business value is strictly monitored. In this sense, enterprise program governance helps ensure that projects are being executed as planned and that the funding is being used as advertised.

If programs stray off course, many organizations are able to leverage the funding process to realign the initiative. The realignment may mean rescoping the project, extending the schedule, or modifying the budget requirements. Of course, management may also elect to stop or reduce funding depending on the current perceived value of that program. The funding disbursement process is the governance mechanism that ensures programs perform according to plan. Many large programs are only funded assuming that they continue to meet governance requirements. Thus, if the project is a $1 million initiative, it may only receive an initial tranche of funding, perhaps $250,000, thereafter to be incrementally funded quarterly based on program performance. This is not uncommon for large programs. The relative size of programs also dictates whether they go through enterprise governance reviews as well. Projects over $100,000 in total value, for example, may have to undergo enterprise governance, while projects over $500,000 must be reviewed monthly. These governance limits help focus attention on mitigating risks and ensuring invested capital is used appropriately.

Relationship to Governance Processes

The funding and budgeting process is sometimes called the "ultimate governance mechanism." Enterprise funding and budgeting ultimately determines the relative alignment of programs and projects to corporate and IT strategy, as well as the IT strategy to the business strategy. The act of funding a program indicates that senior management agrees that the program supports business and IT strategy, that the program is important enough to fund over other initiatives, and that such a capital deployment is a worthwhile use of funds that might otherwise be used elsewhere to generate an anticipated return on invested capital.

Technology Acquisition Process

The technology acquisition process is the high-level process of meeting enterprise requirements and demand for new business, technology, and services solutions. The technology acquisition model is essential to understand as it relates to SOA and services, and more likely than not acquisition and procurement professionals will require training in order to begin incorporating SOA and services concepts into the contracting process.

The bottom line is that acquisition for "services" and supporting SOA tools and capabilities is different than acquiring packaged software, hardware, and other solutions. SOA acquisition challenges are similar to the challenges posed by acquisition of software-as-a-service (SaaS) solutions versus software licenses. These challenges include issues of such as service level agreements (SLAs), quality of service, maintenance and support issues, and related performance metrics. SOA raises the stakes for acquisition models.

Enterprise Program Management/PMO Process

Enterprise program management is the process by which large programs are monitored to ensure they are being executed according to plan. Program management is the execution process for programs and projects that have been approved in the strategic plan for implementation in the planned execution year, normally the following fiscal year. This process has strong ties to the enterprise funding and budgeting process, since large investments in high-risk enterprise programs will be monitored or "governed" to ensure appropriate use of invested capital and appropriate execution of the project plans. Depending on the size of the organization, there may be a PMO function established at the enterprise or corporate level whose responsibility is oversight for major enterprise programs of specific investment thresholds, higher risks, or strategic business impact. Similarly, in federated structures, the enterprise PMO function may run the enterprise governance process by which such large programs are monitored, as well as provide oversight for smaller programs that are being pursued within various operating units or business units within the organization. An extension of this model may include a smaller embedded PMO within the business unit to manage appropriate programs and projects at the operating unit level.

Relationship to Other Governance Processes

Many organizations assign the PMO team to manage enterprise software delivery processes, methodologies, and outsourcing relationships. In this mode, the PMO function is not only responsible for governing large programs, but it also implements and administers the governance process itself, including the SDLC process of the organization. The relationship of PMO to funding and budgeting processes should not be overlooked, as there is often a direct relationship between enterprise funding, program size, and PMO governance. The enterprise PMO function can play a critical role in managing governance activities across a large enterprise, and its potential role in SOA governance should not be overlooked.

TIER 2: SOA OPERATING MODEL GOVERNANCE TIER

The SOA Operating Model Governance tier is an important one that is often overlooked in organizations. SOA operating model governance focuses on development and execution of various SOA-specific processes and capabilities in alignment with the SOA strategy. These are essentially the

SOA extensions to enterprise and strategic governance processes that are necessary to manage and govern a SOA initiative.

We call it SOA operating model governance because these processes effectively instill a SOA operating model in a given organization, including repeatable execution of key SOA processes and disciplines to support the ongoing generation of SOA value for the organization. SOA operating model governance activities are processes and enforcement mechanisms that reflect your eventual "SOA steady state." Certainly most organizations will not have these SOA operating model governance processes in place early in their SOA adoption, but they should most certainly plan for them as there will be dependencies in migrating from your incipient governance model to a more mature SOA governance model over time.

Field experience shows that these SOA steady state processes are most often overlooked and, in many cases, are not even under consideration in most organization's plans. SOA operating model processes are usually neglected in favor of buying SOA tools as well as placing undue emphasis on the provider side of the SOA/Services SDLC process. A recent trend, however, is too much emphasis on service portfolio management when organizations have few to no services implemented, nor have they developed a robust service taxonomy model to categorize and specify the expected services within their enterprise. Exhibit 3.7 depicts the processes that comprise the SOA Operating Model Governance tier.

SOA operating model governance processes mirror many processes identified as enterprise/strategic governance processes. We like to separate them out because an SOA initiative is so important that it merits having its own SOA governance processes separate from enterprise/ strategic governance. It is likely that over time SOA operating model governance processes will be absorbed into various enterprise/strategic governance processes as organizational maturity and SOA capabilities advance. However, over the first few years of SOA strategy execution, we advocate keeping SOA operating model governance separate until there truly is a set of SOA steady state processes online and functioning properly.

Exhibit 3.7 SOA Operating Model Governance Processes

SOA Opportunity Management

Most organizations struggle with their SOA initiatives for one fundamental reason: lack of focus and misapplication of SOA principles. SOA opportunity management is the process of identifying the appropriate SOA opportunities across your enterprise value chain, and then focusing on execution of a few high-value, low-risk opportunities through which your organization gains experience and demonstrates SOA value. Ultimately, an SOA opportunity management process will provide an ongoing means of identifying, prioritizing, selecting, and executing SOA initiatives that support the SOA strategy and drive clear organizational value.

SOA opportunity management should establish two "roadmaps" for the organization: First, you should establish an *SOA Opportunity Roadmap*, which is a list of potential SOA opportunities that offer SOA value and pose relatively lower-risk profiles. This is not a service roadmap. SOA opportunities are larger than that, such as business areas, business processes, or large programs or systems that offer a major SOA contribution. An appropriate SOA opportunity could be decomposed into multiple processes and many services as well as multiple smaller SOA opportunities.

An additional artifact from SOA opportunity management processes should be an *SOA Anti-Opportunity Roadmap*, which is a list of business or process areas where SOA will not be pursued. Some organizations, for example, limit their initial SOA opportunities to internal services instead of externally facing customer services. This decision is often made based on the relative immaturity of SOA security standards and solutions. In financial services, many firms avoid applying SOA to high-volume transactional environments, where speeds and feeds drive the business execution model. In these opportunities, the processing overhead of XML Web services limits their usefulness for these high-performance areas of these businesses. Exhibit 3.8 depicts a model to help identify and manage your SOA opportunity portfolios as you ramp your SOA efforts:

The combination of an SOA Opportunity Roadmap and SOA Anti-Opportunity Roadmap, as well as a prioritization and evaluation scheme to help select the target opportunities, will help ensure the alignment of SOA opportunities to the SOA strategy and goals by repeatable criteria. The SOA Opportunity Roadmap and Anti-Opportunity Roadmap will also help you avoid higher-risk SOA challenges, which could derail a SOA initiative in its incipient stage.

SOA opportunity management is related to these governance processes:

- Enterprise requirements and demand management
- Program and project identification and selection
- Funding and budgeting processes

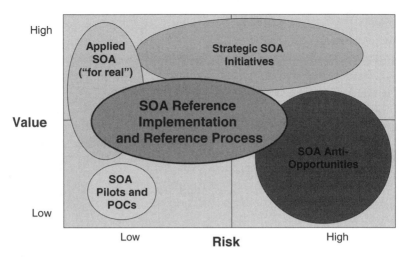

Exhibit 3.8   SOA Opportunity Portfolio Model

- Portfolio management
- Process re-engineering, modeling, and decomposition

SOA and Service Requirements and Demand Management

SOA steady state must accommodate the process of developing and prioritizing service requirements and services demand, and then feeding these prioritized services requirements into the SOA SDLC. Service requirements and demand management processes are essential to drive reuse of services in an enterprise. This governance process establishes a repeatable model for capturing services demand, balancing that demand against a services portfolio, and determining what new services are required to satisfy demand for those services.

Service requirements must be captured in ways that evaluate service utility and benefit to the organization from a service consumer's perspective, and yet balance service provider value through reusability and development efficiencies. Too often services requirements are established bottom-up and from a legacy technology perspective, which makes services very difficult to reuse and share as enterprise SOA assets. Service requirements should be identified in a manner that encourages broader perspectives and an enterprise view. As such, service requirements should be publicized and advertised for broader organizational review and comment prior to beginning services modeling and design. Announcing a new service and a requirements review/comment process will elicit shared requirements and help identify additional potential consumers prior to beginning construction. If new service consumers and potential reusers of services are identified early enough, there is a stronger likelihood of being able to generalize service requirements to encourage reuse and sharing.

Service requirements and demand management is an input to the service portfolio management process. Service demand must be reviewed and vetted against the existing service portfolio as well as the enterprise services roadmap to see if there is already a service available to reuse or extend to meet the new requirements, or if there is a service in development that can be used to meet the new services requirements. If there is not an existing service in the service portfolio, and there is not a similar service already in development, then the new service requirements must be captured as service use cases and the following decisions will be made:

- New service requirements are added to the SOA/Services SDLC backlog as a services work order, and the service will be built from scratch, or . . .
- New service requirements are added to the SOA/Services SDLC backlog as a services work order, and the service will be exposed from an existing legacy system, or . . .
- New service requirements can be satisfied by renting a commercially available service from an outside service provider, or . . .
- New service requirements can be satisfied by acquiring commercial software tools.

Service requirements and demand management are essential to formalizing the process of capturing new services requirements and aggregating that demand into reuse opportunities prior to beginning service development activities. Reuse of services begins with reuse of requirements and aggregation of services demand. When closely tied to the service portfolio management process and the technology acquisition process, service requirements can become the driving force for enterprise reuse and optimized asset leverage for the organization.

Service Candidate Identification

SOA governance ultimately facilitates the creation and consumption of services, which are the substrate of a SOA initiative. Identifying candidate services is often a difficult challenge for many organizations, primarily due to a lack of SOA methodologies and approaches that allow for various types of services to be built and integrated into an overall SOA reference architecture. There are a number of ways to identify candidate services, including process modeling and decomposition approaches, entity data modeling and core entity modeling techniques, ontological and semantic approaches, and legacy services enablement.

Often, process-centric approaches are the preferred approach based on the tendencies or predilections of the SOA core team. However, a data-centric approach to services is also very common, based on either a core entity modeling approach or a semantic ontology-based approach. These two disciplines—process-centric and data-centric—are two very different "cultures" in an organization, and thus they view the world differently. In an SOA context, the same dynamics hold true. However, there is a very clear relationship between the process-centric and the data-centric services approaches, which must be documented and understood by all SOA stakeholders. The connections are often based on processes requiring data based on process events and triggers, so the data-centric services approach should expose data services and map them to processes that consume that data.

Business and mission processes are the fundamental units of service consumption in an enterprise. Business processes can be re-engineered into service compositions, or collections of services organized to conduct business processes and transactions. Process re-engineering, process modeling, and process decomposition are essential SOA activities for two primary reasons:

1. Process re-engineering, modeling, and decomposition are critical processes for identifying candidate services in a top-down logical approach.
2. Business process management and process orchestration tools today are built to exploit discoverable services in a SOA context.

Therefore, business process analysis and modeling concepts are critical to both the analysis and decomposition of business processes into their respective services, and also to re-engineer and optimize business processes based on services and the business process management (BPM) tools available today. Ultimately, business processes will be composed of the available services in an organization, and thus the business process re-engineering, modeling, and decomposition activities will serve to accelerate the business process composition based on services once those necessary services are built or exposed and published into a registry for consumption.

Service identification and modeling is an emerging discipline in SOA. The challenges of services are well known, such as service scope and granularity, as well as various service implementation patterns. Many service identification approaches begin with process analysis, and we concur with this. However, rarely if ever do organizations perform extensive business process analysis for all of their business processes for the purposes of identifying and modeling their services in a SOA initiative. A more likely scenario is to perform business process analysis, re-engineering, modeling, and decomposition activities on those business processes that have been deemed as high priorities by the organization based on the SOA Opportunity Roadmap described above, as well as by their support of and alignment to the business and IT strategies. Therefore in this model, business process modeling and analysis will follow SOA opportunity road mapping, and will be a key step in the process of identifying services in an enterprise. Service identification and modeling should follow this top-down logical process based on targeting key business or mission processes, which again support key initiatives and align to the SOA strategy.

Service Portfolio Management

Service portfolio management is the process by which services and other SOA assets are leveraged to increase reuse, repeatability of delivery, and related cost savings from software maintenance and reduced application development. Service portfolios are groupings of "like" services based on a predetermined domain model, services city plan, or some similar service taxonomy and domain ownership model. Service portfolio management has one primary objective: maximize the reuse of portfolio assets while optimizing the number of assets in the portfolio. In other words, service portfolio management should provide the most organizational value possible through building, maintaining, and rationalizing the service portfolio, and ensuring maximum reuse of existing services. Service portfolio management is not an exercise in increasing the size of the service portfolio. Service portfolio management is an exercise in optimizing the portfolio to support maximal process consumption and organization benefit from services. The following activities are aspects of service portfolio management:

- Managing services as products
- Maximizing service reuse and enterprise consumption of services
- Prioritizing and triggering services work orders based on new requirements and demand
- Representing service portfolio stakeholders through requirements and demand management, enforcement of reuse, and retiring of services based on enterprise consumption
- Optimizing service consumption, minimizing service costs and delivering maximum total return services to the organization

Service Version Management

Service version management is an extension of service portfolio management focused on managing services through their lifecycle as new requirements are introduced, and as services are maintained, revised/updated, deprecated, and ultimately retired. Service version management requires forethought as to how major and minor versions of services will be introduced, as well as how the ongoing communication with service consumers will be managed to update them regarding new services, new versions of existing services, and the impact of modifications to existing services on their service-enabled applications and business processes.

Service Ownership Management

Service ownership management is an extension of service portfolio management focused on assigning and managing the ownership and stewardship of services as they are built, consumed, managed, and retired over time. The first responsibility under this governance activity is to assign preliminary ownership to classes of services based on some kind of enterprise services taxonomy. Typically, this is a layered view of services that is associated with the SOA enterprise architecture artifacts. Exhibit 3.9 is an example.

A service taxonomy model is useful for two fundamental purposes: First, it identifies the service "layers" as part of the SOA enterprise architecture process and artifacts you must develop to establish baseline architecture governance for your SOA initiative.

Second, a service taxonomy model helps in identifying owners for these initial service "portfolios" as a launching point into preliminary portfolio management for services. The service ownership model will begin with one to few portfolios, normally owned or "governed" by the SOA core team until a more mature SOA effort is established.

Once the initial service ownership model is established and you begin building or exposing services according some your enterprise services roadmap, you will over time modify ownership and stewardship of services based on actual consumption and demand profiles. Below are some anticipated examples of service ownership:

- **Service Promotion to Enterprise Service Portfolio.** A service is built by a business unit and made available as an enterprise service, but is paid for and operated by the individual business unit. Over time, the service is consumed by many other organizations across the enterprise, such that the management and maintenance of that service is beyond the resources of an individual business unit. In this scenario, the service may be promoted to an enterprise portfolio with enterprise funding and

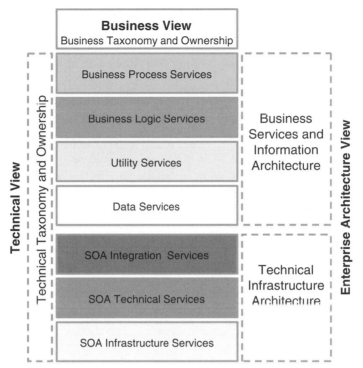

Exhibit 3.9 Service Taxonomy and Domain Ownership Model

support. Potentially, existing support resources and funding will also move to the new ownership model along with the service.

■ **Service Demotion from Enterprise to Business Unit.** The reverse scenario is where an enterprise service is mature and is experiencing declining consumption, to the point where perhaps only one business unit is consuming that service. The enterprise may elect to demote the service to a business unit service, and the business unit will have to fund and support the service going forward, since it no longer is a true enterprise asset.

■ **Service Portfolio Transfers.** Similarly, as your SOA matures and you have many services available, the ownership and portfolios of services will change and adapt as the organization changes and reorganizes. You must anticipate the process of migration or transferring services from one portfolio to another, either as peer portfolios or from enterprise portfolios to business unit portfolios.

Service ownership management will eventually become part of service portfolio management. However, a process or management model must look across all enterprise portfolios to ensure the appropriate ownership and stewardship for services of the enterprise. This responsibility cannot be embedded within a single-service portfolio, but requires instead an enterprise portfolio manager to determine the service ownership models that are best suited for your enterprise.

SOA Enterprise Architecture

SOA EA includes all SOA-specific extensions to the existing IT EA process of your organization. In the SOA EA case, this means developing the following kinds of artifacts for your enterprise to effectively implement services per an SOA strategy and roadmap:

- SOA reference architecture
- SOA design and runtime platform architecture
- Services reference model
- Service design and interoperability standards
- SOA data architecture, semantics, vocabularies, data models, schemas, message exchange standards
- SOA security architecture as an extension of your enterprise security model
- Service consumption models for various application frameworks (e.g., portals, composite applications, dashboards, rich Internet applications, etc.)
- Others as you see fit

The bottom line is that you must implement a process for extending the EA to accommodate SOA, including its subcomponents such as services, SOA platforms, tools and infrastructure, middleware, security, and so forth. The SOA EA must also feed architecture policies into a SOA governance model, as well as mechanisms for SOA policy definition, policy provisioning for enforcement, and enforcement at design time, run time and more.

SOA EA is a critical initial activity that will set the stage for all subsequent SOA implementation activities. Do not shortcut the time and effort needed to establish a solid SOA EA process and develop the appropriate SOA EA artifacts to guide your efforts and establish initial architecture and services policies.

Service Capacity Planning

Service capacity planning is a critical governance activity that must be performed early and often during the services planning and design processes.

We place this process in SOA operating model governance because we explicitly want the operations community involved in services planning activities, as well as playing a governance role during design-time governance reviews.

The service capacity planning process focuses on assessing service requirements and demand, and determining impact on current capacity, including compute power, network bandwidth, and storage capacity. Service capacity planning applies at design time as well as during service contract/SLA negotiations. This process should also receive data from services currently in production, including enterprise service management data on current consumption levels, SLA performance, and so on.

Service capacity planning, combined with service operations reviews, provide an operational input and governance view of services as they transition from planning into design, quality assurance and testing, and eventually into production. Your SDLC governance processes and reviews must explicitly involve the operations stakeholders to ensure runtime governance and total visibility to critical operational and runtime factors involved in building and operating services.

SOA Funding and Budgeting

SOA funding and budgeting is an SOA-specific offshoot of enterprise funding and budgeting, but clearly with an emphasis on SOA initiatives, SOA platforms, tools and enabling technology, and of course, the substrate of SOA services. SOA funding and budgeting must establish SOA-related project and services initiatives as valid projects with unique funding requirements of their own separate, at least in the initial stages, from other IT and business initiatives. SOA funding and budgeting must consider three scenarios in general:

1. SOA initiative funding at an enterprise level, including SOA infrastructure, platforms and tools, as well as seeding the initial projects and pilots to begin the organizational learning process. These funding efforts might provide SOA messaging platforms, registries, repositories, and services management tools that are available to be leveraged by the business units without any tax or chargeback scheme, to incentivize use of services and SOA concepts.
2. SOA funding at the project, program, or business-unit level to encourage business- and mission-aligned efforts at the operating-unit level of an organization. Again, these funding efforts are meant to achieve focus, early learning, and rapid organizational value through quick wins.

3. Services reuse funding, which essentially helps to offset reuse through funding of the incremental costs incurred by a business unit expanding a service from a business-unit scope to an enterprise-level scope. This scenario can be implemented in a variety of ways. One model is to establish a pool of funding to fund service reuse deltas such as the scenario described above. Another model is to establish an SOA funding pool that can be accessed to fund any SOA requirements as long as they meet pre-specified conditions and support the SOA strategy.

There are other SOA funding and budgeting considerations as well. When more formalized service portfolios are defined and require portfolio management discipline, there will be an increase in SOA costs associated with implementing these roles and processes. In addition, assigning SOA portfolios may require migrating ownership of systems and other enterprise or IT assets, as well as their budgets, to the newly-assigned portfolio managers.

Furthermore, once services are being consumed and provisioned across the enterprise, there will be a natural promotion and demotion of services from the enterprise to business units, or vice versa. The inevitable service promotion-demotion cycle will also bring with it certain funding and budget transfer requirements. It is wise to plan ahead for these scenarios with a SOA funding and budgeting model, although implementing these processes will most likely be a few years away.

Service Realization and Utilization

Service realization and utilization is simply the process of going from zero or few services to many services assigned to various service portfolios, and then ensuring that those services are used and reused to drive organizational value. Service realization builds out the enterprise service roadmap that should be defined as part of an SOA strategy. Service realization and utilization together build out the enterprise service portfolio and ensure that the services that are built will be consumed. The service realization and utilization process is an interim process that will most likely be absorbed into other SOA operating model governance processes over time. However, early in the SOA initiative, this role is critical for ensuring discipline of service planning, execution, delivery, and consumption. Of course, no organizational value will be realized until services are consumed by business processes, applications, and organizations.

Service realization and utilization consists of three processes, which are critical early in the SOA initiative and most likely will be absorbed into other processes over time:

1. **Execute the enterprise services roadmap** to build targeted services that will be contributed via multiple projects across the enterprise. The enterprise services roadmap consists of service candidates, prioritized for implementation, as well as the services planned for implementation during the current execution cycle. These planned services will begin to fill out the service portfolio as they are provided and published into a services registry.

2. **Maintain the enterprise services roadmap** and the initial service portfolio until enough services exist to merit formal service portfolio management. This is a critical role early in the SOA initiative. We suggest that organizations pursue this model at least until such time as there are enough services across various portfolio categories that merit formalized service portfolio management discipline.

3. **Ensure consumption and reuse of services** being provided via the SOA/ Services Development Lifecycle (delivery pipeline). This aspect of the process is challenging because it is the interface between service requirements and demand management and the consumers of services in a SOA. However, it also serves as the gateway to SOA value by ensuring that services provided are indeed valued, consumed, and reused over time.

SOA Process and Operations Reviews

SOA process and operations reviews are just that—reviews of the SOA operating model, its constituent processes, and overall operations to ensure desired SOA results are being delivered. These reviews should focus on key processes that affect the SOA initiative, including Enterprise/ Strategic Governance, SOA Operating Model and SOA/SDLC Governance processes.

SOA and Services Management and Operations Reviews

SOA and services management and operations reviews are essential to ensure a well-tuned operational environment for SOA. These reviews focus on the infrastructure, services management, and runtime operations aspects of SOA initiatives, and are critical feedback mechanisms to service providers and consumers to ensure that SLAs are adhered to, that the enterprise infrastructure can support anticipated service consumption levels, and that there are well-defined processes that manage the progression of services from the provider side of the SDLC to the consumer side, with appropriate testing and quality assurance, appropriate security, and a provisioning model to deploy services into production.

From an SOA governance perspective, it is important that the SOA operations and services management personnel are involved in the architecture and services design reviews to ensure operational readiness for services when they are ready for consumption.

Service operations and management should be considered from both a service provider perspective and a service consumer perspective. Service providers of course have to manage and monitor their services for their consumers, and need the necessary processes and tools to ensure reliable performance of services per the service contracts. From the consumer side, reliance on external or internal services may merit adding additional monitoring processes to ensure service contract compliance. This is especially true if the service consumer is actually a service provider to another consumer or end-consumer in a value chain. Thus, they are both a service consumer and a service provider, and need appropriate service management and operations processes in order to fulfill their responsibilities to their consumers, and in order to monitor the performance of services they consume from their service providers.

SOA Strategy Review

SOA strategy reviews provide an opportunity to assess and refine your SOA strategy based on defined performance goals and SOA performance against those goals. In our experience, most organizations have not spent enough time developing an SOA strategy that is clear, documented, and actionable. Until an SOA strategy is developed and aligned to the IT and business strategies, there will be no strategic context under which services and SOA initiatives may be pursued and measured.

SOA strategies do not have to be intergalactically complex endeavors. However, they must be formal, encompass strategic context and business goals, and provide the business context for implementing SOA. Once an SOA strategy is being executed, the annual SOA strategy reviews can provide valuable feedback so the SOA strategy can be tuned and iterated based on actual results.

TIER 3: SOA AND SERVICES DEVELOPMENT LIFECYCLE TIER

The SOA and SDLC tier focuses on the processes that produce services for consumption by enterprise consumers. This chapter provides a brief overview, with more detailed coverage of SDLC governance following in Chapter 8. We break the SOA and Services SDLC into two sub-lifecycles: the provider side and the consumer side. This explicit decoupling of the

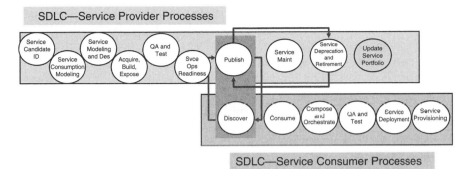

Exhibit 3.10   SOA/Services Software Development Lifecycle (SDLC)

provider and consumer aspects of the SDLC is important so that you understand that realizing the value of SOA is more than just publishing services into a UDDI service registry, or being good at the provider side of the SDLC. Achieving SOA value demands that services be consumed. Few organizations are mature with their consumer-side processes of their SDLC. SOA is about driving business transformation via consumption of reusable services, with the emphasis on consumption. No consumption of services effectively limits any potential value of SOA. Exhibit 3.10 depicts a generic view of an SOA/Services SDLC.

Provider-Side SDLC Processes

The provider side of the SOA/Services SDLC includes all activities from a service demand request (a business or IT requirement calls for a service that has not already been built). The following processes should be considered.

Service Candidate Identification   Services must be defined in the context of the processes that consume them or the information that services provide. One of the most popular methods for identifying and modeling services is through analysis of business processes, modeling the new process based on a services composition, and then transitioning into formal services modeling, design, and development. Normally we expect this analysis to take place prior to beginning service development. However, putting the process early in the provider side of the SOA/Services SDLC offers an opportunity to tune or validate the service process context.

Service Consumption Modeling   A critical modeling exercise early in the provider side of the SDLC is to ensure that planned service consumption scenarios are understood and well-defined as an explicit modeling task. Service consumption modeling ensures that all consumption contexts are under-stood prior to services design and development, whether a service is part of a business process execution language (BPEL)-orchestrated process flow, a composite service, or consumed by a composite application or a portal. Knowing the various consumption scenarios explicitly will force consumer-side thinking for services by the service providers. In our opinion, most organizations are not mature with understanding the consumer demand aspects of their SOA/services delivery processes.

Service Modeling and Design   Service modeling and design involves the iter-ative steps of transitioning from a service use case or specification to a tech-nical design for services. Services modeling and design involves all activities required to specify a service and smoothly transition into development or exposure of the service from an existing application. Service interfaces are defined, schemas and semantics are defined, service operations are specified, and service security is specified. Upon completion of service modeling and design, a service should be developed that meets the consumption model and also meets reuse goals of the organization.

Service Realization (Development, Acquisition, Exposure)   This step in the SOA/Services SDLC is essentially a decision step as to how the service will be constructed to meet the service demand request. Once the service has been modeled and designed, the specification can be handed to developers, who will build it from scratch or expose the service from an existing legacy or commercial application implementation. However, many organizations are looking at ways to acquire or implement services from third-party service pro-viders. All of these scenarios can be explored once the process modeling, con-sumption modeling, and services modeling and design have been completed.

Service Testing and Documentation   Upon completion of service realization, whether you built, exposed or acquired the service from a third party, you still must perform unit testing and provide appropriate documentation of the service(s) before publishing them into your service registry. Testing and quality assurance are critical aspects of the SOA/Services SDLC, and you must explicitly incorporate unit and integration testing into the develop-ment lifecycle. Documentation of the service entails providing metadata about the service, so potential consumers can determine at a glance what the service is, what it does, who the service provider is, and how to gain access to the service.

Service Operations Readiness   This process is a final review by the opera-tions team to ensure that services are certified, tested, and ready to go into production for their intended consumers. Based on the capacity planning process conducted during the SOA operating model governance process described above, the service operations readiness review should ensure that service design, quality assurance and testing, and other operations readiness criteria have been met before a service is allowed to be registered and made accessible to consumers via a service registry or some other means of discovery and advertising.

We advocate developing formal criteria for evaluating operations readiness of services, supported by requiring operations management stakeholder participation on architecture reviews, design reviews, and other appropriate upstream design-time governance activities as needed.

Service Publishing and Registration   Once the service is tested and documented, it must be published and registered into a service registry. The service registry provides the means for consumers to find and connect to services that they are interested in. The registry is the means by which new potential service consumers can discover all available services, by role and authorization, and negotiate service contracts with the service provider to consume the service for their particular business needs. Many organizations have mistakenly assumed that implementing a service registry solved their process requirements for registration, publishing, and discovery of services. While a registry and supporting repository are necessary tools to support design- and runtime service governance, they are only as good as the processes that they will support. Many organizations are good at the provider side of the SOA/Services SDLC, and most are not as good at the consumer side.

Service Version Management   During the provider side of the SOA/Services SDLC, the determination is made whether the service is a new version of an existing service or it is a completely new service. If a change to a service breaks existing service contracts, it probably constitutes a new service. If adding a new service operation is necessary, and it does not break current contracts, that might be a new version of the service. However you proceed, you must define rules and policies for minor and major versions of services, as well as for what constitutes a new service, and also define and implement mechanisms for communicating to current and potential consumers.

Service Deprecation and Retirement (and Update the Service Portfolio)   As services approach the end of their useful life—as they cease being useful to the organization or are replaced by newer or more functionally rich services—they must be smoothly versioned, deprecated, and retired to minimize the impact on existing service consumers. New services that replace existing services must be regression-tested to ensure processes and applications that are dependent on those services continue to function properly. SLAs and service contracts must be validated, and overall service performance and behavior must be ensured.

Service deprecation processes must establish dates for service retirement and the cutover to new services, and allow enough time for the consumer community to test and ensure their applications still function properly. Notification to service consumers of pending changes, new versions, and deprecated services must be sent well ahead of time to allow for regression testing of applications dependent on those services.

Ensuring smooth versioning, deprecation, and retirement of services will be as critical to SOA success as developing and implementing your initial services. Do not underestimate the criticality of service version management, notification processes between your providers and consumers, and managing the contracts between them.

Portfolio Management (Update Service Portfolio)   As new services are developed, the various service portfolios must be updated. Portfolio management processes are thus continuous processes, managing the portfolio from a capability, prioritization and funding perspective, inputting service demand requests to the SOA/Services SDLC services delivery team or organization, then receiving the resultant services as inputs into their service portfolios.

From the provider side of the SOA/Services SDLC, as new services are developed, tested, and published into the service registry for consumption, the services portfolios will be updated and these services will be managed as products. As service consumers provide feedback and new requirements, the service portfolio managers must aggregate new service demand and new requirements and balance these against the business and IT requirements, the available funding allocated across the service portfolio, and then make decisions for new service investments, maintenance, and updates to existing services.

Consumer Side SDLC Processes

As we have noted, most organizations are not as strong at the consumer side of the SOA/Services SDLC as they are with the provider side. This is a function of the early stages of many SOA initiatives being led by IT organizations without business or process input. As organizations mature their SOA adoption and capabilities, the focus will shift more to the consumer front-end of the SOA/Services SDLC. Below we briefly detail processes included in the consumer side of the SOA/Services SDLC.

Service Discovery One of the most critical aspects to incentivize consumption of available services is to advertise them to potential consumers via a discovery mechanism such as a service registry. Consumers, and potential consumers, must know they can go somewhere to find services that may potentially meet business requirements. And when they search for available services, they should be able to consume them, register with service providers and/or negotiate a contract to consume them, or try non-contractual versions of services on a trial basis.

The key to service consumption is discovery of available services. The key to reuse from a developer perspective is finding services that may be reusable. Discovery is the fundamental SOA technical capability that allows service consumption and reuse, which for many organizations represents one of the key value propositions of their SOA initiatives.

Negotiate Service Contract with Service Provider Once you have discovered available services that may meet your business requirements, you will have to contact the service provider to negotiate a service contract in order to consume that service. This is a key point that is often overlooked by many organizations. Discovery of services does not mean you can immediately consume them, especially for a mission-critical business or process requirement. Therefore, consumers must negotiate with service providers to ensure the service contract and service-level agreements are suitable for the consumer's business requirements for availability, response time, security, and even price. This overall service contract negotiation is a must in order to establish a trust-based contract between service consumers and service providers.

You must bear in mind that consumer–provider contracts are necessary between internal consumers as much, perhaps more, as with external service providers. Internal consumers must be extended the same courtesy and professionalism as are external consumers, or customers. Thus negotiating the service contract is not to be taken lightly.

Service Consumption Once the contract is negotiated between service consumers and service providers, the services can be consumed according to the terms of the service contract. Assuming those terms and conditions are met, the consumer-side applications, processes, and business needs will be met and life is good. The ongoing management of the relationship between service consumers and providers, as well as monitoring of service performance, billing, and maintenance, continues as long as the services are needed by the consumer, and as long as the provider can furnish the desired level of support.

Service Composition and Orchestration   Consumption of services can take many forms. The individual service in and of itself can be consumed by a portal, an application, or a business process, or by another service. Or the service can be orchestrated into a business process flow comprised of other services, or it can be composed into a composite service or composite application. Whatever the consumption context required by the service consumers, these requirements will have been negotiated with the service provider up front.

Quality Assurance and Integration Testing   While services consumed will have been unit-tested prior to publishing into a service registry, the composed application or process must also be tested in its entirety to ensure that the process or application behaves as expected. This level of testing is the responsibility of the consumer. As services are versioned and maintained by the service providers, consumers will also have to assess whether those changes will require regression testing for their consuming processes or applications. Again, this responsibility falls on the shoulders of the consumer organization.

Service Deployment   Service deployment is an important consideration for the reality of SOA and services. Service deployment takes into consideration the physical distribution and topology of SOA infrastructure and networks based on the actual business and mission context of the consumers. For example, if the services are consumed by a process where network bandwidth is constrained, what are the impacts on the service deployment? Should services be persisted nearer the consumers physically? Will there thus be duplicate services running, and therefore added overhead in order to manage this environment? What about the concept of federated service registries to accommodate similar requirements?

Service deployment is an additional step in the consumption side of the SOA/Services SDLC, where the reality of network bandwidth, latency, service performance intersects with the operational consumption of services to execute business processes and transactions. In defense industry applications of SOA, where war fighters at the edge are always a central consideration, the physical deployment of services and supporting SOA infrastructure impose additional demands on the planning, development, delivery, and support for services.

Do not overlook the consumption deployment dimensions of services. Be sure to consider where and how consumption of services will occur, and establish a robust service deployment model to satisfy these requirements.

Service Provisioning   Service provisioning is the act of allowing access to services that are available to be consumed. Service provisioning encompasses multiple consumption side processes in order to ensure appropriate service usage by authorized users, metering, and billing to track actual consumption and provide billing metrics for invoicing and/or chargebacks, and of course services management and monitoring to ensure proper performance of services in accordance with the service contract.

Service provisioning is an immature discipline in the SOA sense, but many of these challenges are being addressed by infrastructure vendors, software tools, and standards bodies. Web services security is a very broad area that impacts service provisioning, authentication, and authorization. Metering and billing are necessary as well, and many organizations are extending their Web services management platforms to allow them to tack internal services usage to support chargeback models. As your SOA maturity evolves, service provisioning will continue to move to the forefront of the list of challenges.

Services Operations and Management (Tie Back to SOA Operating Model Governance) Service operations and management are critical aspects of services consumption, although they are fundamentally the responsibility of service providers. Service consumers may have to implement services management and monitoring processes to ensure their service providers are reliable and that services are conforming to the service contracts. This is especially the case when service consumers are also service providers.

Process and Service Portfolio Management As service consumers leverage services to create new processes, business applications, and composite services, there will be portfolio management activities associated with service consumption. New processes will add to process portfolios. New applications will be added to application portfolios. Composite services will have service interfaces that will be added to service portfolios. SOA and services add new requirements for portfolio management that are more complex than before. Plan for robust portfolio management processes as your SOA initiative progresses.

TIER 4: SOA GOVERNANCE ENABLING TECHNOLOGY TIER

The final tier, the SOA Governance Enabling Technology tier, is detailed in Chapter 9. In Exhibit 3.11, we show the SOA Governance Enabling tier being expanded into a technology reference model for SOA governance.

The tools and technologies of SOA governance are detailed in Chapters 6 and 9, and thus will not be discussed here.

SOA Governance Reference Model v.2.0

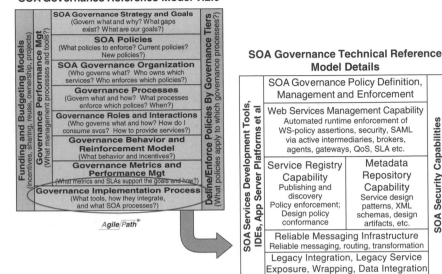

Exhibit 3.11 SOA Governance Enabling Technology

SUMMARY

The Four-Tier View of the SOA Governance Reference Model helps operationalize the concepts of SOA governance in relation to other enterprise and IT governance processes. The Expanded Four-Tier View provides additional detail as to critical governance focal points for the assessment and development of your enterprise SOA governance model. What should be clear is that SOA imposes and extends many enterprise and IT governance processes in order to manage the complexity of SOA and services. The SOA Operating Model Governance tier is meant to explicitly add SOA-specific extensions to IT governance. Over time, these processes will mature into steady state processes, and may even be reabsorbed into enterprise and IT governance processes. In our view, that is what we expect to happen as SOA becomes the de facto model for IT delivery in global enterprises. The Four-Tier Model will help you inventory your existing governance processes and capabilities, map those to various enterprise and IT governance processes, and determine what critical gaps must be closed to realistically implement SOA governance.

The processes we have described may be too fine-grained for your enterprise, or you may add new ones to augment our list. Regardless, enterprise SOA governance demands a holistic enterprise approach, while focusing on the key processes that will enable your SOA efforts to produce business value. Do not be intimidated by these processes. Focus on the few core processes that are critical to your enterprise.

Notes

1. Wikipedia, http://en.wikipedia.org/wiki/Enterprise_architecture.
2. Scott A. Bernard, *An Introduction to Enterprise Architecture*, AuthorHouse, 2005.
3. Todd Datz, "Portfolio Management: How to Do It Right," *CIO*, May 1, 2003.

CHAPTER 4

Organizing Your SOA Governance Toolkit

The objective of this chapter is to build your Service-Oriented Architecture (SOA) governance toolkit so you can assess your current governance model, determine your governance requirements for SOA going forward, and then devise an appropriate SOA governance model for your organization. This SOA governance toolkit will ensure alignment of your governance model to your business, Information Technology (IT), and SOA strategy, and map to your current stage of SOA adoption. Your SOA Governance Toolkit is comprised of two major categories of tools:

1. Governance Assessment Tools. Understanding the current state of governance through assessments, gap analysis, and SOA adoption maturity and SOA governance maturity analyses of your organization.
2. Governance Model Design Tools. Defining your target SOA governance model based on the assessment, gap analysis, and business goals.

These will be supported by governance implementation and governance performance management and evolution processes. All of these tools and processes will be necessary for your SOA governance journey. You must realize that SOA governance is not a single event or a milestone on a project plan. SOA governance is a lifestyle change for most organizations. Those organizations manifesting some fundamental governance competencies will have an easier migration to SOA governance than those without those competencies. Organizations without basic governance capabilities of any kind will most likely struggle with SOA governance.

This chapter will not give you all the answers, because the reality is that governance is still more art than science. This chapter will, however, provide some proven guidance for applying tools and techniques to implement SOA governance in your organization, aligned and tuned to your culture and business.

SOA GOVERNANCE ASSESSMENT TOOLS

The first activity you must do is capture the as-is state of governance in your organization. You will need to assess what your organization's current governance competencies and processes are, what you are governing and what is not being governed, and what the current state of SOA is in your organization. The following tools will be useful in the assessment phase to jumpstart your SOA governance assessment process.

SOA MATURITY ASSESSMENTS

We offer a variety of maturity tools for consideration in this section. You may modify these tools to suit your purposes, and you may also aggregate them into your own comprehensive assessment framework. The following SOA maturity assessment tools will help you understand where you are along a number of critical SOA dimensions:

- SOA Adoption Maturity Model (What is your overall SOA adoption progress?)
- Overall SOA Maturity Model (How evolved is your organization along various SOA maturity dimensions?)
- SOA Funding and Budgeting Maturity (How mature is your SOA funding process?)
- SOA Governance Maturity (How mature is your current SOA governance model?)
- Organizational Structure Diagnostic (How centralized or distributed is your organization, and where is it trending?)

Each of these is discussed below, and again, we offer them as possible tools for your toolkit. Use them only if they help.

SOA Adoption Maturity Model

A very useful tool for you to consider is an SOA adoption maturity model. This tool is used to assess your organization's progress in its overall SOA realization and adoption. Where are you currently? Where would you like to be by when? These maturity models will help define actionable strategic plans and objectives, as well as inform you of what sort of SOA governance steps should be taken. Presented first is an overall SOA adoption model, which quickly identifies where an organization is in its current SOA rollout. Are you just starting? Do you have a formal SOA strategy? Have you developed and implemented SOA governance?

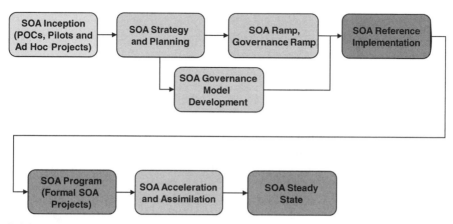

Exhibit 4.1 SOA Adoption Model

Exhibit 4.1 depicts major phases of SOA adoption, from SOA pilots and proof of concepts to SOA steady state:

- **SOA Inception.** Initial SOA pilots and proof of concepts (POC) occur in this initial SOA phase, where the emphasis is on early learning and gaining valuable SOA experience for your SOA core team.
- **SOA Strategy and Planning.** This phase follows the SOA inception phase and attempts to align SOA activities into a coherent strategy and roadmap for execution under the sponsorship and leadership of a corporate executive. Our experience from the field shows that many organizations skip SOA strategy development and instead proceed directly to the next phase, SOA governance model planning. We advise doing them in parallel.
- **SOA Governance Model Development.** This phase involves the assessment, development, and implementation of an SOA governance model that aligns to and supports the realization of an organization's SOA strategy, goals, and objectives. As mentioned above, often the SOA governance phase is started before an organization has defined its SOA strategy. Thus, the first gap to close in order to implement effective SOA governance is the development of an SOA strategy.
- **SOA Ramp and SOA Governance Ramp.** This SOA adoption phase is focused on preparing for the formal, programmatic execution of an SOA initiative in an organization. SOA ramp activities include training the core team; developing reference architecture artifacts, service design, and interoperability standards; specifying and acquiring the SOA development, testing, and run-time platforms; defining the SOA development lifecycle; and implementing SOA governance processes,

organizations, and artifacts. The ramp activities prepare the organization for SOA execution according to the defined SOA strategy and the oversight of the SOA governance model.

- **SOA Reference Implementation.** The SOA reference implementation phase is a milestone phase. Once the organization has done its preparation and ramp activities, it can begin to implement its first true SOA project. This project should be carefully selected, planned, and executed such that, on a small controlled scale, it represents your SOA end state. This is what we mean by a SOA reference implementation. It represents your end-state SOA implementation from a business, process, governance, and technology perspective, and includes or implements most or all of the many facets of SOA that you will require to realize the benefits of SOA according to your SOA strategy and SOA governance model. The SOA Reference Implementation phase represents a major milestone and a major organizational win if it is performed well, and will serve as the nucleus around which your team will iterate and expand its SOA capabilities, processes, governance, and implementations.

- **SOA Program.** In the SOA program phase, SOA has become a standardized and repeatable model for the delivery of business capabilities and solutions via services. SOA is being realized through programmatic execution of your SOA strategy. This phase represents the point at which the SOA strategy is being executed crisply and steadily as a formalized program. SOA governance is robust and guides all SOA activities from strategic planning through sunsetting and retirement of services. This phase represents when an organization should be delivering SOA value through rapid delivery of service-enabled capabilities, where reuse of services is accelerating, and where desired organizational benefits can be measured and demonstrated.

- **SOA Acceleration and Assimilation.** The acceleration and assimilation phase of SOA adoption is where the organization leverages the reference implementation to add new SOA capabilities and new processes, expands the consumption and development of new services, and accelerates the adoption of SOA by its IT and business consumers. The SOA acceleration and assimilation phase is where SOA becomes internalized by the organization as the primary means by which business capabilities will be enabled by the IT organization, and the primary means by which the IT organization will operate. This phase involves rapid iterations around the SOA reference implementation core, expansion of SOA governance, and achievement of a repeatable SOA realization model.

- **SOA Steady State.** By the time an organization reaches the SOA steady state adoption phase, the phrase "Service-Oriented Architecture" and the "SOA" acronym will probably not be in use anymore. SOA will have become the de facto model by which IT services are delivered. There will be no other model except for services. This phase of SOA adoption is a long way off, but it represents some point at which SOA is the clear and assumed model for business and IT. It will have become so ingrained in the organizational culture that services are just a natural way of architecting and delivering business solutions. At SOA steady state, SOA governance will be natural and infused throughout the organization. The SOA strategy will become just another aspect of both the business and IT strategies, and will not necessarily be documented separately anymore. At SOA steady state, the next big IT trend will probably be well on the way, and we'll be solving the challenges that the SOA wave created for us.

There are many SOA adoption and maturity models available. Use this one or pick one you like. Of course, if you are reading this book, chances are you are between the SOA inception phase, where you have completed proof of concepts and pilot SOA projects, and the SOA Governance Model Development phase. This simple diagnostic will help isolate your SOA governance gaps and anticipate challenges you may encounter in each of these SOA adoption phases.

Overall SOA Maturity Model

You can also assess your overall SOA maturity along the seven critical SOA dimensions listed below. This is a supporting model to develop a snapshot of overall SOA maturity based on the major SOA requirements. These categories provide a holistic view of your SOA maturity, and point to weaknesses or major gaps you can begin to address.

1. **SOA Strategy and Vision.** How complete is the SOA strategy? Is there a business vision for SOA, or is it a technology vision? Does it map to the future state, or is it anchored to today's challenges? Does the SOA strategy target business value?
2. **SOA Enterprise Architecture.** How have you extended your current enterprise architecture (EA) process to accommodate SOA and services? Have you developed an SOA reference architecture, and logical and physical views of it? Have you developed a service taxonomy and service design and implementation patterns based on your organization's technical and interoperability standards? Have your design, quality assurance and test, and runtime standards been specified as policies that will feed into an SOA governance model? Do you enforce the SOA EA as rigorously as your corporate EA process? (Our experience is that an

organization with a robust EA process will tend to have an easier migration to SOA than will an organization with a relatively poor enterprise architecture process.)

3. **Services Maturity.** What is the services paradigm for this organization? Is there a services taxonomy defined? How complete is the services vision? How many services do you have currently? How many are reusable? How many are consumed? Do you have a generalized concept of services, or are you only considering Web services? How does your services paradigm support your business objectives and SOA strategy? Is there a mismatch between your services concept and your SOA strategy?

4. **SOA Process Maturity.** How formalized and well-defined are your SOA core processes, such as your software development process or your SDLC, EA, portfolio management, and project management processes? How do you ensure SOA opportunities align with business and IT imperatives?[1] How are services identified and evaluated for reuse and business value? Do you have a SOA- or services-specific SOA SDLC defined? Is your SOA process repeatable and iterative? Can your SOA current SOA processes produce the desired business value?

5. **SOA Governance and Organizational Maturity.** Is there an SOA governance strategy? Are policies defined? Is there an SOA governance organizational model? How is governance implemented? What governance processes exist? Do they work? How are policies enforced? How are governance metrics implemented? Does the governance model affect and guide organizational and individual behavior?

6. **SOA Platform Maturity.** How mature are your SOA platform and supporting enabling technology and tools? What SOA technology elements are implemented or planned for design, run time, and governance? Does the SOA platform include the baseline SOA capabilities to enable the desired SOA value? Is the SOA platform mapped to and derived from the services roadmap, or is it more of a "build it and they will come" SOA platform model? Does the SOA platform align to and support your services paradigm? Does it impose vendor constraints or lock-in? Can you add or subtract elements without major refactoring of the run-time architecture?

7. **SOA Metrics Framework and Business Results.** Are metrics defined for SOA goals? Are the metrics federated (e.g., "SOA Balanced Scorecard?"). Do metrics reinforce the SOA strategy, governance model, and behavioral guidance? How are business results linked explicitly to SOA metrics? Have you realized any SOA-enabled business results? If not, why?

These broad SOA guidelines will help you assess your overall SOA maturity along key dimensions. You may find this to be a very useful device in determining your overall SOA maturity and capability. However, there are more dimensions within the SOA governance category to consider, as we describe below.

SOA Funding and Budgeting Maturity Model

Another diagnostic that may prove useful is to assess your organization's funding and budgeting maturity. Normally, we have observed that SOA funding models tend to be very immature in most organizations. Based on this observation, we suggest that you do not spend a lot of time on funding and budgeting processes early in your SOA initiative. There is lower hanging fruit on which to focus. Eventually you must address the SOA funding model for your organization, but that is best saved for when you have made more progress with SOA adoption, have business engagement, and have a more mature overall SOA profile.

Below is a simple SOA funding and budgeting maturity model you may find useful. It ranges from level 1, incipient to level 5, holistic. A level 1 funding and budgeting maturity rating is immature; a level 5 funding and budgeting maturity rating is mature.

Level 1: Incipient

At SOA funding maturity model level 1, *incipient*, an organization has given SOA no specific consideration separate from how it currently funds business and IT initiatives.

- SOA funding is only project-driven; there is no view of business unit (BU) or enterprise funding for SOA initiatives
- Pilots and POCs are funded by business units or projects within them
- No enterprise SOA strategy or funding model
- No SOA funding process or strategy

Level 2: Opportunistic/Ad Hoc

At level 2, *opportunistic/ad hoc*, an organization is beginning to think about funding SOA initiatives, but only on a preliminary basis. There is a recognized need to address enterprise funding for SOA platforms and tools, and there is also acknowledgement of the need to share resources and tools. However, no formal SOA funding models have been developed or implemented.

- Some common SOA funding requirements identified
- Distributed SOA funding dialog

- Opportunistic funding shared by enterprise and business units
- No consistent SOA funding model yet developed
- Ad hoc SOA funding model
- Informal process, no documentation

Level 3: Pooling of Interests

At level 3, *pooling of interests*, an organization begins to aggregate SOA demand into formal funding requirements. Multiple business units or functions are pooling their SOA interests and are requesting formal funding for shared infrastructure and tools. The SOA funding process is more formalized, and an initial business engagement materializes in the SOA initiative by virtue of formalizing the SOA funding process.

- Shared SOA requirements are identified
- Funding requested by multiple business units for shared SOA assets
- Process for funding shared requirements by business units
- Business sponsorship for SOA begins
- SOA funding model documented and budgeted

Level 4: Shared SOA Funding Vision

By level 4, *shared SOA funding vision*, an organization has a formal enterprise- and business unit-funding model. There is clear delineation of enterprise-funded and business unit-funded processes. The funding model is formalized, has executive sponsorship, and recognizes the criticality of SOA for business success.

- Enterprise SOA funding strategy formalized by enterprise and business units
- Executive business sponsorship for SOA initiatives
- Shared infrastructure funded separately from business services
- A federated SOA funding model is realized, where business units fund unique business services themselves, while enterprise business services and shared SOA infrastructure are funded centrally
- Multi-year funding for SOA strategy and annual review of SOA funding model

Level 5: Holistic

At level 5, *holistic*, the SOA funding model is explicit, maps to SOA strategy, and supports a federated SOA funding model. The holistic SOA funding maturity level recognizes SOA as a multi-year requirement and funds it as such. At this maturity level, the funding model is agile—funding and budgets can be shifted with the promotion and demotion of services from enterprise to business unit based on consumption demand and enterprise value.

- SOA funding model explicitly mapped to SOA strategy
- Clear ownership of SOA assets and funding allocated accordingly
- Centrally funded SOA infrastructure, business-funded services, and clear incentive models for sharing and reuse
- Multi-year SOA funding model
- Agile funding model supporting promotion/demotion of services
- Adaptive funding for emergent SOA requirements

SOA funding and budgeting is a complex topic and one that is fraught with political peril. While IT funding is a root cause issue for governance and SOA governance, we suggest solving basic governance challenges first, gaining momentum for your SOA efforts, and then addressing funding and budgeting when your SOA initiative and your governance processes are more advanced.

SOA Governance Maturity Model

Determining your SOA governance maturity requires a fine-grained view of various dimensions of SOA governance. As SOA governance is one dimension of overall SOA maturity, SOA governance maturity has its own sub-dimensions as well. In order to evaluate SOA governance maturity, you should consider the following major dimensions of SOA governance to assess and rate your SOA governance maturity:

- **SOA Strategy Alignment.** Is there an SOA strategy to inform SOA governance? Are clear business, IT, and SOA goals identified?
- **Goals, Principles, and Policies.** Are there clear SOA principles and policies defined? Are key policy categories (mapped to critical SOA governance gaps) defined? Are goals, principles, and policies related to one another in a clear policy mapping framework? Are business, process, and technical policies defined?
- **Organization and Boards.** What SOA governance boards are in place? Do they have formal charters and clear roles and responsibilities (e.g., defined by a RASI/RASIC chart?). Do they have clear policy enforcement roles and exception management processes?
- **Key Governance Processes.** Are critical SOA governance processes governed? Are there major gaps? How are policies enforced across all of these governance processes? Are key process gaps putting the organization at risk?

- **SOA Governance Tools and Technologies.** What governance tools exist today? What tools can integrate into a SOA governance architecture? Have tools been acquired in hopes of speeding your implementation of governance? If so, might they have become instead the centerpiece of a flawed governance strategy?
- **Policy Enforcement Model.** Are there SOA policies? How are they enforced? What manual and automated enforcement solutions are implemented?
- **Governance Metrics and Monitoring Process.** How will you define and track governance effectiveness? What metrics define SOA success, and what metrics define successful SOA governance? How will you know when governance must be tuned, adapted, or otherwise refined?
- **Governance Process Execution.** How will you establish SOA governance as a sustained and continuous organizational competency? Who will manage and execute governance processes? Who will facilitate governance board meetings, document results, and mediate conflicts?

Exhibit 4.2 depicts an aggregate maturity model for SOA governance maturity according to five levels of relative maturity.

This SOA governance maturity model evaluates governance on a scale ranging from level 1, *little to no governance*, to level 5, *optimized SOA governance*. Narratives below each level characterize where you are. For a more fine-grained SOA governance maturity assessment, consider the SOA governance maturity dimensions below.

Level 1: Little to No Governance (Undocumented)

- No clear governance model, process, or policies
- No accountability for governance; clear ownership and roles undefined
- Key governance processes (e.g., EA, IT governance) poorly executed
- Lack of IT alignment to business; poor business governance

> **Note:** All organizations have some form of governance, as they all make decisions for the use of IT resources across the enterprise. The fundamental questions are how formalized and documented are organizational policies and guidance, stakeholder representation, and transparency of decision making.

Level 2: Informal Governance

- Grassroots or bottom-up governance of key disciplines (e.g., EA, service design)

Exhibit 4.2 SOA Governance Maturity Model

Level 1 Little to No Governance	Level 2 Informal Governance	Level 3 Explicit Governance	Level 4 Collaborative Governance	Level 5 Optimized Governance
• No clear governance model, process or policies	• Grass roots or bottom-up governance of key disciplines, e.g. EA	• Transition to top-down enterprise governance	• Transition from top-down governance to enterprise participation model	• Governance is known, expected, and well understood
• No accountability for governance; clear ownership and roles undefined	• Semi-collaborative; driven by key players; not repeatable; "hero model"	• Policy-driven governance; clear principles and policies aligned to business goals	• Policy-driven governance; clear principles and policies aligned to business goals	• Some governance boards are retired as governance is ubiquitous; self-governance takes hold
• Key governance processes poorly executed, e.g. enterprise architecture, IT governance	• Working group model; not "owned" formally by an enterprise entity	• Emphasis on control and accountability versus "keeping the peace"	• Emphasis on collaborative accountability versus policing and policies	• Governance is enterprise fabric; culture of governance; behavior and incentives are aligned by governance
• Lack of IT alignment to business; poor business governance	• Key governance processes well executed; others are not defined or governed	• Clear ownership, enforcement and accountability for all key governance processes	• Emphasis on governance execution, enterprise performance, and collaborative decision making	• Governance evolves and adapts to changing business priorities

- Semi-collaborative, driven by key players, not repeatable or scalable, "hero model"
- Working group model, not "owned" formally by an enterprise entity
- Key governance processes well-executed; others are not defined or governed
- Relies on key relationships between people "in the know"

Level 3: Explicit Governance

- Transition to top-down enterprise governance
- Policy-driven governance, clear principles and policies aligned to business goals
- Emphasis on control and accountability versus "keeping the peace"
- Clear ownership, enforcement, and accountability for all key governance processes
- Often a difficult transition for most organizations as requires the enforcement of policies that previously have not been enforced

Level 4: Collaborative Governance

- Transition from top-down governance to enterprise participation model
- Policy-driven governance; clear principles and policies aligned to business goals
- Emphasis on collaborative accountability versus policing and policies; blends command and control oversight with community governance and collaborative self-governance
- Emphasis on governance execution, enterprise performance, and collaborative decision making

Level 5: Optimized Governance

- Governance is known, expected, and well understood
- Some governance boards are retired as governance is ubiquitous; self-governance takes hold
- Shift from policy to norms and from policy enforcement to normative behavior
- Governance becomes the fabric of the enterprise; a culture of governance exists; behavior and incentives are aligned by governance
- Governance evolves and adapts to changing business priorities

The SOA governance maturity model can be extended and customized for your own uses, and again, as with all of these tools, only use them if they

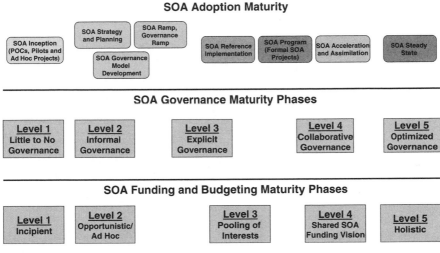

SOA Adoption Maturity

| SOA Inception (POCs, Pilots and Ad Hoc Projects) | SOA Strategy and Planning / SOA Governance Model Development | SOA Ramp, Governance Ramp | SOA Reference Implementation | SOA Program (Formal SOA Projects) | SOA Acceleration and Assimilation | SOA Steady State |

SOA Governance Maturity Phases

| Level 1 Little to No Governance | Level 2 Informal Governance | Level 3 Explicit Governance | Level 4 Collaborative Governance | Level 5 Optimized Governance |

SOA Funding and Budgeting Maturity Phases

| Level 1 Incipient | Level 2 Opportunistic/ Ad Hoc | Level 3 Pooling of Interests | Level 4 Shared SOA Funding Vision | Level 5 Holistic |

Exhibit 4.3   Composite SOA Maturity Summary

help you move forward with your SOA efforts. Do not use them to keep score; use them to inform and plan.

SOA Maturity Model Summary

Exhibit 4.3 depicts a three-part composite view of SOA adoption phases, SOA governance maturity, and SOA funding maturity. Again, this is a way to depict overall SOA maturity as part of your SOA assessment.

This overall SOA maturity map provides a snapshot of your current SOA activity and maturity. This is one view only, and you are encouraged to explore all aspects and tools that help assess your organization's SOA maturity. However, I will emphasize that maturity models are only diagnostics of where you are. They do not inform you of what you need to do from an actionable implementation perspective. If you like maturity models, use one. If you do not like maturity models, focus on the assessment and the target governance model design activities.

The bottom line is that SOA adoption maturity, overall SOA maturity, and SOA funding maturity will provide a fairly accurate view of where you are and where your focus should be to accelerate your SOA efforts in your particular organization.

Organizational Structure Diagnostic

Another useful tool to apply during your SOA governance assessment is to determine the current IT structure and where it is trending. This diagnostic

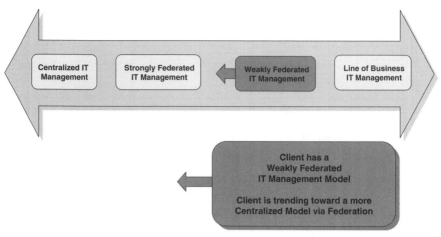

Exhibit 4.4 IT Structural Diagnostic

is a simple one as well, and helps identify expected tensions as organizations migrate from distributed business unit-centric IT organizations to centralized IT organizations, with various degrees of federated IT structures in between. Exhibit 4.4 depicts this diagnostic.

The major IT management models are described briefly below:

- **Centralized IT Management Structure.** All major IT decisions are made centrally by a corporate Chief Information Officer (CIO) or IT executive, including IT funding priorities, project and program investment decisions, business application decisions, and architecture and infrastructure decisions.
- **Strongly Federated IT Management Structure.** Central decision authority for shared infrastructure and enterprise-wide IT capabilities, while business application–and business unit–specific decisions are made by business unit CIOs. Business unit CIOs directly report to a corporate CIO, and report indirectly to the business unit executives. Business unit enterprise architects report directly or have dual reporting to a corporate enterprise architect, and directly to or indirectly to the business unit CIO.
- **Weakly Federated IT Management Structure.** In a loosely federated structure, there is central decision authority for shared infrastructure and enterprise-wide IT capabilities, and like strongly federated structures, business application–and business unit–specific decisions are made by business unit CIOs. However, in this case, business unit CIOs report directly to the business unit executives and indirectly to the

corporate CIO. Similarly, BU enterprise architects report directly to BU CIOs, and report indirectly to corporate enterprise architecture. Corporate IT has less control over business units, and decisions are more distributed.

- **Distributed/Line of Business IT Management Structure.** In a distributed IT structure, all IT decisions are made in individual business units to maximize business unit autonomy. Business unit CIOs enjoy complete autonomy for decision making for their respective business units, and report directly to the business.

The scenario depicted in Exhibit 4.4 shows an organization shifting from a distributed line of business IT structure toward a more centralized model based on a federated structure. In this case, the organization is weakly federated, and while the trend is toward centralization, the preponderance of IT decision making and control still resides within business units or lines of business.

There are naturally other configurations of IT management, such as geographic structures, project management structures, functional structures, and matrixed structures. These can all be mapped into this simple diagnostic. The real purpose of this tool is to assess the current tension level and trend of IT management structures. For example, if the organization is trying to establish more centralized control or IT management in a distributed or federated IT structure, you might expect political tension in the business units as compared to corporate. If a new chargeback cost recovery model has been implemented in the transition from distributed to federated or centralized, you can expect some tension and political push back there as well. This tool will help quickly identify any of these organizational and structural dynamics as inputs into the SOA governance model.

Conducting Your SOA Governance Assessment

A governance assessment is necessary to establish the following baseline information as inputs into your SOA governance model design processes:

- What is the current governance model of your organization?
- What governance policies are currently enforced in your enterprise?
- How are those policies enforced? What policy enforcement mechanisms are currently utilized (e.g., boards, process checkpoints or triggers, tools and technologies?)
- What governance organizational constructs and boards do you have in place? How many? What do they do?

This information will be obtained through a combination of documentation reviews, interviews, and team discussions with various stakeholders across a given enterprise. The nature of this assessment will vary based on business challenges and governance requirements or concerns that are driving the need for governance.

Data Collection and Documentation Reviews   One of the first activities in the assessment phase is to understand your current governance status. You will want to collect as much data as you can regarding current governance processes and activities. This need not be a painful exercise. You are just gathering data regarding current governance processes and activities, as they will have some influence on your SOA governance model.

Documentation Reviews   Gather as much information as you can that pertains to governance in your organization. If your organization is public, much of the data is available through annual reports and Securities and Exchange Commission (SEC) filings. If the organization is public, review the corporate governance model. Determine compliance activities for Sarbanes-Oxley and other compliance oversight processes. Review documentation of IT governance processes and determine the current state of those governance processes as well.

Interviews   Interviews can be very important for determining the existing governance landscape in your organization as well as establishing boundaries, barriers, and other factors that may impact your target SOA governance model design. We suggest developing a basic interview template, which may then be easily tailored to each major SOA stakeholder category, including business unit management, IT management, and even finance management.

The interviews must be structured to provide the following types of information to support the assessment of and development of your SOA governance model:

- Current state of governance in your enterprise
- What governance capabilities exist in your enterprise currently, including:
  - Current governance activities, processes, and mechanisms
  - Current governance organizations, boards, and committees
  - Current governance processes
  - Current policies
  - Current governance tools and enabling technologies

- Overall state of governance at the corporate, enterprise, IT, and SOA levels
- Overall perception of governance, its effectiveness and the culture or behavior it elicits from various stakeholders and participants

Identify SOA Governance Gaps From the assessment, you must identify gaps in your current SOA governance model. If you have no governance at all, you will have major gaps to close. If you have some governance on an informal working group basis, you probably need to formalize those governance processes.

You might perform the SOA governance gap analysis using the Four-Tier Model described in Chapter 3. Exhibit 4.5 depicts the Four-Tier View of Governance that will help you determine your SOA governance baseline.

Perform a quick assessment of your current enterprise, SOA, SDLC, and technology governance capabilities using the Four-Tier SOA Governance Model. Identify the processes, organizations and boards, policies, and enabling technology that fit into each of these tiers.

This brief exercise will help you use an existing framework to identify gaps and evaluate SOA governance process coverage. Exhibit 4.6 depicts a simple assessment graphic and shows how you might communicate your SOA governance gaps to senior management.

Enterprise/Strategic Governance

IT/SOA Strategic Planning, Funding and Budgeting, Business and Technology Alignment, Enterprise Portfolio Mgt., Enterprise Architecture, Tech Acquisition, Reqts and Demand Mgt, PMO

SOA Operating Model Governance

SOA Opportunity Management, Service Portfolio Management, Service Realization and Utilization, Service Promotion/Demotion, Legacy Asset Retirement, Management and Process Reviews

Services Lifecycle Governance

SOA Service ID, Modeling, Design and Development, Publishing, Discovery, Consumption, Composition, Orchestration, Operations, Maintenance, Versioning, Deprecation, Retirement

Governance Enabling Technology

Design-Time, Publishing/Discovery, Runtime

Repositories, Registries, Intermediaries, Policy Engines, Distributed Enforcement Points

Exhibit 4.5 Four Tiers of SOA Governance

Enterprise/Strategic Governance

Immature	Immature SOA strategies, poor business alignment

SOA Operating Model Governance

0%	Little to no consideration of SOA steady state model

Services Lifecycle Governance

Partial Competence	Mostly focused on development to publishing, not consumption activities

Governance Enabling Technology

Partial to Limited Competence	"Registry as Governance Fallacy" and "ESBs are the answer to my SOA challenges"

Exhibit 4.6 SOA Governance Four-Tier Maturity Assessment

You can use this format, supported by a variety of tools, to help communicate your current SOA governance capabilities and gaps, and then to help craft your target SOA governance model.

Prioritize SOA Governance Gaps Once you have identified the SOA governance gaps, you must prioritize them based on your SOA strategy and goals (assuming an SOA strategy exists and formal goals have been defined). Remember, SOA governance fundamentally ensures that the organization's SOA goals will be realized through the execution of SOA planning and services implementation processes. In our experience, most organizations have an SOA strategy gap. That is, they have transitioned from proof of concepts and pilots into a formal SOA governance model definition activity without investing time to explicitly define their SOA strategy and goals. In the first SOA governance gap is to develop a formalized SOA strategy.

Another consideration to bear in mind is that SOA governance gaps vary by relative SOA maturity as well as the stated SOA strategy and goals. Therefore, you must continually assess, review, and refine your SOA governance model, identify SOA governance gaps, and close those gaps by adding, tuning, or removing governance processes, modifying policies, and adapting governance boards and organizational models.

What are the SOA governance gaps based on your progress with SOA adoption? What do you have to govern right now to minimize risk? What governance processes must be implemented to support your immediate SOA requirements?

The prioritized SOA governance gaps will be used to develop the target SOA governance model in the next section.

Information You Must Obtain During the Assessment   Your SOA governance assessment activities must minimally include answers to the following questions:

- Where are you in your SOA adoption or implementation process?
- At what point will you have gathered sufficient SOA strategy documentation?
- What is your estimated SOA maturity?
- What is your SOA governance maturity?
- What are you governing now?
- What are you governing well currently?
- What is not being governed?
- What is not being governed well currently?
- What are your SOA governance gaps? What must you govern now?
- How will you prioritize the SOA governance gaps

These governance assessment tools will help you quickly determine the status of your current IT and SOA governance capabilities. This is essential in order to design and align an effective SOA governance model. Next, we will describe key governance mechanisms you have at your disposal as you consider your target SOA governance model. Chapter 5 puts it all together in a framework to help you structure your complete SOA governance model. In Chapter 6, we present the SOA goals, principles, and policies you will need for your SOA governance model. Chapter 7 focuses on governance organizational models to consider.

GOVERNANCE MODEL DESIGN TOOLS

Designing a SOA governance model is more art than science. That said, we offer this section as a body of concepts, tools, and elements to help you design the appropriate SOA governance model for your organization, based on the assessment process you presumably have already conducted. How effective an SOA governance model truly is hinges on how complete it is. Below are the elements of a complete SOA governance model.

Elements of a Total Governance Model

The following are elements of a complete governance model, with brief descriptions of each. This list comprises what we feel are the core elements of a total governance model.

- **Governance Strategy, Scope, and Philosophy.** What are you governing and why; what is your overall approach to governance; what "style" or "culture" will your governance take (e.g., command and control, collaboration, community model, market exchange)? Define the governance scope, which helps establish an appropriate governance stakeholder model (e.g., enterprise-wide, business-unit focus; process boundaries); the scope of governance stakeholder model will help ensure stakeholder representation in the governance process.

- **Governance Stakeholder Model.** What groups or organizations should be represented in key IT and SOA decisions? (Stakeholders for this step should consist of organizations, groups, or roles, and *not* individuals.) Who has responsibility? Who is accountable? Who supports the effort? Who must be informed? Who has review, concurrence, and approval rights? This model outlines the decision rights allocation process for the stakeholders of critical decisions.

- **Governance Goals, Principles, and Policies (Policy Model).** What are the governance goals? Are principles and policies documented, aligned with business goals, and used to make decisions? Are policies enforced? Are they detailed enough to be enforced?

- **Policy Enforcement Model (PEM)/Policy Provisioning Model (PPM).** Provisioning, allocation, or assignment of polices to various policy enforcement mechanisms, including processes and reviews, governance boards, or automated tools. Policy provisioning and policy enforcement are relative new concepts in the industry, but are essential to migrate to a holistic model of governance based on policies, rather than on guidance or decree.

- **Governance Process Model, Governance Threads, and Activities.** What are the various governance processes that actually implement policies or enforce policies? How are multiple processes linked together into a "governance thread" that enforces a policy at multiple enforcement points in an organization? What activities, events, and triggers cause policies to be enforced? How are policies enforced across various governance processes?

- **Governance Organizational Model.** Do you have necessary decision boards and committees that represent stakeholders? Is the stakeholder model representative of the entire organization, or the scope of the governance decisions? Does the board provide forums for gaining stakeholder input, reviews, approval/sign-off, and ongoing policy enforcement, exception management, waivers, escalation, and appeals? The governance organizational model includes details of specific boards, names of boards, composition, charters, chairmanship, and meeting schedules. The governance organizational model may be documented using organization charts, RASIC charts, swim lanes, activity diagrams, and process flow charts.

- **Governance Enabling Technology and Tools.** How can various governance tools and enabling technology solutions be deployed to support, complement, or automate enforcement of various types of policies?
- **Governance Exception, Waiver, and Escalation Process.** How will exceptions and waivers be handled? How will escalations and appeals be managed? Who has final say for key decisions that may be controversial? How will you learn from exceptions (e.g., add new policies, update old or ineffective policies)?
- **Governance Metrics and Behavioral Model.** What metrics, monitoring, and visibility mechanisms will be used to determine the effectiveness of your governance model? How will you gather data? How will you tie metrics and performance to organizational and individual behavior? How will incentives and rewards be incorporated into the governance metrics and feedback models?
- **Governance Feedback and Review Process.** How will you obtain feedback from governance stakeholders and participants on the effectiveness and value of governance? What feedback processes will be used? What management and process reviews will be used to continually assess and refine the governance model?
- **Governance Communication Model.** How will new policies and updated policies be communicated to stakeholders and affected organizations? Will there be a collaboration process for two-way interaction between policy boards and consumers of policies?
- **Governance Performance Management and Sustainment.** How will governance be established and maintained as an ongoing competency, rather than a milestone to be checked off a list? What sustaining processes will endure beyond the initial preparation, implementation, and roll-out of SOA governance? How will policies, processes, and organizational models be tuned, refined, and adapted to your gradual SOA maturation?

In our view, if you have a governance model that includes all of these elements, you will have a successful governance model that will more likely achieve its desired results. Absence of one or more of these key elements will put your governance model at risk.

Governance Model Design: Four Key Design Dimensions

SOA governance model design essentially boils down to four sets of tools, as identified below:

1. Governance Strategy, Scope, and Stakeholder Model
2. Policy Model
3. Governance and Policy Enforcement Model
   a. Governance boards and organizational model
   b. Governance processes, policy enforcement checkpoints and triggers
   c. Governance tools and technologies to automate policy enforcement
4. Governance Execution Model
   a. Governance exceptions
   b. Governance metrics and behavioral model
   c. Governance communication and feedback
   d. Governance performance management

Governance Strategy, Scope, and Stakeholder Model

Remember our definition of SOA governance: ensuring we are doing the right SOA things, in the right ways, for our stakeholders. The stakeholders on your SOA initiative are essential to ensure support, commitment, and eventual usage and consumption of services. Stakeholder involvement is a fundamental aspect of SOA and IT governance that is most often misunderstood. Governance is all about ensuring stakeholder involvement for key enterprise decisions involving allocation and distribution of assets, most often funding. Stakeholder mechanisms drive the governance model and the organizational model. If there are no stakeholders required to make a decision, you do not need governance. That is a management activity. If stakeholders are necessary to ensure alignment and concurrence with a key decision, then that is a governance activity, and a stakeholder model or organizational model is essential. The following activities are elements of developing the governance scope and stakeholder:

1. **Governance scope.** What is the decision scope of the governance requirements? Enterprise-wide? Business unit? Business region? Process or technology? What decisions or resources are you governing? What do we have to govern better to support the business, IT or SOA

strategy? The governance scope definition will help determine the stakeholder model used to allocate decision rights and enforce policy for key SOA dimensions.

2. **What stakeholders must be involved?** This defines organizational model and decision-making mechanisms, as well as stakeholder input, review, approval, and exception management processes.

3. **Determine governance scope.** Is our focus enterprise-, business unit-, geography-, process-, product- or technology-specific? What resources are we governing?

4. **Allocate stakeholder decision rights based on processes.** These processes might include stakeholder input, stakeholder participation (responsible; accountable; support; inform; consult), stakeholder reviews, stakeholder approval or sign-offs, and stakeholder communication.

5. **Stakeholder input.** Your governance organizational model must include decision-making boards and processes that provide a means for stakeholder involvement in key decisions. The initial stakeholder engagement process will gather their input for key decisions.

6. **Stakeholder review and approval.** Your governance organizational model must also allow stakeholder review and approval for key decisions, most often through governance boards of some kind. If key stakeholders were not involved in the input process, they must be involved in the review and approval process. We suggest you provide processes and mechanisms for both.

7. **Stakeholder sign-offs.** In conjunction with holding governance board meetings to obtain stakeholder input, review, and agreement for key governance decisions, you must also obtain sign-offs from those stakeholders as well. Sign-off processes put symbolism behind governance and demonstrate that the stakeholder representatives assigned to the governance process will take their roles and responsibilities seriously. Sign-off processes and documents can add important weight to governance activities in your organization.

8. **Stakeholder exception management.** One of the most important activities of SOA governance boards is managing exceptions. Exception management is perhaps the most critical dimension of governance to address; as how your organization manages exceptions will determine how effective your SOA governance process will be perceived by your organization.

The SOA governance scope and stakeholder model is an essential tool establishing the governance boundaries and stakeholder participation in key decisions. These are critical inputs into the other aspects of your SOA governance design process.

POLICY MODEL

SOA goals, principles, and policies are the beginning of your SOA governance model design process. In order for any governance to be effective, you must establish the policies that will be enforced in order to govern key processes. No policies, no governance. Without policies, it may be possible to achieve visibility and information sharing around certain governance domains. With policies, you can clearly define the parameters for all key governance concerns, and then enforce conformance to them. Policies, however, must be within the context of the organization's business, IT, and SOA goals. Policies are expressions and reflections of organizational intent, and thus must derive from the strategic intent of management. Bridging the gap between strategy and goals to actionable policies are SOA principles. Principles are essentially aspirational statements that reflect strategy and goals and facilitate decision making.

Chapter 6 provides a detailed overview of goals, principles, and policies, so we will not repeat them here. Suffice to say that your SOA goals, principles, and policies are the foundation on which you will structure your SOA governance model.

We will focus here on an interesting aspect of policies, and that is the decision around what policy enforcement mechanism should be utilized. The goals, principles, and policies process can be summarized as follows:

- Define business, IT, and SOA goals (from SOA strategy document, if it exists).
- Identify IT and SOA principles that support those business goals. These are broad statements of intent that align with and support the business, IT, and SOA strategy.
- Define policy categories that support or implement the principles. These may include:
  - Business policies (e.g., regulatory, Sarbanes-Oxley, compliance, outsourcing, vendor management, acquisition Health Insurance Portability and Accountability Act, and industry-specific policies)
  - Process policies (e.g., SDLC process enforcement, governance thresholds, governance enforcement triggers)
  - Technical policies (e.g., service design-time governance, quality assurance and test policies, service runtime and operations governance, SOA security policies)
  - Security policies (e.g., business-level security policy, security process policies, security policies at service design, and runtime security enforcement)

- Service performance and behavior policies (e.g., service-level agreements (SLAs), quality of service (QoS), mediation policies, selective versioning policies)
- Define policies that operationalize, enforce, and can measure relative conformance to the stated policy.
  - Generate policy statements for manually enforced policies
  - Generate policy assertions for automated enforcement of technical policies
- Determine policy enforcement model for all policies by policy category (e.g., business, process, technical, run-time, security, etc.)

Chapter 6 provides a detailed discussion of SOA policies and various policy enforcement models for policies. This high-level overview of the SOA goals, principles, and policies sets up the following discussion of policy enforcement mechanisms.

GOVERNANCE AND POLICY ENFORCEMENT MODEL

As you transition from the SOA policy model to enforcement of policies, you must consider three broad policy enforcement mechanisms for your enterprise: (1) a governance organizational model, including boards and committees; (2) governance processes, enforcement triggers and events; and (3) automated policy enforcement via governance-enabling technology and tools.

Integrating these three broad categories of policy enforcement mechanisms forms a holistic fabric of SOA governance and policy enforcement for your enterprise. Exhibit 4.7 depicts the concept of an integrated policy enforcement model.

The mechanisms must be integrated into a comprehensive and holistic governance model without being too oppressive and overbearing, and yet they must provide policy enforcement coverage for critical policies across critical SOA processes for your enterprise.

As you develop the policy enforcement model, you must consider two initial scenarios for various policies: automated policy enforcement via SOA enabling technology and tools, and manual policy enforcement via governance organizations, boards, and committees. These are the two extremes, with the potential for technology-enabled policy enforcement as a middle ground approach. The tools and technologies of SOA governance are very immature, and the industry standards for SOA policy are similarly works in progress.

Exhibit 4.8 depicts the bifurcation of policy enforcement scenarios into manual and automated enforcement approaches for related policies.

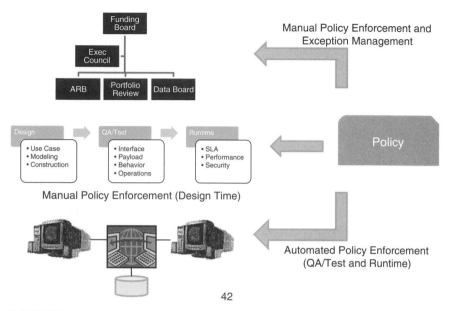

42

Exhibit 4.7   Integrated Policy Enforcement Model

Exhibit 4.8 depicts both manual and automated policy enforcement as two extremes to immediately consider. More interestingly, the exhibit demonstrates how related multi-level policies can be enforced both manually and automatically using tools. The example shown is SOA security, where

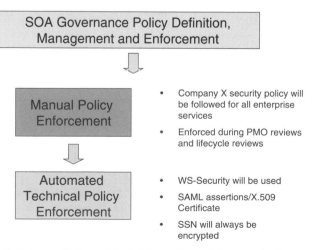

Exhibit 4.8   Policies are Enforced Both Manually and Automatically

enforcement at the enterprise or corporate level is mandatory for compliance purposes, and service security is enforced at run time via security appliances and supporting policy enforcement tools to enable reliable service access and operations for internal and external consumers.

As you develop the policy model for your enterprise, you will quickly realize that some technical polices can be automated, yet you may not have sufficient technology and tools implemented to support automating the enforcement of these policies. Examples here include service design policies, quality assurance and testing policies, and runtime enforcement of security policies, SLAs, and other policies. If you do not have appropriate tools implemented, you will be forced to manually enforce service design policies through architecture or technical design reviews, artifact and code reviews, and the like.

Similarly, for policies that are manually enforced, such as reuse or architecture policies, you will determine what processes and events will trigger governance boards and review teams to convene to provide oversight and policy enforcement for key programs or projects.

Once you have defined your SOA goals, principles, and policies, as well as the policy categories that help close key SOA governance gaps, you can begin to establish your SOA policy enforcement model. Enforcement of policies can be accomplished via a variety of means, much as SOA governance will require multiple approaches to implement. Again, some SOA policies will be obvious candidates for manual enforcement via governance boards and review processes.

Policy enforcement is established based on the types of policies you require to achieve your SOA governance goals and close the critical SOA governance gaps. In general, the following rules of thumb will help you frame your policy enforcement model:

■ **Policy Categories Will Determine Governance Enforcement Mechanisms.** In general, the type of policy will indicate how it will be enforced, whether manually through boards and reviews, or automatically, using governance tools.

Exhibit 4.9 illustrates how various policy categories are enforced using governance policy enforcement mechanisms.

Based on the policy category and type, this exhibit shows how you can begin to develop a governance policy enforcement model by assigning policies to be (1) manually enforced using a governance organizational model and board structure, or (2) using governance enforcement processes for some policies, such as architecture and design policies, or (3) using completely automated processes and mechanisms to govern security and service level agreements, for example, or (3) using completely automated processes

Policy Enforcement Mechanism	SOA Policy Category	Multi-Level Policies
Governance Organizational Model and Boards	Business Policies Process Policies	Security Policies Reuse Policies
Governance Boards and Governance Processes	Architecture Policies Technical Policies Design Policies	Reuse Policies Security Policies
Governance Enabling Technology and Tools	Design Policies QA/Test Runtime Policies	Security Policies

Exhibit 4.9   Governance Policy Enforcement Model

and mechanisms to govern policies such as security, service level agreements, or quality of service.

Below we summarize some of these concepts with policy enforcement best practices.

- **Business policies are manually enforced via boards.** Business policies will almost always require manual governance board oversight. These are very difficult to enforce using automated tools, and thus their enforcement is normally accomplished by governance boards, working group reviews, sign-off mechanisms, and the like. However, some business policies translate into fine-grained policies that can be enforced using tools, as in the case of multi-level policies. Be sure there is traceability between the higher-level policy and the lower-level, automatically enforced policy.

- **Process policies are predominantly manually enforced but can be automated or augmented by process automation tools.** Process policies can be manually enforced, and most often are, but many can be automated by augmenting manual governance checkpoints with business process management tools. For example, an SDLC can be automated with various checkpoints and reviews for a PMO process, but most often the SDLC is manually executed and thus the PMO enforces the governance process by ensuring projects go through appropriate governance at the required times.

- **Technical policies and design policies are often enforced manually and should be supported by tools.** Technical policies can be enforced using many of these enforcement mechanisms, and can also benefit from SOA tooling and run-time governance solutions. Technical policies in general are policies that are more easily automated than business policies. Most often, these relate to design-time policies for services design conformance, as well as run-time policies for security, such as SLA monitoring and enforcement.
- **Runtime policies must be automated for audit, security enforcement, and performance reasons.** Runtime policies are almost always automated since we are essentially running code and enforcing security, performance, and ensuring SLAs are being met.
- **Multi-level policies will mostly be enforced manually, and may require dedicated, focused governance boards.** Some SOA policies apply to all three governance process tiers of the SOA Governance Four-Tier Model described in Chapter 3. Security is one of these, as is a reuse policy. They both are examples of policies that are enforced as business policies, process policies, and technical policies. Thus, enforcement of these policies will require orchestration and coordination across multiple governance enforcement processes. This is a concept we describe as a *governance thread*. A governance thread is coordinated enforcement of a multi-tier SOA policy across multiple SOA governance tiers (i.e., Enterprise/Strategic tier, SOA Operating Model tier, and the SOA/Services Lifecycle tier). Governance threads are discussed in detail in Chapter 6.

The SOA governance policy enforcement model is a critical governance model design process. Getting the policy enforcement model correct will lead to complete policy and process coverage for critical SOA governance requirements. In the sections below, we explore various ways to design and implement your SOA policy enforcement model.

SOA Governance Policy Enforcement Mechanisms The remainder of this chapter will present a variety of governance tools and mechanisms to consider for your particular SOA governance requirements. With SOA governance, there is a finite list of governance requirements, but there are a host of different combinations of governance mechanisms and policy enforcement approaches that can work for your organization.

Your SOA governance toolkit includes a variety of governance mechanisms that all serve different and yet related purposes. You will end up using a variety of these mechanisms as you design your initial SOA governance model, and your organization will use others as it matures and its SOA governance capabilities evolve. This section provides an overview of the many governance mechanisms you have at your disposal. We have categorized these into functional groupings, but as you will see, there are overlaps here. Again, this demonstrates the art aspect of governance versus the science aspect of governance. At least we make it more scientific for you.

By way of introduction, Weill and Ross[2] identify three broad categories of mechanisms for implementing IT governance:

1. **Decision-Making Structures.** Organizational units and roles responsible for making IT decisions, such as committees, executive teams, and business/IT relationship managers.
2. **Alignment Mechanisms.** Formal processes for ensuring that daily behaviors are consistent with IT policies and provide input on which to base those decisions. These include IT investment proposal and evaluation processes, architecture exception management processes, service-level agreements, chargeback, and metrics.
3. **Communication Approaches.** Announcements, advocates, channels, and education efforts that disseminate IT governance principles, policies, and the results of IT decision-making processes.

Weill and Ross go on to declare five principles for designing and selecting effective governance mechanisms, perhaps the most important of which is to draw from all three categories:

Choose mechanisms from all three types. Decision-making, alignment, and communication mechanisms have different objectives. All are important to effective governance.[3]

A bit of commentary here: First, Weill and Ross have established an initial set of ideas regarding IT governance that were sadly lacking in the industry prior to their important work. However, in many regards, their work is only the beginning of the IT governance dialog, and many new concepts are developing, in part because of the intense interest in SOA governance.

SOA governance will place incredible strain on an existing IT governance model if you are not careful, and it most certainly will expose weaknesses in your current IT governance model. IT and SOA governance are more complex than the three broad categories of governance mechanisms identified by Weill and Ross. In fact, decision-making mechanisms are secondary to determining what key IT or SOA decisions require stakeholder involvement in the first place. Weill and Ross assume those decisions are universally understood, and that there are only five areas of stakeholder involvement (mentioned in Chapter). In addition, a separate category of governance mechanisms for alignment seems redundant or recursive, since governance is all about ensuring stakeholder involvement and alignment with key IT and SOA decisions.

Finally, Weill and Ross spend little time on the concept of policy-based governance, policy definition and management, and the subsequent enforcement of policies. While one of the key IT decisions relates to developing IT principles, often in collaboration with business stakeholders, they do not take this topic into the realm of policy enforcement. Governance is not only making decisions, but ensuring enforcement and accountability for compliance to those choices and decisions. This is an area that is emerging in the SOA industry, and one we spend many pages on in this book.

What we will advocate instead is a more complete model for designing, implementing and sustaining IT and SOA governance.

Governance Organizations, Boards, and Committees Establishing your SOA governance organizational model is a critical activity for your governance model. In general, most governance beginners will begin with the board structures and committees that will implement governance, yet they will not fully understand the entities' purposes and missions. Governance boards are not a governance model in and of themselves, as we have indicated. Governance requires oversight for decisions, and policies that guide or inform those decisions. Governance boards provide that oversight and also provide face-to-face opportunities for stakeholders to actively participate in the governance process.

A governance organizational model is an integrative element of governance that links governance processes and enabling technology to exception management boards via policies. In addition, the governance organizational model provides a means for governance stakeholders to participate in the governance process. Stakeholder participation is a critical aspect of the governance organizational model. Below are the roles and responsibilities of a governance organizational model:

- Integrates governance processes and tools with governance boards and stakeholders for decisions and exception management (people along with process and technology); implements an integrated "governance fabric" that blends all three policy enforcement mechanisms into a cohesive governance framework.
- Provides a stakeholder participation model for active involvement in the governance process.
- Provides a means to maintain senior executive sponsorship for SOA and for governance, which is a critical success factor.
- Ensures exceptions and escalations have a transparent and accelerated pathway for mediation and resolution via executive stakeholders.

As you can see, the governance organizational model is essential for
many reasons, yet we must be careful not to assume that the governance organizational model alone is the entire governance model. That is not true.
Do not mistake a governance organizational model or board structure with
governance.

In *IT Governance*, Weill and Ross identify six fundamental political archetypes from their research. These archetypes form the basis for IT governance decisions rights in Weill and Ross's governance framework. The six
political archetypes are:

1. **IT Monarchies.** IT-driven decision by individuals or groups of IT executives. Common IT-only decisions made by IT monarchies include enterprise architecture and IT infrastructure decisions.
2. **Business Monarchies.** Business-driven decision by individuals or
   groups of business executives; excludes IT executives acting
   independently.
3. **IT Duopolies.** Decision is made by IT executives and one other non-IT
   group, business unit, or process/function; excludes business or other
   groups acting independently.
4. **Federal.** C-level executives and representatives of business units; may
   include IT representatives as peers at the C-level and at the business unit
   level.
5. **Feudal.** Business unit owners, functional or process owners, or their
   delegates.
6. **Anarchy.** Individual users make their own choices.

These political archetypes are actually high-level governance organizational constructs that serve as entry points into SOA governance policy enforcement. These archetypes are really high-level stakeholder models that,
at least in Weill and Ross's framework, either provide input into a governance decision or make a governance decision. However, there are many
other considerations for your SOA governance organizational model.

Consider the following questions as you formulate your governance organizational model:

- **Will the boards be permanent standing boards or virtual boards?** Virtual board meetings are triggered by a governance event, while standing
  boards are permanent structures.
- **Will the boards meet on a regular schedule or only as needed based on a
  governance enforcement event?** Will they have regularly scheduled
  meetings? How often? If the board meetings are event-driven, what
  governance reviews or events will be cause to trigger a board meeting?

- **What will the boards do?** Make decisions and arbitrate conflicts and governance exceptions, or review conformance to policies and make recommendations to a decision board?
- **What will the composition of the board be?** How many members, from what organizations, and what roles or seniority will be required? Will surrogates or delegates be allowed?
- **Who will chair the board?** Will there be one chair, as we advise, or will you consider a multi-chair model, such as a dual-chair or tri-chair model, to enable appropriate stakeholder representation?
- **Standing boards.** Will you establish permanent standing governance boards for critical policies and governance decisions? If you do, these should be kept to a minimum and should integrate with other governance or oversight management boards that already exist.
- **Virtual boards.** Virtual boards are triggered by governance process checkpoints, triggers, or policy enforcement events, as dictated by your governance model. Virtual boards meet when necessary and are not permanent or standing boards. Often, virtual boards are cross-functional in composition and reflect the stakeholder model for decision rights for particular decisions or oversight of particular enterprise resources (e.g., funding, asset ownership, portfolios, etc.).
- **Working groups.** Working groups can be established at any time to focus on a particular challenge, policy, or conformance issue as it arises. Many times, a working group can focus on a specific technical challenge or project, in order to develop recommendations or guidance that a governance enforcement or decision board can enact. Working groups are temporary, often virtual, and will disband eventually. Often, working groups are useful in establishing the initial technical and design policies for services, as well as for specifying the SOA enterprise architecture and related policies. Once these are defined, the maintenance and ongoing enforcement will be performed by the enterprise architecture governance process.
- **Review boards.** These include architecture review boards and service review boards, or teams who perform reviews and make pass, fail, or exception recommendations to decision boards.
- **Decision boards.** These boards receive recommendations from working groups or review boards, and make final governance decisions.
- **Exception management/escalation boards.** What are the governance boards that will deal with exceptions and escalations, and will be the final arbiters of policies and waivers?

When it comes to designing a governance organizational model, take care that boards and committees are only implemented as necessary to provide manual policy enforcement and exception and escalation management processes, and to ensure stakeholders are involved in mediating governance conflict. Boards should be integrative and represent the stakeholder model.

Governance Organizational Model Best Practices

Governance boards are manual policy enforcement tools for manually enforced policies, mostly business policies and process policies. Structure and types of boards are not discussed here, but are covered in detail in Chapter 7. The following are governance organizational model best practices for your consideration as you develop your enterprise governance model:

- Boards typically must represent the decision-making structures of the corporation. Thus, an executive board will make funding decisions and be the final arbiter of escalations and conflicts. The EA boards will govern services design, SOA EA enforcement, and security policy compliance.

- Target for three levels of governance boards representing an executive board, a management board, and a technical or enterprise architecture board. Start with two or three "levels" of boards initially and test against the policy model for coverage of decisions and exception processes.

- Ensure the top board is a joint business and IT board, responsible for such executive decisions as funding and budgeting, conflict resolution, and portfolio management.

- Cross-functional boards are essential for business-centric governance decisions where broad stakeholder representation is necessary and they typically will include other business functions and disciplines. Cross-functional boards are critical for alignment and stakeholder representation.

- Ensure that portfolio management includes, or will include, business ownership of the business services portfolio.

- Do not go "overboard" with boards. Too many boards will render the governance model ineffective, overburdening your organization with meetings and making it less able to make decisions.

- Add working groups or domain teams as needed to perform offline reviews, evaluations, and recommendations to the decision boards.

Your governance organizational model is crucial for governance success. However, as we have cautioned, do not equate a governance board structure with governance. Governance boards are integrative enforcement mechanisms that unite policy enforcement with governance processes and technology. They provide a visible forum for stakeholder representation and involvement, and serve as a symbolic reminder that governance is a high priority for the organization. How the boards are named, staffed and the decisions they make will send a strong message to the enterprise that SOA governance is critical to organization's success.

Governance and Policy Enforcement Processes Chapters 2 and 3 provided many of the enterprise processes and management activities required for or involved in governance. These processes represent many of the governance processes and management activities that you will be facing in your enterprise, and offer a way to determine what gaps exist in your current governance framework.

Governance processes are either activities, or sequences of activities, that enforce governance, or they are IT processes that have governance enforcement requirements inherent in their execution. The governance process model provides coverage for activities and processes where key enterprise policies will be or must be enforced. We will focus on key governance processes and enforcement model design best practices in this section.

Establish Your SOA Governance Core Processes You must establish baseline SOA governance processes early in your SOA adoption in order to ensure success of your SOA efforts. Successful governance will provide management oversight and policy enforcement for these core SOA governance processes over time. In order to build your core SOA governance processes, you must focus on the intersection of project execution (e.g., PMO and project management processes), with your core project delivery methodologies and processes, or your SDLC process and delivery.

The reason for focusing on the intersection of project management is that you already have some degree of program or project oversight in place, and presumably you are reviewing enterprise architecture during these reviews. You also have a project or SDLC methodology in your organization that you follow for all IT projects. At the intersection of these processes will fall some of the most critical initial SOA governance processes, key SOA policies that must be enforced during project execution. These include the following:

- SOA enterprise architecture policies
- SOA technical policies for service design, data and schemas, interoperability standards, and runtime policies
- SOA and enterprise security policies
- Service design time, quality assurance/test, and runtime governance policies

- Service utilization, consumption, and reuse policies
- Service capacity planning, QoS, and SLA requirements

This is the intersection of project oversight with project execution, and it is where there is an opportunity to enforce critical SOA policies by either extending existing governance processes or by inserting new processes or reviews within the existing PMO and SDLC processes. Because these are relatively "known" and understood processes, inserting or extending them to add SOA governance will not be as challenging. Mind you, though, it will not be easy.

Key Governance Process Enforcement Concepts As you develop the SOA governance process model, bear in mind that there are many enterprise governance processes available to enforce various policies. Recall the process descriptions in Chapter 3, in which we decomposed the Four-Tier Governance Model into its component processes and activities. As you determine policy categories and policies that close critical governance gaps, you must develop the governance processes that will enforce those policies.

Consider how various policies above will be enforced across the following major SOA processes:

- SOA/service requirements and demand management
- SOA/Services Development Lifecycle process (design time, quality assurance and testing, and run time)
- Service operations and management
- Services Lifecycle Management (concept and requirements through construction, testing, operations, and retirement)
- Service portfolio management

Again, refer to Chapter 3 for a more comprehensive list of enterprise governance processes. As you identify and define your core enterprise governance processes, document them using process modeling tools, activity diagrams, and other documentation and visualization tools.

Ensure Governance Process Ownership, Management, and Facilitation A key challenge for SOA governance is to ensure somebody in the enterprise is accountable and responsible for definition, implementation, and ongoing execution of the SOA governance process.

Often, IT governance processes are facilitated and managed by the PMO function of the enterprise. Similarly, the same organization may own or manage the definition of the enterprise SDLC processes, as well as key enterprise architecture and project reviews across the software delivery process or SDLC.

Regardless of your organization's preference for process accountability, be clear on who or what organization is responsible for SOA governance.

Program and Project Governance via Project Reviews Project review processes provide excellent ways to enforce various policies as projects are executed. After all, projects are the primary means by which strategy is carried out, and are the fundamental unit of IT delivery. Project reviews can be conducted by project managers, by a PMO, or by project sponsors. Regardless, many process and technical policies can be manually enforced using different types of project reviews.

Governance Process Checkpoints Key process checkpoints can serve as SOA governance enforcement points (e.g., key milestones in your SDLC, or production readiness reviews). You should define the critical gates or checkpoints for governance reviews. These reviews are opportunities to enforce core policies for enterprise architecture, service design, security compliance, et cetera. Your policy model and policy enforcement model must be mapped to these core governance processes to ensure coverage and enforcement across all processes.

Governance Events and Triggers Policy enforcement can be accomplished by events and process triggers that call for a particular governance enforcement review. Examples here include project scope change, budget overruns, and other significant changes that would potentially impact key policies. Below are examples of governance events and triggers:

- SDLC Process Reviews
- Exception Conditions (e.g., project schedule overruns, additional funding requests, architecture exceptions, customer complaints)
- Offline Working Group Artifact Reviews: Many policy enforcement activities can be accomplished manually by offline reviews of design artifacts, architecture artifacts, and other documentation. These can be effective supporting governance processes that feed into the governance boards and support various governance processes. On many cases, senior executive governance boards must have the support of working groups and other supporting teams that are better qualified to assess, investigate, and make governance recommendations to the decision-making board. Offline activities must be planned so that when key governance boards meet, they are making the most effective use of their time.
- Sign-Off Mechanisms by Key Stakeholders: Key stakeholder sign-offs are useful accountability mechanisms for key policies at all levels of an organization. The symbolism of a signature is a powerful signal that

you are accountable for a decision, and it provides a paper trail as well. Sign-offs can be very effective for lower-level policy enforcement. For example, reuse of services is desired by many organizations. One way to achieve this is a sign-off by project managers that indicates they have checked the service catalog or repository before determining the need to build a new service. This sign-off will be visible as the project proceeds through SDLC reviews.

Key Governance Process Considerations

- **Assign a credible SOA governance champion.** Make sure your governance model and process has executive involvement, sponsorship, and support.
- **Focus on critical governance processes first.** There are many IT management, planning, and execution processes to pick from. SOA governance cuts across many of these. The trick is to identity core governance threads that enforce policies across groupings of related or linked processes.
- **Ensure policy enforcement for critical policies across critical processes.** Again, there are many policies to choose from, and your policy model will require prioritization. Develop an A, B, C policy prioritization scheme. All "A" policies will always be enforced with consequences for nonconformance. Make sure these polices are clearly enforced across core governance processes.

Governance Tools and Technologies   SOA and SOA governance have spurred the development and commercialization of many new tools and technologies to support service design and runtime governance. These include such tools as repositories and service registries, which are purported to address many core governance and policy enforcement requirements. In addition, next-generation SOA governance tools include policy management tools and policy engines, which facilitate the development and management of policies, impact analysis, and similar capabilities. The tools, technologies, and standards of SOA governance are covered in detail in Chapter 9.

Many policies in your enterprise are technical policies, security policies, or other performance-related policies. You should explore automating as many of these policies as are appropriate to your current and planned SOA technology solution. Many technical policies must be automated to succeed, in particular security policies, mediation policies, and routing and transformation policies. Business and process policies can be supported by tools as well, but not every enterprise has the tooling, for one, and there is no integrated policy model and vocabulary for aligning business and process policies to automatable technical policies (see Chapter 9 for a detailed explanation of the various tools and technologies of SOA governance.).

GOVERNANCE EXECUTION MODEL

The fourth major dimension of the governance model design process is the governance execution model. This collection of activities is focused on mechanics of governance execution, measurement, communication/feedback, and ongoing sustainment and evolution. The following are the major categories of activities:

- Governance Exceptions, Waivers and Conflict Resolution
- Governance Metrics and Behavioral Model
- Governance Communication and Feedback
- Governance Performance Management

Governance Exceptions, Escalation, and Appeals

A critical function of the governance organizational model is to provide a transparent and explicit process to identify, manage, and resolve governance exceptions. This is one of the most important processes in your governance model, and thus requires considerable forethought. How you anticipate and address exceptions will determine the early credibility and success of your governance model. If you deal with exceptions poorly, you may handicap your governance model permanently. If you anticipate exceptions and have prepared and accelerated pathways to manage them, you will gain support and credibility from all stakeholders.

There are multiple aspects to the exception management and appeals process to consider. First, how will you treat policy violations as they arise? What are the various ways in which policy breaches can be dealt with? You must be clear and consistent in how you treat exceptions. If a project fails a critical review, you must treat it appropriately. If you allow the project exception, conditional upon a future remediation, you must track the follow-up and ensure the project comes back before the governance review board. Exceptions can also be the driving force to update policies and standards. In those cases, exceptions are granted during reviews and the new solution or design pattern is added to the enterprise architecture repository, for example, and policies are either revised, added, or deleted.

Exception Management Mechanisms   As you plan your SOA governance model, you must provision for exceptions and provide clear means to manage and resolve all exceptions. In general, exceptions engender the following decision process:

- **Exception Identified.** Failed review; project must remediate the exception and come back to the review board to demonstrate compliance to existing policy.
- **Exception Identified.** Conditional pass; project is granted a waiver to proceed, but must remediate the exception in the future (by some deadline) to comply with policy.
- **Exception Identified.** Project passes review; project is granted a waiver to proceed; policies are updated or added to reflect a new standard or implementation model.

Policy Exception Alternatives

- Education and coaching about policies, why the exception was triggered, and how it will be remedied
- Funding action (e.g., remove or reduce project funding)
- Educational outreach to an organization, division, outsourcing partner, or leadership of an organization
- Coaching and mentoring for key participants in the process (e.g., enterprise architects, chief information officers, project managers, program managers, technical leads, etc.)
- Reject and re-review
- Kill project
- Personnel action

Remember, your SOA governance organization has two fundamental roles: provide manual enforcement for enterprise policies, and manage exceptions that will always arise as you enforce policies. We urge you to define the exception management process using some of the ideas above, and to ensure a rapid and crisp response to dealing with governance exceptions. A clear exception management model will give your governance model credibility with the stakeholders.

Metrics and Behavioral Model

A critical aspect of your SOA governance toolkit is how you measure SOA results and SOA governance performance. The following are ways to communicate SOA governance effectiveness through metrics and monitoring mechanisms:

- SOA Governance Dashboards
- SOA Metrics and Scorecards (think of a "balanced scorecard" for SOA)
- Traffic Light Reports, e.g. red/yellow/green
- Governance Portals and Intranets
- Web Services Management System Feed into a Governance Portal/ Dashboard

SOA metrics are critical. You need SOA metrics to know where you are and where you are going with your SOA initiatives. In other words, SOA metrics put a steering wheel on your SOA. Very often metrics are the afterthought of SOA initiatives because much of the early focus is on getting the technology implemented and working, then measuring the results later. Sound familiar? We believe that metrics must be built into the SOA planning process, up front, and then assiduously monitored to help ensure goals are met. Below are examples of SOA metrics to consider.

- SLAs and quality of service (QoS) metrics
- Conformance reporting and policy breaches
- Enforcing reuse of existing services versus novel development of new services
- Enforcing "good reuse" versus "bad reuse," or reusing published, proven services and not reusing rogue services
- Enforcement of services design best practices enterprise-wide as opposed to one-time design principles
- Your SOA metrics and governance metrics should be defined in your SOA strategy and roadmap. The SOA governance metrics will thus align to and support the realization of those SOA goals and objectives, according to the performance metrics used to measure progress toward SOA goals.

Managing Individual SOA Behavior: Big Carrot, Big Stick

How are individual behaviors governed within the context of an SOA? Governing behavior requires a combination of clear metrics of the SOA, as discussed, and a means to relate overall SOA metrics to individual and group goals. All of these metrics and goals should be related and reinforce one another. For individual behavior, these approaches should be considered:

- Document SOA performance and behavioral expectations in annual plans for employees and contractors.
- Implement SOA performance and behavioral elements into employee review processes.
- Implement an SOA review process that helps reinforce the expectations and objectives of the SOA overall, as well as the roles of various departments and individuals within the SOA context.
- Build SOA behavioral reinforcement into employee incentives and compensation plans. Consider a profit-sharing approach for costs saved from SOA reuse, and other hard-dollar and soft-dollar business benefits of SOA.

Influencing SOA behavior is going to require embedding enforcement of SOA policies and metrics within all employee annual plans and reviews as well as in compensation and reward systems.

Achieving Political-Cultural Alignment   Often, enterprise SOA governance can succeed or fail based on factors that are unrelated to logic, right and wrong, or ensuring the success of a SOA initiative. That is when the political landscape of your enterprise comes into play. Once you have developed the initial structure of your enterprise governance model, you should begin factoring in the political and cultural influences that can make governance more likely to succeed, or less likely to succeed, based on the internal political and cultural dynamics of your enterprise.

To address these forces, we like to create a "political alignment model" (PAM). PAM simply determines what positive political forces can enhance governance success and reduce the likelihood of failure. Who can champion the SOA governance activities and fly executive air cover? Who can chair key executive boards such that a better probability of SOA success can be ensured? How can SOA funding and budgeting be assured by engaging business leaders in the governance process?

While this topic can take an entire chapter of its own, justifiably, we only offer some ideas for you here. Do give proper consideration for the political and cultural aspects of your governance model, and seek ways to increase the probability of success of SOA governance in your organization. Below are some ideas you can adapt to your organization:

Political-Cultural Alignment Thought Starters

- **Latch onto corporate mantra (e.g., Six Sigma, "Quality is Job One," etc.).** If there is a corporate theme, slogan, or mantra that is recognized and practiced, you should consider aligning to it and integrating it into your SOA governance model. If there is a key corporate initiative underway, for example, lean Six Sigma or some other quality-related program, align to it and adopt aspects of it into the SOA governance model. You can then capitalize on the halo effect of these mantras or business initiatives for the benefit of SOA governance.

- **Political Alignment—Rising Stars.** If there are corporate rising stars— key executives who are fast-tracking in your organization—try to gain their support for SOA and SOA governance. Recruit them to lead or participate on key governance boards; make them supporters of the SOA initiative.

- **Political Alignment—Structural Accordion Winners and Losers.** Recall the IT structural accordion model discussed earlier in the chapter—the continuum between centralized and distributed IT organizations. As the accordion contracts and expands from centralized to distributed, there will be organizational winners and losers. Use the structural accordion model to identify potential and emerging power bases, and align SOA governance to the winning organizations and winning executives. Plan ahead, and take a long view in this analysis. You may be able to map the evolution of your SOA governance model to anticipated changes in the organizational and leadership structure of your enterprise.

Governance Communication and Feedback Mechanisms

Other critical ingredients in a governance model are a communication strategy and process, and mechanisms for receiving input and feedback from the stakeholders and "consumers" of governance—those being governed. These communications processes provide outbound information to the community involved in or under the coverage of the governance model, while creating a channel to receive feedback from those stakeholders as well. You must plan a two-way communication model for your governance model, and implement supporting tools and processes to sustain the bidirectional communication model. Use newsletters, portals, emails, company meetings, and education and awareness tools to get the message out about governance, updates, changes, and other relevant news. Develop inbound feedback mechanisms to receive feedback, to incorporate innovations from users and others into the governance model, and to "take the pulse" of governance and its effectiveness for your enterprise.

Governance Performance Management and Sustainment

A final critical aspect of governance execution is the process of adapting, managing, and sustaining governance over time. It is surprising how often organizations leave out planning for the sustained operation of the governance function in their enterprises. Governance performance management is the process of sustaining, evolving, and managing governance processes through time. Governance performance management requires metrics to track success, ongoing management and "ownership" of the governance process to ensure its integrity and ongoing sustainment, and a mechanism for managing and evolving policies as the governance model adapts to changes.

SUMMARY

This chapter presents the governance analysis and model design tools you will need to begin your SOA governance journey. The new governance toolkit presents a very modern view of policy-driven governance, with an emphasis on SOA governance, but with clear recognition that this model can be applied to all governance requirements of any enterprise: corporate governance, enterprise governance, IT governance, SOA governance. This chapter will help ease the transition into the steps of governance model design presented in Chapter 5.

Notes

1. For a detailed discussion of business and IT imperatives, see Eric Marks and Michael Bell, *Service-Oriented Architecture: A Planning and Implementation Guide for Business and Technology,* John Wiley & Sons, 2006.
2. Peter Weill and Jeanne Ross, *IT Governance: How Top Performers Manage IT Decision Rights for Superior Results,* Harvard Business School Press, 2004, p. 86.
3. Ibid., p. 115.

CHAPTER 5

SOA Governance Model Design Process

This chapter presents a replicable Service-Oriented Architecture (SOA) governance model design and management framework that will facilitate the assessment, design, implementation, and ongoing management of your SOA governance model over time. We will walk you through key decisions you must make with respect to governance processes, organizational models, and policy enforcement approaches based on the dynamics of your particular organization. In the last section of this chapter, we will offer guidelines and best practices for "rightsizing" your SOA governance model for the most effective and yet least intrusive approach. This SOA governance model design framework can apply to any form of governance in fact, from corporate governance to Information Technology (IT) governance, from enterprise architecture (EA) governance to SOA governance. It is scalable, reproducible, and effective.

The biggest confusion about SOA governance and governance in general is the intermixing of governance concerns, governance processes, enforcement mechanisms, and policies. For example, when is a governance board required? What purpose does a governance board serve? While we believe that the organizational and structural aspects of governance are critical, one must not begin with the governance organizational view. This tends to result in governance boards looking for something to do. We subscribe to a view that continuously asks what has to be governed, what policies are necessary to govern that concern effectively, and then when, where, and by what means are those policies enforced. The "when" refers to the processes or events that trigger governance reviews or enforcement points. The "where" refers to the various project execution processes across which projects are executed and during which various governance enforcement points are invoked to ensure policy conformance. The "means" refers to various enforcement mechanisms that may be utilized to enforce policies. Enforcement mechanisms can include governance boards, offline artifact reviews, working groups, automated enforcement tools, reviews, and more.

This brings to the fore the confusing landscape of enterprise SOA governance. Because SOA is a relatively new discipline that extends and affects current IT governance processes, enterprise SOA governance demands attention to these new SOA dimensions.

There is a finite list of critical SOA governance concerns based on various SOA maturity profiles. Furthermore, there are a finite number of ways to govern these concerns across various enterprise planning processes and program and project execution processes. The SOA governance model design framework will help you identify your critical SOA governance concerns, and determine how best to establish governance for those concerns.

GOVERNANCE MODEL DESIGN PREREQUISITES

Before you begin working on SOA governance, you must have an established baseline. In Chapter 4, we presented a governance assessment process to help establish your current state SOA governance capabilities.

That baseline is a critical input into the SOA governance model design process in this chapter. If you are reading the book in order, please do continue. If you are skipping around from one part to another, be sure to read Chapter 4 prior to reading this chapter. The following prerequisites are necessary before performing the activities described in this chapter:

- SOA Governance Assessment is Completed
- SOA Governance Gap Analysis is Completed
- Prioritized Gaps–Critical Processes and Gaps to Address

Review the Complete SOA Governance Model Checklist

The governance model design framework is a replicable process for designing a governance model of any type: enterprise governance, corporate governance, IT governance, or SOA governance. The elements of a complete and integrated enterprise SOA governance model are:

1. Governance Strategy, Scope, and Philosophy
2. Governance Stakeholder Model
3. Governance Goals, Principles, and Policies (Policy Model)
4. Policy Enforcement Model (PEM)/Policy Provisioning Model (PPM)
   - Governance Process Model, Governance Threads, and Activities
   - Governance Organizational Model, Boards, and Committees
   - Governance Enabling Technology and Tools
5. Governance Exception, Waiver, Escalation, and Appeals Process
6. Governance Metrics and Monitoring Model

7. Governance Feedback Processes and Management Reviews
8. Governance Communication Model
9. Governance Performance Management and Sustainment Process

SOA Governance Strategy, Scope, and Philosophy

To begin the SOA governance model design process, you must first establish a high-level context for your governance model. The governance context consists of your SOA governance strategy, philosophy, and governance scope.

SOA Governance Strategy, Scope, and Philosophy and Style What is the overall approach and strategy for your governance model? What goals will it accomplish for your organization? How will you justify the cost and effort to implement enterprise SOA governance?

What is your governance philosophy? Will you implement a kinder, gentler governance model or one with explicit policies and hard-line enforcement of them? Will governance be tied to individual performance and compensation? How will governance be integrated into behavior and culture and norms of your enterprise? What will be the tone and style of governance: collaborative, hard enforcement, informational, guidance?

Policy Enforcement Approaches and Styles
Policy-Driven
The policy-driven governance style is predicated on a defined body of policies that codify principles and goals of the organization. The body of policies will be enforced explicitly to ensure alignment and conformance to the policies. The governance model concepts in this book are examples of the policy-driven governance style.

Collaborative/Encouragement
This is a more mature governance style, where the governance process is explicitly designed to be, or evolves to be, collaborative in its interactions and enforcement of policies across the enterprise. This approach can be implemented in a more middle-out fashion that engages bottom-up and middle-down to create collaboration and a two-way exchange model that ensures participation of more potential stakeholders in the governance process. In addition, this approach can link top-down, edict-based approaches with mid-level decision makers and stakeholders to help tie together a broader slice of the organization.

Visibility/Participation
This is a governance style that seeks to encourage participation and compliance by providing more visibility into decision making and governance

processes. In many implementations of federated governance models, early success can come simply from making decisions, and their rationales, visible. Once greater participation of the enterprise is achieved, more collaboration, and eventually a self-governance model, can be realized.

Governance by Decree (Top-Down Edicts)

This is a top-down model of governance that attempts to establish governance by issuing decrees and edicts to lower levels of the enterprise without establishing buy-in or more holistic governance stakeholder models. The "governance by decree" approach establishes an "us versus them" perception in the enterprise, and, being a top-down model, is a one-way model, as opposed to the bidirectional, feedback approach that we prefer.

Community-Based Self-Governance

This form of governance is more collaborative and community-centric than other approaches where polices and enforcement are necessary to meet governance objectives. Self-governance through community models is a very effective approach to governance, as demonstrated by the open source community governing the many open source projects in the IT industry today. The principles and approaches of community governance models offer insights for governing SOA based on combinations of policy-driven governance, supported by a community-centric construct that augments the policy-driven models.

Kumbayah/Faith-Based Governance

The kumbayah style of governance is our description for a naively optimistic style of governance based on the assumption that good people will always make good decisions for the greater good of the enterprise. This is similar to a style called "faith-based governance," in which hoping it will work is enough to make it so. Faith in our people will result in good governance. While these labels are a bit tongue in cheek, they do represent perspectives of some governance practitioners. Avoid these approaches, as they do not scale, and they do not work as realistic governance approaches.

SOA Governance Scope Another key parameter is to determine what scope of governance you need to meet the goals. Are you focused on the entire enterprise or on a single business unit or business region? Another aspect of governance decision authority is the scope of oversight. Does this decision authority span the enterprise, or is it within a division or strategic business unit (SBU)? For some aspects of governance, and depending on the IT and corporate structure, there may be mirrored organizations at the enterprise level, or there may be a federation model to ensure visibility and alignment to the enterprise. Regardless of the organization and structure, the governance decision authority must be clearly defined and supported organizationally for appropriate governance to be possible.

Governance Thresholds

Another decision is what thresholds will trigger various governance oversight and policy enforcement processes? What issues, decisions, or actions must be subjected to the governance process? Many times, IT governance will trigger for large projects of a certain size in total cost, resource commitment or complexity. Initially, you may force 100% of projects to go through your governance. process, and relax it to a threshold model based on size, impact, or cost. Along with governance scope, governance thresholds will help establish some initial parameters from which you can build your SOA governance model.

The key questions here are determining how wide of a governance net to cast, and what is the focal point of governance. What criteria will be used to ensure appropriate projects go through governance at all, and what are the governance enforcement points that will trigger ongoing governance reviews?

For example, most IT governance tends to take place at a project level as the governance focal point. EA is enforced during initial project planning, business case review, preliminary approval, and then across the project delivery lifecycle. Program management office (PMO) reviews focus on project management disciplines related to budget, schedule, and scope control. Is the project within the budget or is it over? Are we on time or late? Is the project still going to deliver what it promised, or has the scope changed?

Many organizations establish filters for various tiers of governance based on project size, scope, impact, and risk. If a project's budget is $100,000 or more, it must go through enterprise architecture reviews. If a project is $500,000 or larger, it must be reviewed by PMO and EA, and signed off by a joint business and IT executive team. PMO governance is applied to all enterprise initiatives.

There are many options here. You must determine the governance focal point, the limits for applying various governance enforcement activities, and the entry point into the governance process.

Key Questions to Answer

- What is the scope of governance? What critical decisions require stakeholder input (e.g., funding decisions, enterprise architecture decisions, application investment decisions, staffing or organizational decisions)?
- What resources must be governed or allocated with stakeholder involvement?

- Are governance thresholds appropriate for key governance concerns? In other words, will governance capture 100% of all projects or will you set project parameters that will determine which projects will go through governance and which ones do not (e.g., based on project cost, size, impact, risk, or other criteria)?
- Will all projects or initiatives go through governance, or only enterprise projects?
- What is the focal point for governance? Do you govern at the project level? Do you govern at the program level? If the project is the focal point for governance, have you integrated the more fine-grained concepts of processes and services into the project planning process?
- What is the governance entry point? What triggers the requirement for a project, program, or initiative to go through governance?
- What events or project delivery process activities trigger various governance reviews?
- Who has decision authority for the governance concern? Does one person or one organization "own" the responsibility?
- Is there a single decision maker, or should stakeholders be involved? Does the decision maker require input from others?
- What organizational scope does the decision authority have? Enterprise-wide? Business unit only? IT only? The governance scope must be defined in order to ensure appropriate decision authority and stakeholder input and representation.
- What governance style are you planning for? Command hierarchy? Collaborative model? Market exchange model? Community model?

Governance Stakeholder Model

For key SOA governance concerns, you must determine who is or should be the decision authority. Using EA as an example, who is responsible for defining, managing, communicating, educating, and enforcing EA conformance for Enterprise IT consumers? For some critical SOA governance concerns, there may be a single "owner" of the decision, while for others, key stakeholders may require representation, a "seat at the table", so to speak. Stakeholder representation will most likely require a board structure supported by working groups to establish the governance requirements, policies, and enforcement mechanisms, all to ensure appropriate representation for their respective interests.

Governance Stakeholders   In order to govern any critical SOA governance concern, you must determine who the stakeholders are. Stakeholder analysis is a natural outgrowth of determining the SOA governance decision authority, as described above. Governance requirements with multiple stakeholders will almost always require governance board structures in order to obtain stakeholder input into the decision, as well as to ensure stakeholder participation in the oversight for that governance concern.

Stakeholders will vary depending on the governance dimension in question. For example, who are the stakeholders for EA? Depending on the organizational structure, it might include business unit executives, project champions, project managers, tech leads, development managers, IT executives, EA leads, and a chief architect.

Every governance concern will have different stakeholders, and you must evaluate how the appropriate governance model accommodates stakeholder input, communication, and decision making. Many governance concerns will require overlapping membership on working groups, boards, and reviews. Creating overlapping committee membership is a recommendation made by Weill and Ross[1] to ensure effective and aligned governance.

Remember, if the stakeholders are limited, or the decision authority resides in one organization, you may be able to simplify governance to a communications model rather than an active decision making and oversight model. Stakeholder models can complicate your SOA governance model, but remember what the purpose of governance is—ensuring you are doing the right things the right way for your stakeholders. For critical governance concerns, stakeholders will demand at least a voice, and most likely a seat at the table with voting rights and participation in the decisions.

Key Questions to Answer

- What governance concerns require stakeholder involvement?
- What governance concerns require stakeholder input and representation only?
- What governance concerns require stakeholder input and also have stakeholder decision authority?
- Do all stakeholders have an equal voice in governance, or are some more influential than others?
- How will you communicate with stakeholders in a bidirectional fashion to gather input and requirements, and then disseminate governance decisions and policies?

Goals, Principles, and Policies (Policy Model)

We have explained the SOA goals, principles, and policy model already. This section will not repeat, but will offer concepts and best practices.

Define Policies and Processes Before Organization   In our SOA governance framework, we advocate defining policies and processes first, then determining the organizational model that will integrate it all and manage exceptions, escalation, and appeals. You can remember this easily by using the acronym PPOT, or by using the mathematical expression PP/OT, which stands for "policies and processes over organization and tools."

Never define the governance organizational model or implement governance tools before you understand the governance scope and stakeholders, the policies to be enforced, and the governance processes necessary to enforce those policies. Once these elements of your governance model are clearly articulated and understood, you can layer and integrate the governance organizational model with the policies and processes, and of course the technologies, of governance. Remember the expression "PP/OT" and your governance model will not get out of sync.

Policy or Policies To Be Enforced   We have covered the challenge of SOA governance policies already. In order to structure and implement SOA governance, we have stressed the critical need for defining and enforcing a body of polices at all levels of the enterprise—the business level, the process level, during design, publishing, discovery, and run time for services. We have discussed the concepts of policy granularity and multi-level policies, as well as the need to integrate all polices in both an SOA governance and IT governance context.

From the policy derivation process described in Chapter 6, you must determine what policies are essential based on the two-pronged approach described. Establish the body of policies and classify them into business, process, security, architecture, services, design, and run-time policies.

Next, determine the policy enforcement model for those policies, based on the policy classification scheme. Where will the respective policies be enforced? By what governance process or processes? Rank and prioritize your policies by a simple three-level scheme: A, B, and C.

"A" policies are critical and must always be enforced. Exceptions will be rare if at all. These policies are the backbone of your SOA governance model.

"B" policies will be enforced, but exceptions are more likely. "B" policies are important yet less mission-critical than "A" policies.

"C" policies are points of emphasis, guidance as it were, but they are not iron-clad policies.

Your SOA policies are ultimately expressions of how you will achieve SOA business value for your organization. Policies are a translation mechanism to ensure achievement of business and mission results from your SOA efforts.

Key Questions to Answer

- What critical SOA policies are essential to achieve your SOA goals?
- What second- and third-level policies will supplement your mission-critical "A" policies?
- How are mission-critical aspects of security, architecture, services design and interoperability, and run time factored into your SOA policies and supporting policy enforcement model?

Major Process Steps

1. Define your IT and SOA goals
2. What principles support these goals?
3. Define policies that implement the principles
4. Start with policy categories
5. Develop the policies from the categories
6. How many policies are necessary? How many principles? (As many as required to close the gaps.) Now, how many manually enforced policies are realistic?
7. How many architecture, technical, design, QA/test, and runtime policies can be enforced? (Automated governance tools will offload the enforcement burden of the many technical policies you will require for SOA and services governance.)

Policy Enforcement Model (Assign Policies to Various Enforcement Mechanisms)

In this step, we essentially define the overall PEM that implements your governance model. The policy enforcement model is the deployment, assignment, and provisioning of the policies to various policy enforcement mechanisms in your governance model, such as technology solutions, governance processes, and governance boards.

As discussed in Chapter 4, the type of policy will help in determining how to best enforce it. We differentiated between business policies, process policies, architecture policies, technical policies, design policies, QA/test policies, and runtime policies. As you define these policies and determine how and where to enforce them, you will begin assigning them to various processes, tools, and boards for enforcement, as well as define how to manage exceptions and waivers for key policies.

The SOA policies and policy enforcement model will determine the necessary policy enforcement mechanisms to ensure conformance to critical SOA policies. You must frame the policy enforcement model using the "A",

"B", and "C" rating for policies, and must consider the potential risk from *not* enforcing various policies.

The following governance policy enforcement mechanisms may be considered as your SOA governance tool kit:

- Key executive (e.g., chief information officer [CIO], chief technology officer [CTO], president, business unit leadership committee)
- Governance boards
- Governance board reviews (permanent or virtual)
- Working groups
  - Reviews
  - Analysis and recommendations to decision board
- Automated policy enforcement (SOA runtime governance, automated security enforcement)
- Service design reviews, artifact reviews, and checklists
- Governance event triggers (e.g., process checkpoints, exception conditions, governance re-reviews)
- Sign-offs by key stakeholders and accountability executives

Chapter 4 describes the various tools in your SOA governance toolkit, and so there's no need to repeat them here. In choosing and implementing a variety of governance and policy enforcement mechanisms, be sure to align all governance activities.

Key Questions to Answer

- What mix of automation, software tools, processes, and manual oversight is necessary to provide governance coverage for the most critical policies of your governance model?
- How will you integrate the policy enforcement using a combination of enforcement mechanisms, such as governance boards, processes, and tools?
- How will you align SOA governance to the corporate culture, political forces, and organizational dynamics of your enterprise?
- How will the current corporate structure and organization impact your SOA governance model? Can you effectively govern SOA without changing the structure?

Key Points

- Ensure coverage for all key policies
- Ensure multi-level policies are integrated into the PEM

- If orphan policies, orphan boards, or unnecessary processes are discovered during this process, iterate the governance model design process and eliminate redundant, duplicate, or unnecessary policies

Policy Provisioning Model   A policy provisioning model is a new concept based on either a process or a technical solution that can actively "provision" or deploy policies into an active enforcement status based on effectivity dates or other criteria that implement policies. A policy provisioning model could be an automated process using technology, or it can be a manual process of announcing new policies and their effectivity dates. Either way, you must define and put into enforcement new policies, or new versions of existing policies, or retire outdated or deprecated policies so that they are no longer actively enforced.

For manually enforced business and process policies, the policy provisioning process is manual, normally done through communications to stakeholders via email, portals, and other information dissemination channels. These policy announcements will state what the new policy or revised policy is, as well as when it will begin to be enforced (effectivity date). If the new or revised policy requires documentation or artifacts to be completed for a governance review, new templates may be distributed or made available via a portal as well.

However, for technical policies that can be enforced using automated enforcement tools and enabling technology, the provisioning model is different. In this case, policies can be defined or managed in a policy management tool, then put into effect and "downloaded" or "provisioned" into enforcement by disseminating it to various policy enforcement points in the governance architecture. For example, a security policy may be defined in a policy management engine, then provisioned to multiple enforcement solutions, such as a quality assurance and testing tool, an application router, a security appliance, and an identity management solution. Similarly, a service-level agreement (SLA) for response time could be defined and provisioned to a Web services management tool with distributed agents that actually enforce the policy in conjunction with the other governance tools on the SOA network.

Such policy provisioning tools are a relatively new concept. In order to realize automated definition, provisioning, and enforcement of SOA policies, a number of gaps or challenges must be overcome.

First, there is no industry-agreed standard for a unified policy grammar, vocabulary, syntax, or integration standard for the interoperability of SOA policies. This gap applies to all policies, including business, process, compliance, and technical policies, as well as their decomposition into fine-grained versions that are enforced at design time, quality assurance and testing, and at run time.

Second, there is no accepted policy model to unify multi-level policies that require vertical integration across boards and automated tools. Multi-level policies may include enterprise compliance policies that may decompose into fine-grained technical policies implemented as software or technical solutions, or enterprise security policies that break into multiple versions of finer-grained security policies enforced at multiple levels vertically, as well as horizontally across the services/software development lifecycle (SDLC) of an enterprise.

Finally, there are many tools and technologies that claim to play a role in policy management and policy enforcement. This is especially true with the rise of SOA governance these days. As you define your SOA governance model and policy enforcement model, give strong consideration and care to the governance-enabling technologies and tools you will deploy as part of your overall policy enforcement model. Do not buy the tools first without understanding the full scope of governance and policy enforcement.

Governance Processes: Policy Enforcement Triggers and Events

A key aspect of your SOA governance model is defining what the governance triggers are for key SOA policies. What events, conditions, processes, or activities trigger critical SOA governance reviews or policy enforcement events? Your governance processes must identify key reviews, policy enforcement events, governance activities, and other events that will merit the invocation of a governance board or a policy enforcement event. These governance triggers are what integrate the governance organizational model with various governance processes. Below are examples of governance triggers and events:

- Key process checkpoints (e.g., SDLC reviews [EA and portfolio reuse], PMO reviews [cost, schedule, scope], and strategic reviews [project or program still aligns and supports strategy])
- Project events/changes/degradations (e.g., project changes, such as scope changes, funding requirement changes; schedule slips, exception conditions)
- Project re-reviews to address previous exceptions/fail conditions

Governance triggers and events are either scheduled as regular events that occur in the normal sequence of a governance process, or they are triggered by exception conditions or unexpected events. Governance processes can be automated or supported by enabling technology and tools as well. Regardless, the governance process model must integrate with the governance organizational model, as various governance triggers and events initiate governance boards to convene to review projects, manage exceptions, and enforce policies.

Governance Threads: Linking Governance Processes via Policy Enforcement

Another governance process dimension to consider is the concept of governance threads. A governance thread is a series of related governance processes that are linked in order to govern various business policies. A good example of this is a reuse policy. Most organizations desire to achieve reuse of services in their SOA initiatives, although very rarely are policies for reuse established such that it is really enforced well. Exhibit 5.1 illustrates a notional view of a reuse governance thread that unifies several governance processes.

Reuse is an enterprise policy that requires coordinated enforcement across many interrelated governance processes, including enterprise requirements and demand management, strategic planning, project and program planning, EA management and maintenance, and project execution across SDLC by a PMO organization. There are multiple policies that may require coordination across multiple governance processes. Portfolio management is another example. Service portfolio management requires coordination with other portfolios, such as the application portfolio, the EA portfolio,

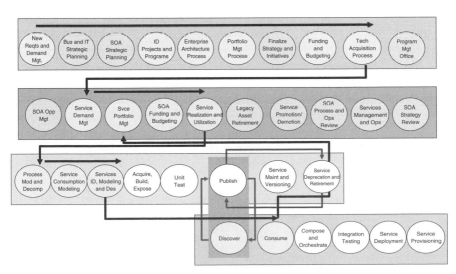

Exhibit 5.1 Sample Governance Thread

process portfolios, and the overall technology portfolio. Technical policies require coordination across the horizontal lifecycle process that span service design, quality assurance and testing, and run-time operations.

Key Questions to Answer

- How do you provide governance coverage for all governance concerns and requirements?
- How are key governance concerns related, and can they be aggregated into one governance process?
- Are multiple governance processes linked by key business policies? Can these be linked into a governance thread?
- Have you identified major SOA governance threads that provide governance for enterprise policies?

Implement Governance Processes to Close Critical Gaps

Once you have determined the SOA governance gaps and governance concerns, you can begin to define the SOA governance processes that will enforce key SOA policies within the structure and spirit of your SOA governance model. What governance processes are needed to ensure conformance of key policies? Can existing governance processes be extended or modified to suit your SOA governance requirements?

You must also consider the interconnections of multiple processes in enforcing policies. The concept of governance processes and governance threads are presented here based on the overlap and interdependent nature of many governance activities.

A governance process is a sequence of activities, events, and other triggers that results in governance over a specific discipline or concern. As discussed in Chapters 2 and 3, there are many governance processes you may consider to achieve an effective and appropriate SOA governance model. However, there are some core governance processes that should receive consideration. Below is a list of key SOA governance processes to consider:

- SOA strategy and opportunity management
- SOA enterprise architecture process (across the SOA SDLC)
- Services design and interoperability standards
- SOA SDLC process for services design, QA/test, and run time
- Service portfolio management (during planning and following the SOA SDLC process)
- SOA funding and budgeting

Define Your Governance Organizational Model, Boards, Stakeholders

You should develop your policies and process models first, then design the governance organizational model that integrates it. We created the PP/OT or (Policies + Processes)/(Organization + Tools) expression to encapsulate this concept. While we cannot tell you how to design your SOA governance organizational model, we can offer insights and best practices for it.

Below are recommended steps to help in designing an appropriate governance organizational model that will not waste time and resources, nor create negative perception of the new SOA governance model.

1. Design the preliminary organizational model (based on assessment).
2. Define policy enforcement roles for each board or committee; map and assign/provision policies to boards based on their criticality to the enterprise; ensure no policies are orphans, and no boards are orphans.
3. Define and plan your exception management and escalation/appeals process; you will need this early and often as your governance model matures.
4. Integrate the governance organizational model with governance processes, triggers, and events; ensure a minimalist approach for events that trigger governance boards to convene. Less is most definitely more.
5. Refine your governance organizational model based on feedback from stakeholders; communicate early renditions of the governance organizational model to critical stakeholders to obtain their buy-in.
6. Define boards, names, charters, chairs, and composition/membership.
7. Validate governance organizational model against policy and process models to check for gaps, orphaned policies, or processes.
8. Communicate governance model, processes, and boards to the community; soft-launch governance at first, as opposed to big splashes; get early wins and successes with governance before expanding to the enterprise.

Governance Organizational Model Considerations   The following are aspects of your enterprise SOA governance organizational model, along with recommendations, best practices, advice, and considerations to bear in mind as you develop your enterprise SOA governance organizational model:

- **Naming Boards and Aligning to Culture.** Be careful with names of boards, as the names can create an expectation of the board's purpose and intent. This is definitely more art than science. In addition, it must align with the governance scope and stakeholder model.

- **Charters.** Define a clear charter for the governance board, identifying its purpose, what policies it is concerned with, and how often it will meet.
- **Membership.** Must reflect the SOA governance stakeholder model, and ensure appropriate stakeholder representation for key governance decisions (e.g., input, review, approve, consult, inform).
- **Chairmanship Models.** Assigning the chair of a governance board can be a tricky activity. There are symbolic, political, and stakeholder representation challenges to the determination of a board chair. There are also dual-chair and multiple-chair techniques, with rotating chairmanship models occasionally mixed in as well.

Other supporting tools may be useful as you document your governance model. In addition to descriptive narratives, you may elect to utilize other industry-accepted modeling techniques to document your governance model. Common tools include:

- Swim lanes and process models
- Activity diagrams
- Value chain models
- RASIC/RASCI Models

Implement SOA Governance Enabling Technology and Tools

Once you have established the other elements of your governance model, you should determine how to integrate various tools and enabling technologies into your governance model. Many of the tools and enabling technologies are those you may already have implemented for your SOA development and run-time platform. These tools may already have some ability to support design-time governance and run-time governance. However, depending on how sophisticated your organization is and how mature your SOA efforts are, you may begin exploring higher-level governance solutions such as policy engines, registry and repository solutions, and so forth.

Chapter 9 discusses in detail many of the tools and technologies of SOA governance, and these will not be discussed here. Exhibit 5.2, however, presents an SOA governance technical reference model that represents the many categories of tools and technologies that potentially contribute to SOA governance policy definition, management, provisioning, and enforcement.

A critical concern in the SOA industry is the relative immaturity of standards and interoperability between SOA platform vendors and the integration and standards surrounding SOA governance.

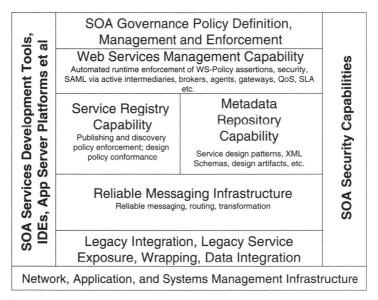

Exhibit 5.2 SOA Governance Technical Reference Model

Key Issues

- Define your SOA policies and processes before selecting governance tools and technologies.
- Defining your policy enforcement model and policy provisioning model before you select tools will help inform your tool selection and implementation process. Understand how well your target vendors integrate together into a coherent governance platform.
- Be sure to "integrate" governance tools and technologies into the other elements of your enterprise governance model, including governance processes, organizations and boards, and overall policy management and policy enforcement models.

Governance Exception, Waiver and Escalation, and Appeals Process

A critical dimension of your SOA Governance model is how you will anticipate and deal with governance exceptions. Exceptions to your governance model are not only to be expected, but they are important for evolving your policies and overall governance model. Exceptions provide the means by which your governance model "learns" as it wrestles with scenarios, policies, and standards that your original model may not have considered. And this is a good thing. Exceptions do not have to be negatives, just adjustments by the governance model and your organization over time.

Exceptions and waivers are natural results of policy enforcement. As exceptions are identified, your governance model must provide explicit means to address them quickly. If there is a policy nonconformance during an architecture review for example, the following decision making process might apply:

- **Pass/Approve.** Continue project as planned.
- **Fail.** Kill project (project cannot be fixed, is out of alignment, etc.).
- **Fail.** Re-review in three months or after addressing policy nonconformance.
- **Second Fail.** Remove funding; performance reviews.
- **Exception–Conditional Pass/Waiver.** Issue waiver due to customer requirement or mission-critical requirement; begin project to address exception condition.
- **Exception–Conditional Pass/Update EA or EA Policy.** Issue waiver for project to proceed, and update or revise EA policies and design patterns to reflect learning.

Escalation and Appeals: Resolving Conflicts   The fundamental reason for a governance organizational model is to provide stakeholder input and participation, and to provide a means to escalate and resolve conflicts. That is why there are multiple levels of governance oversight and escalation, ultimately mediated by either a senior IT executive or a business executive.

Key Issues to Consider

- Design your governance exception management processes very well. The first exceptions will have to be aggressively managed, and you want to demonstrate that you are serious about governance and that exceptions will be addressed explicitly within the parameters of your policies and supporting policy enforcement model.
- Plan for exceptions and escalations. These are natural and expected results of governance.
- Governance exceptions are not all negative. Often, exceptions provide opportunities to add, revise, or improve policies, and result in better overall governance for the enterprise.

Establish Governance Metrics and Monitoring Model

Governance must be based on metrics to be successful. Recall that governance, or SOA governance, is a process of ensuring appropriate use of enterprise resources to drive targeted goals and outcomes. The desired SOA outcomes must be identified early in the SOA strategy and planning process. To reinforce this emphasis, we have created the SOA scorecard model, which is a metrics approach to defining "federated metrics" for an SOA. By federated metrics, we mean applying balanced scorecard thinking to the variety of metrics that will be necessary to successfully migrate to and manage the success of an SOA.

Governance metrics should be added to this scheme as well. Examples of SOA governance metrics to consider include:

Governance Coverage

- Number of projects/services that go through the SOA governance process
- Percentage visibility of in-scope projects or services

Governance Effectiveness

- Ratio of conformance to nonconformance
- Number of exceptions granted

Policy Effectiveness

- Number of reusable services planned, in development and in production
- Number of retirement opportunities based on reusable services
- Savings from reuse and sunsetting
- Architecture alignment

We suggest that you select a few meaningful initial metrics to use as your SOA governance processes take hold, and gradually formalize them via scorecards and dashboards over time.

Below are metrics that are under consideration for the technology organization. These should be woven into the SOA governance metrics framework, as well as align the SOA governance model with the technology strategy.

Architecture Metrics

- Number of platforms/applications/systems (annually)
- Total cost of ownership of architectural stack (by component) (annually)
- Percentage of IT spend on technology strategy (quarterly)
- Number of exceptions requested/granted (monthly)
- Number of projects compliant with architecture standards (quarterly)

- Number of systems retired (quarterly)
- Total cost of ownership (TCO) savings from standardizing on common architecture components (annually)
- Percentage of data elements standardized (annually)
- Reduction in technology interfaces (annually)
- Number of components reused by more than one segment (quarterly)
- Percentage of revenues/transactions processed through SOA (annually)

Security Metrics

- Number of applications/systems compliant with policies and standards (quarterly)
- Number of exceptions requested/granted (monthly)
- Number of security violations (by type) (monthly)
- Revenue and IT costs due to fraud (quarterly)

Governance Feedback Processes and Management Reviews

This step of the SOA governance model design process explicitly builds self-evaluation, external feedback, and management reviews into the model. Any governance model must feature a bidirectional process between its stakeholders and participants.

Establish Governance Communication Model

A critical success factor for SOA governance is establishing a robust governance communication model. Such a mechanism will provide a means to communicate with all governance stakeholders and participants. Your governance communication model must be a multifaceted approach that supports all modes of governance—explicit, policy-driven governance, collaborative governance, as well as community governance.

Governance communication models serve multiple purposes for your enterprise:

- **Communication and Awareness.** Communicate governance updates, new policies, new processes, and other developments to the stakeholder communities through portals, newsletters, awareness briefings, company update meetings, and the like.
- **Feedback and Input from Stakeholders.** Establish a means to receive feedback from governance participants and stakeholders, as well as to harvest governance ideas and innovations from business units and

projects and incorporate those innovations into the policy model. Governance feedback and collaboration can be facilitated through collaboration tools, surveys, and other feedback mechanisms.

- **Support the SOA Business Engagement Model.** Governance communications provide a mechanism to help bridge the gap between technology and the business stakeholders in an SOA governance model. Often, SOA initiatives struggle when they push from the center of gravity or core team out to other business units, or from the technology core to business process stakeholders. This business engagement chasm can be bridged through a variety of communication, awareness, and educational programs, all of which must be premeditated and rolled out during SOA planning.

As mentioned, a number of governance communications techniques and tools may be employed, and most likely will be utilized as your governance model and processes mature. The list below is a sampling of the variety of communication and feedback mechanisms at your disposal:

- Portals
- Newsletters
- Education and awareness programs
- Surveys
- Collaboration tools
- Governance repositories and service registries

Utilize a combination of communication strategies in support of your governance model. They will also provide concurrent support for the SOA business engagement model as well.

Governance Performance Management and Sustainment Process

Governance performance management is the process of sustaining and evolving governance over time. Governance performance management is a new discipline that recognizes the strategic important of governance and thus creates a governance process owner and execution oversight for governance processes and activities of an organization. Governance performance management does not exist today. We have named it as such because we feel that performance is a critical dimension of governance. Governance is about ensuring corporate performance. SOA governance is about ensuring SOA performance. The following activities are essential to governance performance management:

- ▪ **Governance Process Ownership.** Ensures an enterprise owner of governance processes and policies, with clear executive oversight for the ongoing execution of enterprise governance processes, and activities.
- ▪ **Goal, Principle, and Policy Management; Policy Provisioning, Versioning, and Retirement.** Ensures the body of policies enforced via the governance model is aligned with enterprise goals and principles; oversees the provisioning of policies to the policy enforcement model; implements a versioning, retirement, and affectivity process to maintain policies over time.
- ▪ **Governance Performance Metrics.** Develops a metrics and scorecard framework to ensure governance metrics are aligned with corporate objectives; monitors effectiveness of governance and policies while ensuring effectiveness of processes being governed.
- ▪ **Governance Process Evolution and Change Management.** Ensures the governance model, policies, and processes are adapted and evolved to your enterprise over time; performs change management to support evolving governance;
- ▪ **Governance Sustainment and Ongoing Execution.** Ensures governance is a sustained competency and discipline; provides ongoing ownership and process execution to avoid the "one and done" approach to governance. Develops a career path for governance professionals.

Governance performance management is essential for ensuring an ongoing governance capability in your enterprise. Consider the logical "owner" of SOA and enterprise governance in your organization, and how best to implement a sustained governance competency center. Sustaining and evolving governance will be essential to your SOA success.

GOVERNANCE MODEL VALIDATION, REFINEMENT, AND IMPLEMENTATION PLANNING

The sections below describe critical activities you should perform to validate your enterprise SOA governance model, refine the model as need, and begin preparations for implementation and roll out of the finalized enterprise SOA governance model.

Governance Model Validation: Walk through and Test the Model

A key aspect of a useful governance model is a validation process to ensure policies actually work, are enforced per the policy enforcement model, and support business and technology objectives. In the governance model validation step, we are making sure the model is appropriate and right-sized, and that the policies and enforcement mechanisms all work in concert to achieve the desired outcomes. The following processes should be performed in validating and rightsizing the governance model:

- Validate governance strategy, scope, and stakeholder model
- Validate policy model
- Validate policy enforcement model (PEM):
  - Validate governance processes
  - Validate organizational model, boards, and composition
  - Validate governance tools and enabling technologies
- Walk through the model and test it against multiple scenarios, including exception conditions
- Test and validate exception management processes via governance board structure

Iterate and Refine the Governance Model   Another critical aspect of governance is to evolve, adapt, and mature your governance model through time. There is no such thing as a perfect governance model, and you almost never get it all right the first time. Accept that fact and plan to adapt and evolve your model. Plan multiple iterations of the model and multiple phases or thresholds of governance capabilities. Close critical gaps in the first phase of governance implementation, and implement fundamental SOA capabilities.

Governance Implementation Roadmap   During the implementation of your SOA governance model, we advocate developing a governance implementation roadmap. This SOA governance implementation roadmap should consist of between two and four phases that will allow you to "grow" into your governance model.

In this approach, we recommend that the first phase be relatively short, perhaps six months, and focus on the critical SOA governance gaps you identified during your governance assessment. The first phase of the roadmap should focus on lower hanging fruit, and relatively critical yet less difficult governance processes to implement.

For example, while services portfolio management is an important process for your SOA initiative, most organizations are not mature enough to implement this process well in the early stages of their SOA initiatives. In fact, most organizations do not have any portfolio management disciplines implemented, yet they feel as if they can establish services portfolio management early in their governance model implementation. This scenario should be avoided. In the first phase of the governance implementation roadmap, focus on easier governance gaps and obvious SOA policies first.

Key Considerations

- Devise SOA governance implementation roadmaps to help plan your governance rollout in broad phases of capabilities or maturity
- Make the first phase relatively short and high-impact, with a high probability of success
- Add increasingly challenging governance processes, policies, and enforcement models in phase 2 or phase 3, after you have had some experience and success with governance
- Do not lead with governance tools; sequence them in parallel with or following the implementation of governance processes and other policy enforcement mechanisms.

Governance Change Management

Part of a successful governance model implementation is supporting the transition from governance model design to implementation. In addition, as your SOA initiative matures and you evolve and adapt your governance model, you will have to manage changes to the governance model over time. Governance change management is a critical process to managing your governance implementation and assimilation.

Governance Education, Awareness, and Training

Governance education, awareness, and training are critical dimensions for your governance model framework. Supporting your governance model with appropriate governance education, training, and awareness will help ensure a successful rollout of governance, as well as a broad understanding of the governance process and rationale. As you implement the initial phase of governance, determine the various participants and stakeholders, and determine who requires training and education as opposed to awareness. How can you support the dissemination of governance information to the community of stakeholders using the governance communication model? What communication channels can augment the education, training, and awareness campaigning?

Governance Coaching and Mentoring

As you implement and execute your governance model, you must plan to perform ongoing coaching and mentoring for various stakeholders in your enterprise. Governance coaching and mentoring will be especially critical when managing exceptions at the project, organization, or even individual level. Depending on the exception, and whether escalation and appeals are required, you may have to perform additional education and training for business units or their management teams.

Determine the coaching and mentoring model you may use for various scenarios of governance exceptions. Plan for individual and group mentoring, but also use the coaching and mentoring as augmenting approaches to support the governance training, awareness and educational process.

SOA GOVERNANCE MODEL DESIGN FRAMEWORK CHECKLIST

This section will help you ask the appropriate questions and make appropriate choices for your SOA governance model.

Once you have completed the SOA governance assessment activities, you can begin to design your target SOA governance model. Key activities in this phase are listed in Exhibit 5.3.

EXHIBIT 5.3   SOA Governance Model Design Checklist

Governance Requirements Checklist	Example(s)	Comment

Governance Concern, Gap or Requirement (What must be governed now?)	• SOA enterprise architecture (EA) extensions and supporting artifacts
	• Services, service interfaces, payloads, design standards
	• Data model, schemas, and canonical form
	• SOA platform and tools
	• SOA/Services SDLC
	   o Design time—provider
	   o Design time—consumer
	   o Composition, orchestration, application assembly
	   o Runtime governance
	• Services management, runtime governance, and service operations	

Governance Decision Authority and Scope	Enforce conformance to EA across enterprise for all projects > $100,000 in total cost that impact or consume EA products	
Governance Gap/ Requirements Stakeholders	Business execs, project champions, project managers, CIO, CTO, chief architect, EA leads, PM, development mgr, operations manager	If many stakeholders, a governance review board will be necessary

(Continued)

Governance Requirements Checklist	Example(s)	Comment
Governance Process(es) or Threads	Reuse, portfolio management, EA, etc.	
What is the unit of governance? What gets governed? What are the thresholds?	All projects, programs, services? Programs or projects of a certain size or scope?	
What policies will be enforced?	• Reuse policy • EA conformance • Services design conformance	A policy can be a business policy, a process policy, or a technical policy, or a WS-policy.
Policy Enforcement Mechanisms	• Governance board reviews • Working group reviews, who submit recommendation to governance boards for final decisions • Automated governance enforcement • Offline artifact reviews and checklist • Governance event triggers, e.g. process checkpoints, exception conditions, governance re-reviews, major project changes	
Who owns governance process and governance execution?	• PMO organization owns governance process, facilitates governance reviews • Enterprise governance team owns and facilitates the governance process	
Governance Event Triggers	Key process checkpoints, e.g. SDLC reviews (EA and portfolio reuse), PMO reviews (cost, schedule, scope), strategic reviews (project or program still align and support strategy) Project Events/Changes/ Degradations, e.g. project changes, such as scope changes, funding requirement changes; schedule slips, exception conditions. Re-Reviews to address previous exceptions/ fail conditions	

Governance Decisions and Feedback	Pass: proceed per project plan; everything in compliance Fail: change or modify architecture; come back for EA review. 2nd fail: remove funding; performance reviews Exception: fail, but make exception (complete EA waiver form) Exception: pass, make exception, add solution to EA portfolio Other Governance Feedback Mechanisms: education and training, performance reviews Promotion/demotion Recognition – good Recognition – bad Reward – bonus Reward – recognition Reward – promotion	
Governance Exceptions and Waiver Management	Fail – kill project (cannot be fixed, out of alignment, etc) Fail – re-review: re-review project after it has addressed shortfalls, noncomformances, flags Pass – continue project as planned Conditional pass/waiver: issue waiver due to customer need, mission critical; fix project later Conditional pass EA/portfolio revision: issue waiver to proceed, add new EA pattern or solution to EA/Portfolio, remove waiver Conditional pass/policy change or revision: issue waiver, change, add or update policy, then remove waiver	
Escalation and Appeals Process	Appeal governance decision, request waiver • Appeal to higher IT governance board • Appeal to OCIO team • Appeal to CIO council • Appeal to business head/CIO team • Appeal to corp. executive council	

SUMMARY

This chapter presented a repeatable enterprise SOA governance model framework to help you design your target SOA governance model based on the assessment and analysis tools provided in Chapter 4. The elements of a total governance model were discussed, and an enterprise SOA governance model design checklist was also presented as a potential tool to help ensure you have full coverage for your enterprise SOA governance model. In the chapters that follow, we will dive deeper into the critical concepts of SOA governance policies, governance organizational design approaches, and governance enabling technology and tools. All subsequent chapters will leverage the SOA governance model design framework discussed in this chapter.

Note

1. Peter Weill and Jeanne Ross, *IT Governance: How Top Performers Manage IT Decision Rights for Superior Results*, Harvard Business School Press, 2004.

CHAPTER 6

SOA Governance Goals, Principles, and Policies

One of the rapidly developing areas of Service Oriented Architecture (SOA) governance is the domain of policies. While governance and policy enforcement are fairly immature, the concept of policies is still emerging within the context of enterprise governance. What are policies? How do you identify and enforce the right ones? How are policies enforced? How does policy-based governance differ from previous approaches to governance? Governance and policy are immature disciplines and need a lot of work from both a technology as well as an industry standards perspective.

This chapter provides a framework and model to transition from your SOA strategy to a governance model and a complete body of enforceable policies. This is the goal of SOA governance, of course. The domain of SOA policy is an emerging one, yet it is fraught with challenges. The standards of SOA policy are volatile. The tools and technologies are repositioning for SOA governance, runtime governance, runtime policy enforcement, and policy provisioning.

Yet, with all this focus on automating technical SOA policies for security—authentication, authorization, credential passing, and trust domains—there are as many (probably more) challenges around business and process policies. The challenges here relate to the fact that these are primarily behavioral policies, the enforcement of which is accomplished via governance boards, manual policy enforcement processes, and behavioral reinforcement mechanisms.

I would argue that the most challenging arena are these business and process policies, since there is currently no way to automate the enforcement of these policies. Sure, they can be defined in tools such as metadata repositories, and they can be codified in business process management (BPM) tools, but nonetheless they represent behavioral issues.

Furthermore, in many cases, there are direct relationships between business, process, and technical policies. After all, security is a critical business policy that has Sarbanes-Oxley compliance implications from a corporate perspective, business implications from a revenue and customer trust perspective, and process implications from the ways in which security threads through all business and Information Technology (IT) processes. Ultimately, security is described using WS-Policy and WS-Security, XML standards for security, and is enforced using the SOA runtime infrastructure.

The relationship between corporate, business, process, and technical views of security policies has not been explored well enough. We will do so in this chapter, although we will not claim to have all of the answers. At the very least we can propose concepts that map and align business goals to SOA goals, IT and SOA principles to SOA policies, and then define a policy enforcement model that ties together the Four-Tier view of SOA governance described in Chapter 3.

OVERVIEW OF THE GOALS–PRINCIPLES–POLICY CYCLE

SOA governance is most effective when the SOA policies are derived from and aligned to an SOA strategy and its supporting goals. These SOA goals form the basis for defining SOA principles, which are critical inputs in defining SOA policies. Thus, there is an ongoing cycle of defining, managing, and updating SOA goals, principles, and policies, as well as assessing policy impacts on existing services, consumers, and providers. The SOA enabling technology must support the critical policies, and the SOA governance model must provide organization and process for enforcing manual policies. Taken together, an SOA governance model must integrate governance organizations, people, processes, and technology into a coherent policy enforcement fabric.

The SOA governance goals, principles, and policies cycle is summarized below:

- Define business, IT, and SOA goals (from the SOA strategy document, if it exists).
- Identify IT and SOA principles that support those business goals. These are broad statements of intent that align with and support the business, IT, and SOA Strategy.
- Select governance processes and/or concerns that impact the principles.
- Define policy categories that support the principles, such as the examples below:
  - **Business policies** (e.g., regulatory policies, Sarbanes-Oxley, compliance policies, industry specific policies for example HIPAA, outsourcing policies, vendor management policies, acquisition policies)
  - **Process policies** (e.g., Services/Software Development Lifecycle (SDLC) process enforcement, governance thresholds, governance enforcement triggers)
  - **Technical policies** (e.g., service design-time governance, service runtime governance, security policies)

- **Security policies** (e.g., business-level security policy, security process policies, security policies at service design, and runtime security enforcement)
- Define SOA policies that operationalize, enforce, and measure relative conformance to the stated intent.
  - Generate policy statements for manually enforced policies.
  - Generate policy assertions for automated enforcement of technical policies.
- Determine policy enforcement model by policy category (e.g., business, process, technical, runtime, security). Which policies must be manually enforced and which must be automated using various SOA tools and technologies?
- Determine the policy provisioning model and process for ongoing policy management, impact analysis, versioning, deprecation and retirement.

This high-level overview of the SOA goals, principles, and policies sets up the following discussion of policy enforcement mechanisms.

SOA STRATEGY AND SOA GOALS

As emphasized earlier, SOA governance must govern according to some guiding compass. That compass is the SOA strategy. Often, an organization begins developing its SOA governance model before an SOA strategy has been developed. SOA governance must have an SOA strategy to provide the direction, strategic alignment, goals, and objectives, and of course the associated roadmaps for services, SOA opportunities, and SOA technology. The SOA goals in the SOA strategy must align to the IT strategy, which in turn must align with and support the organization's business strategy.

Once the SOA goals have been defined in accordance with the SOA strategy, they must be translated into SOA principles and SOA policies. Exhibit 6.1 depicts this translation process from goals to principles and ultimately to a body of SOA policies that will be enforced to implement your SOA governance model.

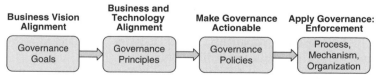

Exhibit 6.1   Deriving SOA Governance Goals, Principles, and Policies

The goals/principles/policies translation process is essential to maintaining the alignment and relationship between business, IT and SOA goals, and the principles and policies that will lead to the realization of those goals.

SOA GOVERNANCE GOALS

SOA goals come from the SOA strategy and serve as the master compass for the SOA governance model. These goals directly inform how SOA governance must be implemented to support them. We find this essential alignment and mapping is often missing in SOA governance projects, which leads to a focus on technical governance challenges at the expense of business and process policies. SOA goals must represent and reflect business goals. The following sample of business goals are often cited in informal or formal SOA strategy documents:

- Become an agile business.
- Maximize revenues and profits.
- Reduce time to market for products, services or capabilities.
- Develop a holistic view of the customer.
- Present a singular view of the company to customers.

These business goals become the substrate for formulating the following SOA governance goals:

- **Increase Agility.** We must improve its ability to support new products and services. This requires implementing real-time event driven SOA-enabled processes supported by a flexible SOA. It means shedding legacy heritage systems through an aggressive application rationalization program. Finally, it means enabling our information assets to support SOA and data services.
- **Emphasize Enterprise Architecture.** Establish enterprise architecture processes to deliver an enterprise view of business, technology, and resources to enable a decision support mechanism for internal and external business and technology communities.
- **Rationalize, Reuse, and Retire Legacy Assets.** Identify, define, and plan for the alignment and consolidation of functions, data, and systems. Deliver consistent and qualifiable services and products in a reusable manner to the business and public domains.
- **Achieve Organizational Effectiveness and Accountability.** Identify, establish, and execute strategies, policies, and plans for SOA interfaces.

SOA interfaces include organization, operator, process, hardware, software, and environment.

- **Leverage Shared Services.** Identify, reuse/buy/build and deploy SOA business/data/technology services, tools, and infrastructure that deliver accessible, reliable, discoverable, and secure services to the business, and public domains.

Exhibit 6.2 depicts a mapping of enterprise goals to SOA governance goals. The goals of SOA and SOA governance must align with the enterprise and IT strategies, objectives and goals. Using a table as shown will help crystallize the mapping of SOA governance goals to the enterprise goals.

Exhibit 6.2   Mapping SOA Goals to Business Goals

#	Organizational Goals	SOA Governance Goals
1	Become an agile business	• Enterprise architecture • Rationalize, reuse and retire legacy assets • Organizational effectiveness and accountability • Shared data services
2	Maximize revenues/profits	• Enterprise architecture • Rationalize, reuse and retire • Organizational effectiveness and accountability • Shared business/data/technology services
3	Reduce time to market	• Enterprise architecture • Rationalize, reuse and retire • Organizational effectiveness and accountability • Shared business/data/technology services
4	Develop a holistic view of the customer	• Enterprise architecture • Organizational effectiveness and accountability • Shared business/data/technology services
5	Present a single view of the company view to a customers	• Enterprise architecture • Organizational effectiveness and accountability • Shared business/data/technology services

In the following section, SOA governance goals represent the initial derived set of goals to establish an SOA baseline and direction, while providing a framework for identifying measurable objectives. A list of derived SOA principles follows, and finally the SOA policy and associated enforcement mechanisms are identified. The enforcement mechanisms are not separately called out because they are specified in the organizational and process models defined earlier.

TURNING SOA GOALS INTO SOA PRINCIPLES

SOA principles are derivatives of business goals. While SOA goals are expressions of how an SOA initiative or strategy will enable or support the business and IT strategies, SOA principles are higher level guidelines that provide the basis for making decisions. SOA principles are aspirational in some regards and help provide high-level decision making criteria to facilitate and guide actions. SOA principles are reflections of business, IT, and SOA strategy goals. They are an essential bridge to translating SOA strategy into tangible implementable guidance for SOA services and technologies that will support the business objectives of the SOA initiative.

DERIVING SOA GOVERNANCE PRINCIPLES

SOA governance principles set the strategic role for IT and articulate expectations to support your business strategy and goals. The principles in Exhibit 6.3 are derived from a set of fairly typical SOA goals. In addition to these principles, we have highlighted expected categories of policies that would support or enforce those principles.

From our experience, it is useful to begin with policy categories first before delving into a fine-grained policy model comprised of specific policy statements and policy assertions. The use of policy categories will simplify the derivation of your SOA policies from SOA principles.

Also, remember that SOA policies are derived from two related analysis streams: First, they are derived from the top-down goals-principles-policies cycle we described above. Second, there are also some "policy absolutes" that will and must be governed, and these are related to SOA reference architecture and the SOA extensions to your enterprise architecture. For example, some SOA governance policy absolutes might include:

Exhibit 6.3 SOA Governance Principles and Policies

#	Principles and Expected Policies
1	We will create an enterprise view of the organization based on the businesses it supports.
	Expected Policies: Enterprise architecture (EA) policies must be developed in support of this principle.
2	We will create data and informational views of the data assets and make them available as consumable products and services.
	Expected Policies: EA Policies, data architecture policies, and data services design standards and policies required.
3	IT/SOA/acquisition lifecycle will be centrally planned to support a multi-channel execution path based on the types of products and services being delivered.
	Expected Policies: Requirements management policies; services reuse policies, e.g. reuse first, acquire next, then expose/develop services.
4	We will identify, build and manage a single portfolio of enterprise business services, which will be visible to and leveraged by all Traveler's consumers.
	Expected Policies: Service Portfolio Management policies; reuse policies; publishing, discovery and consumption policies; retirement policies.
5	There will be a single set of business enterprise services that encapsulate and allow for the seamless elimination of redundant data stores, application rationalization and legacy heritage retirement.
	Expected Policies: Service reuse policies, application portfolio management policies, and legacy heritage retirement policies.
6	Standards for enterprise architecture, technology, business and infrastructure services, and data and data services will be defined, implemented, monitored, and sunsetted in cadence with industry standards.
	Expected Policies: EA policies, SOA and services design policies, IT standards and policies, technology acquisition policies.
7	We will have a consistent enterprise canonical data form. The enterprise data format achieves consistent definitions, names/tags, and structure.
	Expected Policies: Data model policies, XML schema policies, service payload policies, and general services design policies, e.g. doc-literal.
8	Our enterprise architecture will treat external service consumers and internal service consumers identically. There will be no functional difference in how SOA accommodates internal or external service consumers.
	Expected Policies: EA policies, SOA runtime policies, services design policies.
9	We will eliminate batch processes and replace them with real-time or near real-time event-driven services.
	Expected Policies: Service design policies; data services design policies; SOA/EA enabling technology policies.

(Continued)

10   We will use our SOA efforts to achieve reuse, application rationalization, and retirement of legacy heritage systems. We will use SOA principles of requirements, reuse, rationalization, refactor/replace/wrap, and retire to help guide acquisition and portfolio management decisions.

Expected Policies: Reuse policies, application rationalization policies, legacy heritage retirement policies, portfolio management policies.

11   For every reusable service identified and built, they will map to legacy retirement opportunities.

Expected Policies: Reuse, Legacy heritage retirement policies.

12   We will eliminate batch-based processing and instead implement real-time/ near-real time solutions event services. This will reduce batch created latencies and dependencies.

Expected Policies: Service identification and design policies.

- Security Policies
  - Authentication, authorization, and credential management
  - Encryption and signing of confidential content
  - Passing credentials within and across trust domains
- Service Design and Implementation Policies
  - Service interface design standards
  - Service payload standards
  - Service integration and interoperability standards
- Semantic, Data, and Schema Governance policies
  - Schemas and semantics
  - Canonical data models
  - Data governance
- SOA Platform and Operations Policies
  - Specification and implementation of your SOA development and run-time platform
  - Management and operations of services via the SOA platform
  - Operational and management policies for runtime
  - Quality of services and service level agreement (SLA) policies
- SOA/SDLC Policies
  - Defined and consistent overall SOA SDLC delivery model
  - SOA-enabled application delivery model, or a process to compose or assemble business applications by consuming services
  - SOA process orchestration and composite services lifecycle
  - Service development lifecycle: provider side
  - Service development lifecycle: consumer side

There are many aspects to SOA governance. These categories should always be on your immediate short list of SOA governance processes and requirements, and thus might be considered policy absolutes. These are SOA dimensions that must be enforced using clearly defined and enforceable SOA policies.

SOA GOVERNANCE POLICIES

As stated earlier, policies are the means by which governance is operationalized. Policies are what make a governance model tangible, enforceable, and meaningful for the stakeholders of an SOA. They are what puts 'teeth' in governance from an enforcement and conformance perspective.

Your policies are ultimately expressions of how you will achieve SOA business value for your organization. Policies translate business objectives from your SOA strategy into actionable guidance, principles, rules, and enforcement such that you have a better likelihood of achieving your business goals. SOA policies begin and end with business policies, even though some eventually become fine-grained technical policies. They all ultimately map into the business context and goals of your SOA initiative.

SOA policies are a major source of industry confusion given the relative immaturity and lack of standards, as well as general confusion over runtime governance and design time governance. And what about the lack of corporate governance policy and guidance standards? In this chapter, we will develop a unified policy model to clarify the concept of policies in SOA governance. We hope to set in motion efforts to standardize the integration of business and process policies with technical and security policies.

INTRODUCTION TO POLICIES

SOA governance is realized through the body of policies that drive the overall behavioral model of the SOA participants and ensures the interoperability of services operating in the SOA. The collective behaviors of services and the SOA participants are the real challenge. Policies define the parameters of acceptable behaviors for both constituents.

SOA governance is accomplished by policies. Policies are the specific rules that services adhere to at design and run-time, as well as the behavioral policies that developers and architects adhere to. There are therefore enterprise policies that all SOA parties must adhere to, e.g., "Reuse services before developing/exposing new services," as well as granular technical policies that ensure architectural compliance, such as "avoid RPC Encoded Web services operations," or "use document-centric messaging wherever possible." The nature of the policies is driven by business and technology requirements which feed into the overall goals of the SOA.

While SOA governance is accomplished through the definition of policies, it is critical to understand that defining clear enforceable policies as part of the SOA governance model is not enough. Policies must be enforced during both design time and run time. Enforcement of policies in these offline and online capacities brings into play the technical implementation of policies that comprise the SOA governance model. But what do we mean by offline enforcement versus active online enforcement of SOA policies?

Offline policy enforcement involves manual design reviews, code walkthroughs, and other checks and balances during the development lifecycle that help architects understand how well the SOA policies are being incorporated and adhered to in various IT projects. This is not far from the normal architectural enforcement model of the pre-SOA enterprise. Policies are reduced to documentation, which must be distributed to architects and developers and reinforced to them with active mentoring and ongoing education and training.

However, policies should not be institutionalized as documentation only. Somehow, they must be integrated into the services design, development and deployment processes and the services publishing, discovery, and operational processes. Policies must also be enforced at runtime by consumers and providers. Remember, behaviors are conditioned and shaped for all participants (the human participants as well as the services, applications and enabling infrastructure) and roles in an SOA.

Enforcing policies in an automated fashion using various technology solutions is essential for runtime SOA policy enforcement. SOA policy enforcement requires the appropriate enabling technology, including tools such as Web services management (WSM) platforms, policy validation engines, service registries, and metadata management solutions (for both run-time policy enforcement and manual enforcement during design). For example, consuming a service from an outside provider requires that the service contract, or Web services description language (WSDL) document, be validated for compliance to the consuming organization's SOA policies, such as the security assertions contained in the SOAP message headers, the message encoding specified in the WSDL (e.g., RPC encoded versus document-literal) etc.

However, the IT industry is not ready for fully automated policy enforcement due to immature standards and variable interpretation of standards as implemented in SOA platforms and tools. Most importantly, there is a lack of an integrated approach to policies that unites business policies, process policies, and technical policies.

WHAT POLICIES ARE REQUIRED?

The body of policies necessary to govern your SOA and services comes from two sources: They are derived from your SOA goals and principles, as well as from your SOA reference architecture and supporting SOA enterprise architecture artifacts. The policies derived from SOA goals and principles are often business and process level policies, while those derived from the SOA reference architecture are technical in nature and relate to service design and implementation patterns, design- and runtime governance, and security implementation and enforcement from both a service design perspective as well as a runtime perspective. Some policies are derived from the convergence of both exercises. The resulting policy model will form the basis for enforcing governance for key SOA processes and governance requirements.

Many types of policies must be defined to support your SOA efforts, such as:

- **Enterprise Policies.** Policies that affect all business units, processes and roles such as reuse, security policies, design best practices and standards.
- **Business Policies.** Address business issues, including process policies, SLAs and performance criteria, approval levels, spending limits for external services, and more.
- **Process Policies.** Who is allowed to publish a service? What minimal standards must be adhered to for a service to be published to a registry? How will versioning of services be managed? How many versions will be allowed? How will new versions of services be advertised to consumers? How will deprecation of older versions be handled?
- **Compliance Policies.** Policies that implement regulatory compliance standards and other industry-specific standards, such as HIPAA for healthcare, FIXX and IFX for banking and financial services, and ACORD for insurance.
- **Technology Standards Compliance.** Web services standards also apply here, such as compliance to WS-I, appropriate versions of SOAP, WSDL, and UDDI, as well as other related standards including XML Schema, Xpath, and Xquery.
- **Security Policies.** Policies that implement the organization's security model and technical standards, such as authorization and authentication policies as well as the standards that will be used to implement security policy. For example, WS-Security standards, SAML, XML Signature, and XML Encryption may be specified for specific security requirements based on your corporate or enterprise security policies.

The body of specific policies will be determined by the overall SOA governance model, defined standards, goals of the SOA, and, of course, the nature of the services that will be exposed or developed internally, as well as services consumed from external service providers.

SUGGESTED POLICY DEFINITION PROCESS

Next we turn to the policies or the specific "rules of engagement," for designing, building/exposing, and operating services within an SOA. SOA governance is an exercise in futility without enforceable policies that will drive conformance to the SOA vision, goals, and standards. The policies that will be enforced include specific design-time and runtime policies. They must support and enable the higher-level SOA governance model. The following are major steps in defining enterprise policies that will be enforced in your governance model:

- Define business, IT, and SOA goals (from the SOA strategy document, if it exists).
- Identify IT and SOA principles that support those business goals. These are broad statements of intent that align with and support the business, IT, and SOA strategy.
- Define policy categories that support or implement the principles, such as the examples below:
  - *Business policies* (e.g., regulatory policies, Sarbanes-Oxley, compliance policies, industry specific policies, for example, HIPAA, outsourcing policies, vendor management policies, acquisition policies)
  - *Process policies* (e.g., SDLC process enforcement, governance thresholds, governance enforcement triggers)
  - *Technical policies* (e.g., service design-time governance, quality assurance and test policies, service runtime and operations governance, SOA security policies)
  - *Security policies* (e.g., business level security policy, security process policies, security policies at service design, and runtime security enforcement)
  - *Service performance and behavior policies* (e.g., SLAs, quality of service (QoS), mediation policies, selective versioning policies)
- Define Your Policy Model: Operationalize policies such that they can be enforced and can be measured for relative conformance to the stated policy.
  - Generate policy statements for manually enforced policies.
  - Generate policy assertions for automated enforcement of technical policies.
- Determine enforcement and provisioning models for all policies by category (e.g., business, process, technical, runtime, security, etc.).

Exhibit 6.4 illustrates a high-level model for identifying your SOA policies within the constructs of our governance model design framework explained in Chapters 4 and 5.

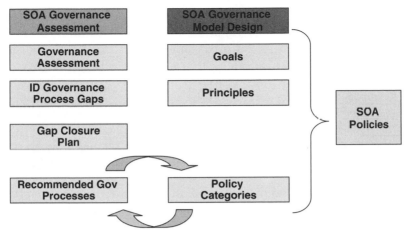

Exhibit 6.4 Deriving Your Policy Model from the Assessment and Model Design Processes

Based on this exhibit, we urge you to identify policy categories first, based on performing an SOA governance assessment and gap analysis. From this assessment, you should identify major policy categories that satisfy or close critical governance gaps. Policy categories will be used to devise the policy model that will be enforced. The policy definition process follows the following steps:

- **Identify governance processes and policy gaps.** In order to determine your policy model, you must perform an assessment of your current IT/SOA governance process and identify governance organization, process, policy, and technology gaps.
- **Identify policy categories (that map to processes and close the gaps).** Next, you should identify policy categories that relate to key governance processes and critical governance requirements. Again, this should be clear from your governance assessment. Policy categories will relate to the Four-Tiered model discussed in Chapter 3, and you must prioritize these categories based on enterprise requirements and governance goals and objectives.
- **Identify SOA goals, principles and policies (unconstrained by gap analysis).** In the governance model design process that follows the governance assessment, you should identify the IT/SOA goals, principles and policy categories that support business goals. This is a three-phase effort:
  1. Define IT/SOA goals.
  2. Derive IT/SOA principles that support those goals.

3. Define SOA policy categories that support the principles, which in turn support the IT/SOA goals.
4. Last, develop the policy provisioning model that enables policies to be deployed to the policy enforcement model—to the governance boards, processes, and tools that will enforce policies at the appropriate points in your enterprise.

- **Establish the policy enforcement model and policy provisioning model.** Translate and decompose the enterprise policy model into enforceable policies; generate policy statements for manual policies, policy assertions for automated policies, and policy artifacts for other technical policies.

- **Provision policies to the policy enforcement mechanisms.** Deploy policies to the various policy enforcement mechanisms, using the policy provisioning model. Instantiate manually-enforced policies for enforcement by governance boards or manual review processes, deploy technical automated polices into various SOA platform solutions for automated enforcement.

DECOUPLING POLICIES FROM SERVICES

In order to truly achieve the loose coupling goals of SOA, we must make greater progress toward decoupling SOA policies from services. Achieving this requires much more effort in the area of SOA policies, services design operations, SOA infrastructure and runtime platforms, and the overall process of design through runtime governance. The realization of loose coupling of Web services, for example, has been limited by immaturity of Web services and SOA standards and by lack of understanding of SOA governance and policy enforcement in general.

From a technical perspective, the lack and relative immaturity of standards around SOA policies has been a primary factor in the failure to achieve loose coupling of services. While simple service implementations have been able to achieve some degree of loose coupling, more complex scenarios involving security, reliability, routing, versioning, and service behavior are more challenging. It is in this domain that immaturity of standards has caused developers to hard code these policy requirements into service implementations and thereby create brittleness and service dependencies.[1]

Another area of discussion involves whether policy assertions should be contained in the WSDL document or hard coded in the service. There has been recent discussion of the need to decouple policies from service descriptions because it is likely that an organization may apply different policies to the same service depending on who is consuming it (internal or external consumer), how it is being consumed, and by what process. Given this reality, decoupling policies from the service contract makes sense so an organization can centrally manage, modify, and update policies in an abstract fashion separate from the WSDL descriptions.

IDENTIFYING TECHNICAL POLICIES

The policy model steps stated above apply to any policies, including business, process, and technical policies of an enterprise. If your focus is only technical policies, we recommend following the same approach described above, and then using these additional steps in the technical policy analysis and implementation. Again, treat this process as a subset of the overall policy model described above:

- Define SOA policies needed based on business and technical requirements.
- Define conformance processes across the services lifecycle (e.g., design, development/enablement, deployment, publishing, discovering, operation/run time, management, and maintenance activities).
- Govern your SOA using the defined policies.
- Measure conformance to the SOA governance model by examining multiple areas of conformance.[2]
  - *Policies.* What are our policies? Where are they described, documented and implemented? How are they enforced during design, development, and run time? Where are the gaps?
  - *Enterprise Services.* What enterprise services are being developed or exposed? How are policies being enforced during development? Is policy enforcement automated during the service's life cycle?
  - *Conformance Status.* Do our services (and others we consume) conform to our policies? What is the impact of nonconformance on service operations or business processes (e.g., security intrusions, SLA degradation, inoperable services)?
  - *Impact Analysis.* What happens to the SOA and associated business processes and business services if a policy is changed (e.g., SOAP policy, adding new metadata to SOAP message headers and message encoding policies, etc.)?
  - *Interdependencies.* How will business processes and operations be impacted by changes to services? What mission-critical processes will

be impacted or fail due to a service change or enhancement? What regression testing processes must be followed when a service changes and other processes or business units rely on that service?

■ *Exception Management*. How will policy exceptions be granted for services used by a specific project? What is the impact of policy exceptions? What minimal tier of policies must always be enforced in order for a service to be consumed? Should there be tiers of policies to handle the exception process?

Even when consuming an internal service, the policies supported by that service should be validated against the SOA policies to verify conformance. This step is important; in some cases, there may not be a solid process for enforcing policies during the development/enablement process and subsequent publishing of the service to a registry. In fact, a service registry or a metadata repository may not even be implemented as part of the SOA enabling technology. Although these registries and repositories can help with the enforcement of policies prior to publishing, there is often debate as to when a service registry is needed to manage a particular volume of services. How many services drive a registry need? How many planned services will drive a requirement for a service registry? These are all decisions that must be made case by case, as there is not enough empirical data to suggest a general pattern.

TOWARD AN INTEGRATED MODEL OF SOA POLICIES

One of the challenges we face in the SOA industry is the integration of SOA governance from an organizational, process, and policy enforcement perspective to the SOA runtime platforms and governance enforcement tools. There are many challenges to developing this integrated policy model.

First, as is often the case, the software vendor community has suborned the standards process to focus attention on those standards related to selling software and solving technical challenges. The technical focus on SOA policies via the WS-Policy Framework has led to a severe lack of attention being paid to the more difficult challenges of SOA—definition and enforcement of business and process policies via various governance processes, manual reviews and governance oversight boards.

Second, the notion of policy-driven SOA governance, or governance of any aspect of business or IT, demands a more scientific approach to what policies are, how they are derived, and how to provision them to various enforcement mechanisms across an enterprise. Once again, there has been significant work done from the technology and tooling perspective, but much less so from an organizational and process perspective.

POLICY TAXONOMY AND VOCABULARY

A key challenge to an integrated policy model is a policy taxonomy and vocabulary for defining, describing, and uniting various business, process, design, security, and runtime policies. While the standards bodies have made great strides with various technical standards for policy definition, policy assertions, and automated enforcement of these policies (called "runtime governance" by many), the same cannot be said for manual policies or for integrating manual policies with automated policies. For example, the Web services policy framework known as WS-Policy is a standard under oversight by the World Wide Web Consortium (W3C). This standard employs the policy terminology listed below:[3]

- **Policy:** A *policy* is a collection of policy alternatives.
- **Policy Alternative:** A *policy alternative* is a collection of policy assertions.
- **Policy Assertion:** A *policy assertion* represents an individual requirement, capability, or other property of a behavior.
- **Policy Expression:** A *policy expression* is an XML Infoset representation of a policy.
- **Policy Subject:** A *policy subject* is an entity (e.g., an endpoint, message, resource, interaction) with which a policy can be associated.
- **Policy Scope:** A *policy scope* is the collection of *policy subjects* to which a policy may apply.
- **Policy Attachment:** A *policy attachment* is a mechanism for associating policy with one or more policy scopes.
- **Effective Policy:** An *effective policy*, for a given *policy subject*, is the resultant combination of relevant policies. The relevant policies are those attached to policy scopes that contain the policy subject.

While this relatively new standard is being adopted by many software vendors for implementation into their tools, there is no corresponding standard for business or process policies, or for the general case where policies are not enforceable using technology and tools.

For example, the concept of "policy assertion" could effectively apply to a manual policy, which is equally "an individual requirement, capability, or other property of a behavior," much as a Web services policy is.

The difference fundamentally is that Web services policies are codified in a policy expression, which is an XML representation of a policy assertion such that it can be enforced using SOA technology and tools via WS-Policy and WS-Security standards. A policy assertion for a business or process policy does not have a corresponding policy expression for XML representation and automated enforcement.

To differentiate between automated technical policies and manually enforced business and process policies, we have resorted to calling these manual policy assertions "policy statements." A policy statement is to business policies what a policy assertion is to a technical policy.

Another aspect of SOA governance that remains to be addressed is the relationship of business and process policies to runtime policies described using the WS-Policy standard. In fact, this chapter will attempt to frame the problem and develop an initial framework for integrating business and process policies with technical policies.

Exhibit 6.5 describes some examples of SOA policies based on their classification as business, process, technical, and security.

A key takeaway from this exhibit is that different kinds of policies are enforced using different governance and policy enforcement mechanisms. Some are automated—for example the runtime governance for security policies. Others are clearly business policies that are manually enforced via governance boards and manual review processes. Perhaps the notion of a policy assertion is appropriate for unifying business and process policies into a single SOA governance and policy enforcement framework. However, given that WS-Policy is so anchored in technical policies and SOA platforms and tools, we will offer the notion of policy statements as the unit of enforcement for manual policies.

POLICY GRANULARITY

SOA implementations almost always trigger discussions about the notion of service granularity—of course referring to the relative coarse or fine-grained size of services and the industry best practices, or lack thereof. What has not been a topic of discussion is the concept of "policy granularity."

Policy granularity refers to certain scenarios where SOA policies span multiple levels of the enterprise and therefore require a multi-level policy enforcement model. Security is a good example of a policy that is enforced at multiple levels, beginning with a simple coarse-grained policy statement and then ultimately enforced automatically at service run time via security appliances and other automated enforcement mechanisms. Exhibit 6.6 depicts the concept of a coarse-grained business policy being decomposed and

Exhibit 6.5   A Policy Meta Model and Policy Taxonomy

Policy Type	Enforcement Mechanism	Example
Business Policy	Governance review board	All projects of $100,000 in size or greater must be reviewed and signed off by the enterprise architecture council (or architecture review board) at key SDLC checkpoints.
Process Policy	SDLC checkpoint reviews	All projects will follow the company's SDLC process and complete all artifacts and deliverables.
Process Policy	PMO oversight	All projects greater than $250,000 will be assigned to the PMO for project execution oversight and reviews.
Technical Policy – Service Design	Service design reviews during SDLC Checkpoints	Web services will use document-literal encoding.
Technical Policy – Security	Service design reviews during SDLC checkpoints	SSN will not be transmitted using clear text; SSN will always be digitally signed and encrypted.
Security Policy – Run Time	Automated security enforcement via security appliance	Verify identity and authorization based on X.509 certificate.

translated into fine-grained policies that can be enforced manually at design time and automatically at run time.

In this case, security is a business policy, a process policy, a technical service design policy and a runtime policy. The business version of the security policy might be written as follows: "All IT initiatives must conform to the corporate security policy. All IT projects must submit the security conformance declaration form, be reviewed by enterprise architecture and the corporate security officer."

The process version of the security policy will essentially describe the security process when reviews will be conducted, what triggers the reviews, what compliance to the policy entails, and what exception management steps will be taken. In addition, the process will specify security

Exhibit 6.6   Decomposing Policies: Manual and Automated Enforcement

implementations across project delivery process and the services/SOA development lifecycle.

The technical security policy would apply to services design as well. This policy might read as follows: "Services will conform to the SOA security policies in alignment with the corporate security policy. SSN will be digitally encrypted and signed in the payload of messages. UserID/password credentials will be passed using SAML."

As you can see from this example, security is enforced at multiple levels of the enterprise, and the coarse-grained corporate security is ultimately decomposed into more fine-grained policies for services design and runtime governance.

The security example demonstrates that there are varying degrees of policy granularity, and that there are multiple levels of policy enforcement. In other scenarios, business policies may be described and enforced using WS-Policy as well.

MULTI-LEVEL OR MULTI-TIERED POLICIES

Multi-level SOA policies are interesting and challenging. As described above, security policies can be defined and enforced as business policies, process policies, technical service design policies, as well as runtime policies. A multi-level policy such as this requires a model for associating the business policy as a parent policy to potential child policies that are essentially more fine-grained derivative policy assertions.

Reuse is another multi-level policy that is common for SOA initiatives. Recall the concept of a governance thread from Chapter 4. A reuse policy will be enforced at multiple levels and across multiple processes in your enterprise. We proposed the concept of a governance thread as a mechanism to link related governance processes together in order to enforce a policy at multiple levels and across multiple governance processes in an enterprise.

VERTICAL AND HORIZONTAL POLICY ENFORCEMENT

Another compelling and complex issue with a unified policy model is the vertical and horizontal enforcement of policies across the enterprise. Vertical policy enforcement refers to multi-level policies that involve integrating governance enforcement processes vertically to enforce a given policy. Reuse is an example of such a policy, where it is enforced during enterprise planning and project approval processes, as well as during service design and service portfolio management.

Horizontal enforcement of policies occurs when a given policy or group of policies are enforced through horizontally integrated governance processes. An example of this is the enforcement of service design and technical policies across the SDLC, from services modeling, design, and construction to quality assurance and testing, run time and operations.

Ultimately, the policy model you enforce is a decomposition of enterprise business polices into fine-grained technical policies and automated policies. The decomposition leads to enforceable policies that can be deployed or provisioned to various runtime tools for automated enforcement, or they can be issued to governance boards or invoked by governance processes for enforcement manually.

POLICY ENFORCEMENT MODELS: MANUAL, TECHNOLOGY-ASSISTED, AND AUTOMATED

Once you have determined the governance gaps to close and have derived policy categories from principles, you must begin to define the policy enforcement model (PEM) for your governance model. Remember, governance is for the critical aspects of your business. SOA governance is meant to focus on the critical aspects of your SOA initiative. The policies you must define and enforce are critical to SOA success and thus will be subject to enforcement.

The real gray area is in determining the overall governance and supporting policy model, deriving the necessary policy enforcement model, and then implementing or provisioning those policies to it for enforcement,

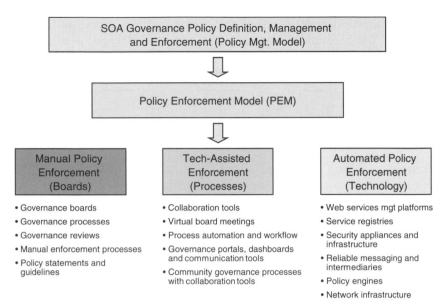

Exhibit 6.7 Policy Enforcement Scenarios

whether manual, technology-assisted, or fully automated. Exhibit 6.7 depicts this challenge at a high level.

Once your governance and policy model are defined, you must then determine the policy enforcement model for those policies. Which policies are business and process policies that will be enforced manually, and which are more technical and thus can be automated via SOA tools and technologies? Once you have defined your SOA goals, principles, and policies, as well as the policy categories that help close key SOA governance gaps, you can begin to establish your SOA policy enforcement model. Enforcement of policies can be accomplished via a variety of means, much as SOA governance will require multiple approaches to implement.

POLICY CATEGORIES DETERMINE POLICY ENFORCEMENT MECHANISMS

Policy enforcement is established based on the types of policies you require to achieve your SOA governance goals and close the critical SOA governance gaps. In general, the following policy rules of thumb will help you frame your policy enforcement model:

- **Business Policies.** Business policies will almost always require manual governance board oversight. These are very difficult to enforce using any automated tools, and thus their enforcement is normally accomplished by governance boards, working group reviews, sign-off mechanisms and the like.
- **Process Policies.** Process policies can be manually enforced, and most often will, but can be automated by augmenting manual governance checkpoints with business process management tools. For example, an SDLC can be automated with various checkpoints and reviews for a program management office (PMO) process, but most often the SDLC is manually executed and thus the PMO enforces the governance process by ensuring projects go through appropriate governance at the required times. The possibility of governance enablement and governance collaboration tools will open up new opportunities to implement robust governance solutions that more tightly link organization and process to automated policy enforcement.
- **Technical Policies.** Technical policies can be enforced using many of these enforcement mechanisms, and can also benefit from SOA tooling and runtime governance solutions. Technical policies in general are policies that are more easily automated than business policies. Most often, these relate to design-time policies for services design conformance, as well as runtime policies for security for example, or SLA monitoring and enforcement.
- **Multi-Tier or Multi-Level Policies.** Some SOA polices apply to all four tiers of the SOA Governance Four-Tier model described in Chapter 3. For example, security is one of these, as is a reuse policy. They are both examples of policies that are enforced as business policies, process policies, and technical policies. Enforcement of these policies will require orchestration and coordination across multiple governance enforcement processes. This is a concept we describe as a *governance thread.*

GOVERNANCE THREADS AND GOVERNANCE PROCESS ORCHESTRATION

Some business and process policies can only be enforced by stringing together multiple governance and management processes, and then enforcing that business policy across these related processes. To accommodate this scenario, we have coined the term "governance thread." A governance thread is coordinated enforcement of a multi-tier SOA policy across multiple SOA governance tiers (e.g., Enterprise/Strategic tier, SOA Operating Model tier, and the SOA/Services Lifecycle tier).

Policy enforcement is established based on the types of policies you require to achieve your SOA governance goals and close the critical SOA governance gaps. In general, the following rules of thumb will help you frame your policy enforcement model:

- **Policy categories will determine governance enforcement mechanisms.** In general, the type of policy will indicate how it will be enforced, whether manually by boards and reviews, or automated using governance tools.

Exhibit 6.8 illustrates how various policy categories are enforced using various governance policy enforcement mechanisms.

Based on the policy category and type, this exhibit shows how you can begin to develop the governance policy enforcement model by assigning policies to be manually enforced using a governance organizational model and board structure, or using governance enforcement processes for some policies such as architecture and design policies, or completely automating the enforcement of policies such as security and service level agreements.

Below we summarize some of these concepts with policy enforcement best practices:

- **Business policies are manually enforced via boards.** Business policies will almost always require manual governance board oversight. These are very difficult to enforce using any automated tools, and thus their enforcement is normally accomplished by governance boards, working group reviews, sign-off mechanisms and the like. However, some business policies translate into fine-grained policies that can be enforced using tools, as in the case of multi-level policies. Be sure there is

Exhibit 6.8 Unified Policy Model by Policy Type and Enforcement Mechanism

Policy Enforcement Mechanism	SOA Policy Category	Multi-level Policies
Governance Organizational Model and Boards	Business Policies Process Policies	Security Policies Reuse Policies
Governance Boards and Governance Processes	Architecture Policies Technical Policies Design Policies	Reuse Policies Security Policies
Governance Enabling Technology and Tools	Design Policies QA/Test Runtime Policies	Security Policies

traceability between the higher level policy and the lower-level automatically enforced policy.

■ **Process policies are predominantly manually enforced but can be automated or augmented by process automation tools.** Process policies can be manually enforced, and most often will, but can be automated by augmenting manual governance checkpoints with business process management tools. For example, an SDLC can be automated with various checkpoints and reviews for a PMO process, but most often the SDLC is manually executed and thus the PMO enforces the governance process by ensuring projects go through appropriate governance at the required times.

■ **Technical policies and design policies are often enforced manually and should be supported by tools.** Technical policies can be enforced using many of these enforcement mechanisms, and can also benefit from SOA tooling and runtime governance solutions. Technical policies in general are policies that are more easily automated than business policies. Most often, these relate to design time policies for services design conformance, as well as runtime policies for security for example, or SLA monitoring and enforcement.

■ **Runtime policies must be automated for audit, security enforcement and performance reasons.** Runtime policies are almost always automated since we are essentially running code and enforcing security, performance and ensuring service level agreements are being met.

■ **Multi-level policies will mostly be enforced manually, and may require dedicated focused governance boards.** Some SOA policies apply to all four tiers of the SOA Governance Four-Tier Model described in Chapter 3. For example, security is one of these, as is a reuse policy. They both are examples of policies that are enforced as business, process and technical policies. Thus, enforcement of these policies will require orchestration and coordination across multiple governance enforcement processes. This is a concept we describe as a *governance thread*. A governance thread is coordinated enforcement of a multi-tier SOA policy across multiple SOA governance tiers (e.g., Enterprise/Strategic tier, SOA Operating Model tier, and the SOA/Services Lifecycle tier). Governance threads are discussed in detail in Chapter 5.

The SOA governance policy enforcement model is a critical governance model design process. Getting the policy enforcement model correct will lead to complete policy and process coverage for critical SOA governance requirements. In the sections that follow, we explore various ways to design and implement your SOA policy enforcement model.

Integrated Policy Enforcement Model

As you transition from the SOA policy model to enforcement of policies, you must consider three broad policy enforcement mechanisms for your enterprise: (1) a governance organizational model, including boards and committees; (2) governance processes, enforcement triggers and events and (3) automated policy enforcement via governance enabling technology and tools. These three enforcement mechanisms form the basis for an *integrated policy enforcement model*. They form the fabric of SOA governance and policy enforcement for your enterprise. Integrated policy enforcement blends these three enforcement mechanisms into a holistic governance and policy enforcement fabric for your enterprise. Exhibit 6.9 depicts the concept of an integrated policy enforcement model.

As you develop your enterprise policy model and your policy enforcement model, you must consider various policy enforcement scenarios based on the policy metamodel above: automated policy enforcement via SOA enabling technology and tools, and manual policy enforcement via governance organizations, boards, and committees. These are the two extremes, with the potential for technology-enabled policy enforcement as a middle ground approach. The tools and technologies of SOA governance are very immature, and the industry standards for SOA policy are similarly works in progress.

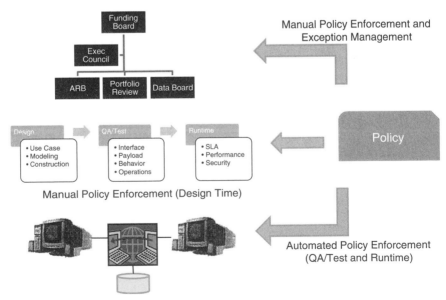

Exhibit 6.9   Integrated Policy Enforcement Model

BARRIERS TO A UNIFIED POLICY MODEL

Given the SOA governance landscape and the requirements for unifying approaches to governance and policy enforcement, there are a number of critical barriers to overcome in order to resolve this challenge. A few key barriers are listed below:

- Lack of industry standards for enterprise governance policies for compliance, business, process, and technical policies.
- Lack of a unified policy model that establishes an ontology and taxonomy of policies, as well as the relationships of policies to one another by category, such that enforcement can be accomplished using an integrated policy enforcement model.
- Lack of technical standards supporting a universal policy model. While Web services standards are evolving for Web services policy enforcement, there are different approaches and vendor proprietary models for network, security, and SLA and QoS policy enforcements among others.
- Lack of integrated tools that support an integrated policy enforcement model. While governance interoperability frameworks have been proposed by vendor consortia, little progress has been made to add non-Web services standards into the picture, much less integrating policy enforcement using manual and process-based enforcement concepts.

In some ways, this chapter is a call to action to address the industry standards for policy enforcement and policy management. However, in the following section we address the other gaps in policy enforcement.

INTEGRATED POLICY ENFORCEMENT MODEL

Based on the concepts of a unified model for policies, we can now proceed to integrating policy enforcement across the enterprise. As we have suggested, there are three fundamental policy enforcement mechanisms available to you when you design and implement a governance model:

1. Governance organizations, boards, and committees
2. Governance processes, triggers, and events
3. Governance tools and enabling technology

These three broad policy enforcement mechanisms must be integrated into a policy enforcement "fabric" that first and foremost ensures coverage for all critical governance processes and policies, and then ensures an integrated policy enforcement model that integrates governance boards with governance processes, and integrates boards and processes with governance tools. The uniting concept, of course, is the unified policy model.

As we have observed earlier, the weaknesses in most governance approaches is that they focus too narrowly on technical governance via automated tooling without considering the enterprise and business policies that support those technical policies. The technical approach to governance tends to ignore the enterprise context that gives value to those technical policies at run time.

The other extreme is when an organization establishes what it believes in a governance model by implementing a number of board structures and an organizational model embellished by charters, supporting artifacts and great fanfare. These models are just as limited because they ignore critical governance processes as well as the tooling enforcement mechanisms that can translate the business and enterprises policies typically enforced by boards into operational, technical, design, and runtime policies.

Our approach is to first unify the policy model for all enterprise policies, and then craft a policy enforcement model that integrates boards, processes and tools into an integrated policy enforcement model. This concept is depicted in Exhibit 6.10.

This illustration depicts the development of a policy model and a PEM, which consists of manual policy enforcement, process-based policy

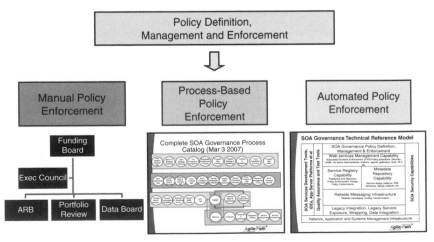

Exhibit 6.10   Policy Enforcement Scenarios: Manual to Automated

enforcement, and automated policy enforcement. These concepts are described below:

- **Manual Policy Enforcement.** Enforcement of policies through manual oversight and reviews by boards, committees, and working groups described in a governance organizational model. Manually enforced policies are often enterprise business policies that cannot be enforced automatically.
- **Process-Based Policy Enforcement.** Enforcement of policies through various governance processes, the execution of which occurs via scheduled reviews, process events and triggers. The governance process model establishes the governance events and triggers that will invoke policy enforcement activities and reviews, and will often convene a governance review board as well. Process-based policies include technical policies such as design-time and enterprise architecture policies, as well as operations and runtime policies that may be validated prior to a service going into production.
- **Automated Policy Enforcement.** Enforcement of policies using various forms of technology and tooling such that the policies can be automatically enforced in real time based on particular governance requirements. Examples include security, QoS and SLA policies. Because of the speed and criticality of such policies, automated enforcement is essential to ensure that those policies are indeed enforced, and that non-conformance is logged for troubleshooting, compliance and regulatory purposes.

Manual, process-based and automated enforcement of policies can of course be supported by governance enabling technology and tools. Exhibit 6.11 depicts policy enforcement models using various tooling scenarios.

In this exhibit, manual policy enforcement remains non-automated, with most of the enforcement driven by governance processes, reviews, and governance boards. Some aspects of this could be automated using collaboration tools, but there still must be governance processes that trigger governance boards, which could be conducted virtually or in person, supported by collaboration tools.

However, this illustration opens the possibilities for technology-assisted policy enforcement using various emerging technologies in support of process-based governance. Some potential tools include:

- Collaboration tools
- Virtual rooms and board meetings

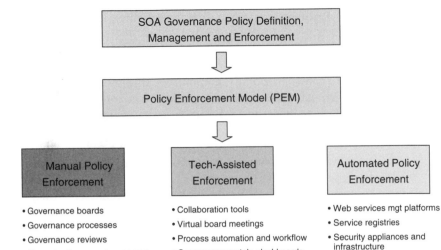

Exhibit 6.11   Policy Enforcement Approaches and Mechanisms

- Business process automation and management tools and workflow management tools
- Portals and dashboards supported by metadata management tools

In the automated policy enforcement category, there is a new breed of tools and enabling technologies on the market that support runtime governance and automated policy enforcement. Again, the motivation here is that at run time, in real time, specific policies demand automated enforcement based on the performance and throughput requirements of running service-based applications and still enforce security policies, ensuring SLA and QoS policies via routing, load balancing, failovers, and dynamic capacity management. In these scenarios, automated policy enforcement is essential. Tools that support automated policy enforcement include some of the following examples:

- Policy engines and policy management tools
- Service registry/repository solutions
- Enterprise service bus/reliable messaging platforms
- Security appliances
- Identity management solutions
- XML accelerators and load balancing appliances

- Distributed policy enforcement solutions based on policy enforcement points and broker/interceptor intermediary solutions
- Web services management tools
- Quality assurance and testing tools

This is a representative list, although there are many specific tools available that lay claim to runtime policy enforcement and governance.

Currently, the IT and SOA vendor community is very far from proposing and integrating their tools to consistently enforce runtime policies using some de facto or industry standards. This lack of vendor standards places the burden of policy enforcement on end user companies to develop and manually deploy policies as they extend their SOA initiative and as they have more and more services, clients and service-based applications in production.

BARRIERS TO INTEGRATED POLICY ENFORCEMENT MODELS

Based on the discussion above, there are a number of gaps and barriers to realizing a truly integrated policy enforcement model at an enterprise level. We already identified the policy challenges above and the absence of industry standards for unifying the total body of enterprise policies. This problem extends to the lack of industry standards for enforcing policies using various vendor tools and enabling technologies.

The following barriers currently prohibit the integrated enforcement of policies, with or without the development of a unified policy model:

- Lack of horizontal integration of tools supporting end-to-end SDLC processes
- Lack of mapping design-time policies to quality assurance and testing and runtime policies
- Poor to no integration of design-time tools with governance tools supporting design, quality assurance (QA)/test and runtime policy enforcement
- Lack of vertical integration of enterprise, corporate, business and process policies with technical policies enforced across a corporate SDLC or project delivery processes
- Lack of integration of key governance processes and tools with project execution tools (e.g., portfolio management tools integrated with Integrated Development Environments (IDE) and software development tools, which may in turn integrate with policy engines and policy repositories)

Again, much as the absence of a unified policy model was a call to action, the barriers above should serve as a similar call to action for industry standards to integrate policy management and enforcement across an enterprise. This discussion leads to new requirements for enterprise/SOA governance based on a unified policy model and an integrated policy enforcement model described above.

POLICY PROVISIONING MODEL (AND PROCESS)

As the industry matures the concepts, approaches and tools for enterprise, IT and SOA governance, we anticipate the development of tools that can automate the development, enforcement and provisioning of enterprise policies according to the policy framework we have mapped out thus far. Three potential solutions work in lockstep to potentially facilitate automation of policy model development, policy enforcement models, and policy provisioning.

Exhibit 6.12 depicts this policy provisioning model concept.

The policy provisioning approach illustrated depends on three technology solutions: (1) a policy modeling solution, (2) a policy enforcement modeling solution, and (3) a policy provisioning solution.

Policy Modeling Solution Gap

A governance policy modeling tool that can facilitate definition, management and version control for all enterprise policies developed according to

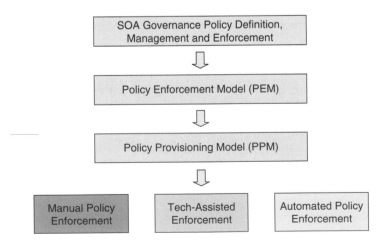

Exhibit 6.12   Policy Provisioning Concept

the concepts of a unified policy model and an integrated policy enforcement model is necessary. Key requirements of such a policy modeling solutions would be as follows:

- Model, align, and map enterprise policies to business, IT, and SOA goals and principles.
- Enable the decomposition of enterprise, business, compliance, and process policies into fine-grained policies that can be enforced via an integrated policy enforcement model based on manual, process and automated policy enforcement concepts.
- Support vertical and horizontal mapping of policies based on a policy ontology and taxonomy, such that there is clear alignment and traceability of fine-grained policy assertions to enterprise and corporate policies.
- Support or implement a standard policy vocabulary, ontology and taxonomy that can be submitted as an industry standard, as well as mapped into current or emerging industry standards for policy enforcement (e.g., WS-Policy, etc.).
- Allow for policy version control, deprecation, affectivity dates and related policy management processes.
- Integrate with a policy enforcement model (described next).

Policy Enforcement Model Solution

A policy enforcement modeling solution is needed to enable assignment of policies from your policy model to various policy enforcement mechanisms. Such a solution might have the following functionality:

- Assign policy categories and policies to a policy enforcement model that includes governance boards, governance processes and governance tools of all types.
- Incorporate an inventory listing of all enterprise policy enforcement mechanisms, including all technology solutions, governance boards and governance processes.
- Allow modeling and simulation of the policy enforcement model to ensure complete integrated enforcement of enterprise policies and total coverage across all critical governance processes.
- Provides visual mapping of policies to the policy enforcement model to, again, ensure a complete policy coverage model.
- Generates policy enforcement metrics that feed into a governance scorecard, governance portal, and dashboard solution.

■ Integrates with a policy provisioning modeling solution (described below).

Policy Provisioning Modeling Solution

A policy provisioning solution will enable the provisioning or deployment of enterprise policies to the various policy enforcement mechanisms modeled in the policy enforcement model. The requirements of such a tool might include:

■ Automatically download industry-standard policy assertions or policy enforcement syntax to the automated policy enforcement technologies and tools based on existing drivers.
■ Generate policy enforcement syntax and code, in an industry standard format, that enables automated policy enforcement across a broad range of technologies and tools regardless of vendors.
■ Generate manual policy enforcement artifacts, templates and supporting policy documentation for manual and process-based policies.
■ Generate business process automation support (e.g., workflow, process triggers and events, review schedules and governance triggers and other process-centric approaches to automating policy enforcement).

Integrated Policy Enforcement Model and Feedback

Finally, there must be a feedback model that closes the loop for all governance processes and policy enforcement processes. Again, establishing a unified policy model and an integrated policy enforcement model will enable the opportunity to achieve closed loop governance and feedback across the horizontal processes of an SDLC as well as the vertical feedback via governance threads.

Exhibit 6.13 depicts such a feedback model.

While many of these concepts are being pondered by the industry, perhaps we can accelerate the realization of an enterprise governance framework that meets some of the requirements stated above. Without addressing the major barriers to both a unified policy model and an integrated policy enforcement model, a complete governance and policy enforcement model is not possible without being heavily tilted toward manual policy enforcement, or the fragmented approach being currently implemented by tools vendors in the industry today. A final barrier must be addressed along the path toward unified policy models and integrated policy enforcement: goal, principle, and policy management processes.

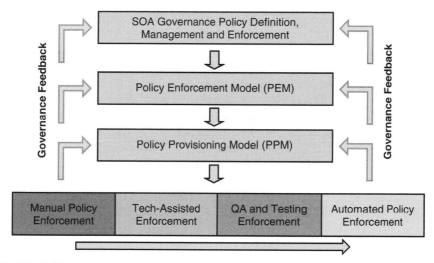

Exhibit 6.13　Integrated Policy Enforcement and Feedback

SOA GOALS, PRINCIPLE, AND POLICY MANAGEMENT

Policies and policy management in general, must be defined, managed, versioned, deprecated, and retired using an ongoing management and oversight process that parallels service portfolio management activities. In Chapter 10, we place this discipline under the heading of "Governance Performance Management." Governance Performance Management is the ongoing process ownership and sustainment of enterprise governance processes and disciplines, as well as the management of the enterprise policy model.

Policies are defined by multiple members of the IT organization who play a role in the definition of the SOA governance model and overall SOA vision and strategy. IT managers, chief technology officers, chief architects, architects, development managers, team and/or project leaders can play a role in defining the policies that will comprise the SOA governance model. Exhibit 6.14 depicts the processes required to implement a sustained goal,

Exhibit 6.14　Goal, Principle, and Policy Management Processes

principle, and policy management capability as part of your governance performance management function.

Ultimately, policies are derived from the business and technical requirements of the SOA initiative and the portfolio of services that will operate in the SOA over time. Therefore, it is likely that an initial body of policies will be defined by an SOA core team to spearhead the implementation of services and SOA in a given organization. In fact, many organizations define their initial policies without calling them policies at all.

Many organizations begin their SOA effort by defining their services design guidelines and best practices within various business process domains. These initial service design guidelines will become the basis for identifying and enforcing specific policies through code reviews and manual SOA governance processes under the oversight of the architects and IT management. Eventually these policies can be implemented as enforceable policies using automation and tools that provide centralized policy definition, management, and policy enforcement across the organization and SOA lifecycle processes.

Enterprise policies must be managed as strategic assets in many respects like the services and processes they help govern. Governance tools and approaches described in this chapter do not currently exist, but may begin to emerge based on many of the challenges in the current enterprise and SOA governance landscape. However, we must discuss one final aspect of policies in this chapter: the concept of policies transforming into behavioral norms.

TRANSFORMING SOA POLICIES INTO BEHAVIORAL NORMS

An emerging research area for SOA governance and IT governance relates to the concept of transitioning from policies to behavioral norms, and how these impact the relative scalability of governance. When SOA governance is initially implemented, most organizations are new to SOA and governance, and are therefore not accustomed to explicit enforcement of policies under a formally defined and explicitly enforced governance model. Explicit policy-driven governance will be difficult for many organizations where the corporate culture is not one of explicit policies and where informal governance dominates current decisions, or consensus based models dominate decision making calculus. The definition and implementation of policy-driven governance will strain current decision-making mechanisms, and will formalize governance processes that have been more collegial to date.

Policy-driven governance can be uncomfortable in its early implementation phases, which is why we urge the development of change management models, education and awareness campaigns, and other approaches to easing your way into it.

That said, once your governance model has matured and policies are known and understood, there will be a magical transformation in your enterprise; suddenly policies will not be "enforced" in the punitive sense of the word. They will be known already, with the expectations understood, and thus policies will become behavioral norms rather than top-down edicts. Once your governance maturity has reached the tipping point where policies have transformed into norms, and policy enforcement is more like normative behavior, we can begin to replace explicit policy-driven governance with self governance concepts, collaborative governance models, and community governance constructs. Your goal with SOA governance should be to accelerate maturation around policy-driven governance so that you can transition to more collaborative community and self-governing concepts. However, in the early phases of your SOA initiative, you must implement policies and supporting policy enforcement mechanisms, all based on integrating governance organizations and boards, governance processes and events, and governance tools and enabling technologies. Hopefully, this chapter gives you hope that there is a stepwise model and framework to work with to achieve your policy-driven governance model.

SUMMARY

Governance is critical to the success of an SOA. Policies are the substrate of governance. This chapter developed some far reaching concepts for policy-based governance and suggested some gaps in industry standards around the unified model of policies and an integrated policy enforcement model. We offer suggestions on how a policy model is defined such that it is enforceable using an integrated policy enforcement model comprised of governance boards, governance processes, and governance tools and technologies. Policies are almost as misunderstood as governance itself. We hope that policies and policy enforcement are now clearer for you, and that you can see how to begin developing enterprise policies that make sense and will help achieve the business goals you seek. Remember, the sooner you achieve policy-based governance, the sooner you can transition into more normative behavioral models and realize collaborative self-governance capabilities.

Notes

1. Toufic Boubez, Layer 7 Technologies: *"Enabling SOA Runtime Policy,"* 2006, p. 4.
2. WebLayers Whitepaper: *SOA Governance,* 2005, p. 11.
3. Web Services Policy Framework (WS-Policy), V. 1.2, www.w3.org/Submission/WS-Policy, March 2006.

CHAPTER 7

SOA Governance Organizational Models

One of the most challenging and misunderstood aspects of Service-Oriented Architecture (SOA) governance is establishing a viable organizational model for governance processes and policy enforcement. One of the most common SOA governance mistakes we see is the misconception that implementing a sophisticated governance board structure is the equivalent of implementing effective SOA governance. It is not. Implementing governance boards without clearly defined goals, principles, and policies, as well as clear definition of the board's role in enforcing SOA policies, will result in lots of meetings but ineffective SOA governance. In fact, effective SOA governance should result in as few boards as necessary to govern your SOA initiative and services, but as many as necessary to effectively govern in order to realize your SOA goals. The right-sizing of SOA governance is an important consideration because from a stakeholder perspective, any SOA governance is too much governance, and will initially be more intrusive than the projects and business units prefer.

Furthermore, adding new governance processes and explicit enforcement will feel like "over-governance" initially. That is the nature of governance. Asserting control over decisions that were made by individuals or business units will often be a painful transition. However, planning for this and having a pre-mitigation strategy to address organizational conflicts and exceptions will go far in smoothing the transition to effective SOA governance.

There are a number of key questions to consider as you plan the organizational model for SOA governance. A partial list follows:

- How do I govern SOA given my current organizational structure and Information Technology (IT) organization?
- How do we integrate SOA governance with existing IT governance organizations?
- When do you use a board versus a working group?
- When should I implement a standing board versus a virtual board?

- How and when should I represent key process stakeholders?
- How many boards do we need for SOA governance coverage?

Key points to consider when establishing governance organizational models are: What do the boards do? What is their scope? What policies or decisions are they enforcing?

Governance boards are expensive and consume resources, thus they must be implemented to govern critical concerns, not aspects of SOA that can be managed offline or using other mechanisms.

FIRST THINGS FIRST: UNDERSTAND YOUR CURRENT ORGANIZATIONAL STRUCTURE

In order to structure an SOA governance model, you must understand how your organization is currently structured. Many business strategists have documented the impact of organization and structure on organizational performance.[1] There is always a dramatic impact of organization and structure on the resulting performance of an organization, and with SOA governance, you can expect the same. In order to design a governance organization, you must begin with the corporate structure and organizational model first. What kind of organization do you work in? Functional? Divisionally structured? Matrixed? Product or geographically structured? This is important, because it has a direct bearing on how your IT organization is structured. Is the IT organization a mirror of corporate structure?

CONWAY'S LAW AND ENTERPRISE SOA GOVERNANCE

As you consider organizational designs in support of your enterprise SOA governance model, you should bear in mind Conway's Law.[2] Conway's Law was coined by Fred Brooks in his famous book *The Mythical Man-Month*. Conway's Law is actually Brooks' application of concepts from Mel Conway's 1967 paper entitled "How Do Committees Invent?" The paper was submitted to the *Harvard Business Review* and rejected, and was subsequently submitted to *Datamation* magazine, the major IT publication of its time, and was published in 1968. The fundamental concept of Conway's papers is:

> *Any organization that designs a system (defined more broadly here than just information systems) will inevitably produce a design whose structure is a copy of the organization's communication structure.*[3]

Simply stated, a system designed by a given organization will reflect the organizational structure of said organization, often to the detriment of that system or software application. It is rare that an organization structures itself, or its software development organization, for the optimal creation of a software product or application.

Applying Conway's Law to SOA and SOA governance, we can say that there is a clear relationship between your organization, both business and IT organizations, and the resultant SOA strategy, governance model and implementation process you employ. Conway's Law applies in a number of ways:

- **SOA is often pursued to create shared reusable services in an enterprise.** Often, achieving sharing and reuse requires an organizational construct that is responsible for identifying, building and enforcing/encouraging sharing of enterprise services. Without an organizational structure to enable sharing and reuse, there will be no sharing and reuse.
- **Conway's Law also applies to ownership and oversight of service portfolios.** How you organize to establish ownership or stewardship for the various categories of services in your enterprise will have a direct bearing on your ability to build, consume and share those services. Service portfolios are reflections of the application portfolio, which reflects organizational structure and funding models. Thus, you cannot escape the inevitable influence of organizational structure on SOA.
- **Enterprise architecture and legacy application portfolios are behavioral artifacts.** The organizational models that generated these artifacts are driven by corporate behaviors and the resultant funding models. Thus, Conway's Law would help explain the relationship between organizational models and IT enterprise architecture and application portfolios of an enterprise. As you consider SOA and the impact of services on your enterprise, consider the impact of Conway's Law on these decisions.

In some respects, enterprise governance and both IT and SOA governance overcome the challenges imposed on your enterprise by various organizational structures. As we know, there are strengths and weaknesses of various organizational designs. Centralized structures are good for clear decision making and accountability, but can be slow to respond to changing conditions. Distributed organizations can more rapidly respond to changing conditions, but can be more difficult to manage due to the decentralized decisions structure and accountability framework. Federated IT organizations are blends and have their own strengths and weaknesses as well.

SOA governance is necessary and critical in any organizational design, but must be designed and implemented in light of, and in many respects, to compensate for weaknesses of your current IT and organizational structure.

Thus, Conway's Law is a useful concept to bear in mind as you structure your SOA governance organizational model and boards. How will they enable your target outcomes and not become burdened by your current organizational model? Be sure your SOA governance organizational model enables your future and is not anchored to your past or current organization structure.

MARKS' LAW? ORGANIZATION REFLECTS FUNDING

A complement to Conway's Law is a phenomenon I have observed for many years: Organizational structures, and thus the IT and enterprise architecture, are reflections of the funding model of the enterprise. As the corporate leadership funds the organization, so do they design the organization. The organization chart of an enterprise is a reflection of the financial structure of the organization. Thus, the Conway's Law upstream corollary is what I will call (tongue-in-cheek of course) Marks' Law: Funding models directly impact organizational models, which directly affect the IT and enterprise architecture of an enterprise, as well as the software systems developed by that organization. The funding model either enables or inhibits an optimal design of a software system by virtue of the organizational model that creates it. Organizations reflect funding models.

ORGANIZATIONAL ANALYSIS STEPS

The following steps should help you analyze and understand your current enterprise/SOA/IT governance model and organizational model's impact on governance.

Current Organization Structure   First, you must understand the way your organization is structured at the corporate level. Review organization charts and quickly determine the corporate structure and how it may impact IT and SOA governance models.

Current IT Organization   Next, how is the IT organization structured? Is it a mirror image of the corporate structure or some variation? Is the IT organization centralized, distributed, or a federated structure, and what is the trend?

Are there divisional chief information officers (CIOs) or line of business CIOs? Is the enterprise architecture function aligned in a similar fashion? What are the IT-specific organizational constructs that have been implemented for your IT model? Are there technology-specific support teams?

Centralized to Decentralized IT Continuum

As you understand your organizational model, consider how centralized or distributed your IT organization is, and where it is headed. Exhibit 7.1 depicts an organizational continuum with two extremes: centralized and distributed.

This simple model shows an IT organizational continuum that ranges from completely centralized IT management model to a completely distributed line of business (LOB) IT management model. In the middle, there are two federated organizational views: strongly federated and weakly federated IT management. Your IT organization and management model is somewhere on this continuum, and it is also trending either toward more centralized IT management or toward a more distributed IT management model. Rarely are IT organization and management models perfectly stable.

Organizations inevitably transition from centralized to decentralized and back to centralized structures over time. As these accordion-like structural shifts take place, you must understand the dynamics and organizational tensions that accompany these transitions. If your organization is decentralized and the IT organization is decentralized, there will be political tension from centralizing funding and decision authority for aspects of IT that used to be under decentralized control. Another aspect of this transition tends to be the implementation of chargeback schemes, which add to the organizational angst about transitioning from decentralized to centralized IT structures. Similarly, the transition from centralized to decentralized IT structures is fraught with similar political organizational dynamics.

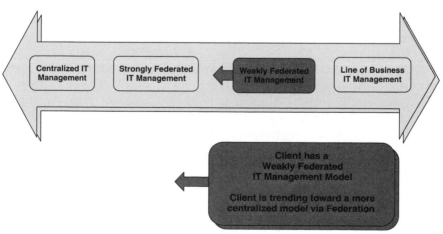

Exhibit 7.1 IT Structural Diagnostic

Determine Your Current Governance Baseline

In defining an SOA governance organizational model, you must understand and document your current governance organizational baseline. What are the current governance organizations, boards, and committees? What do they do? What policies, decisions, or resources do they oversee?

As you document the current governance baseline, organize the information by major governance functions using the following categories of governance:

- Corporate governance
- IT governance
- Enterprise architecture governance
- Program governance/program management office (PMO)

Inventory the governance boards, document the governance organizational model, and identify governance coverage gaps. This baseline will help you develop an appropriate enterprise SOA governance organizational model for your enterprise.

PURPOSE OF THE SOA GOVERNANCE ORGANIZATION

Why do you need an SOA governance organization? What purpose does it serve? These questions are central to establishing appropriate and right-sized SOA governance organizational models. Governance organizations are established for a variety of reasons, but for an SOA governance model, they play crucial roles.

- **Alignment.** SOA governance boards provide a mechanism to ensure alignment of business and IT, as well as internal IT alignment to SOA goals and decisions. Alignment is accomplished by creating boards comprised of business and IT leaders for example, or by establishing other cross-functional teams to make sure every stakeholder has a voice and a seat at the table.
- **Stakeholder Representation.** SOA governance boards provide key stakeholder involvement in those critical SOA governance decisions that impact multiple stakeholders. This is one of the most fundamental reasons for a governance organizational construct—to obtain stakeholder input and maintain their involvement in all decisions related to a particular SOA governance concern.

- **Manual Policy Enforcement.** Governance boards play a role in the manual enforcement of policies that cannot be automated or should be enforced by boards.
- **Exception Management.** Governance boards play a critical role in managing exceptions to governance policies. Exception management must be explicitly defined in the SOA governance model. This means anticipating possible exceptions, and having alternative pathways for dealing with exceptions. In this manner, you can pre-mitigate for many exceptions ahead of time. The exception management role of a governance board will also involve the next primary purpose of a governance board: escalation and appeals.
- **Escalation and Appeals.** A major reason for establishing a governance board structure is to provide a means to manage exceptions and enable dialog around those exceptions. If a governance board makes a decision that a business unit disagrees with, a process must be defined to escalate the decision by appealing to more senior or higher level boards. Your governance organizational model must plan for exceptions, escalation, and appeal procedures so that there is a clear and unambiguous decision path that will always be followed.
- **Information Sharing.** SOA governance boards can provide an information sharing forum, but we urge you not to establish a governance board merely for information sharing purposes. That can be accomplished in an offline forum or via other communications mechanisms. If the board is established for more valid reasons, then the information sharing benefit is an incremental benefit.
- **Signal Clear SOA Intent and Commitment.** A final reason for establishing SOA governance boards is to send a clear signal that SOA and policy enforcement are so important that senior management will be meeting once or twice per month to ensure alignment, involvement, and clear decision making with respect to SOA initiatives. If no other purpose is achieved, this outcome is worth its weight in gold. However, we believe you can achieve all of these benefits with a right-sized SOA governance organizational model.

GOVERNANCE ORGANIZATION PATTERNS AND BEST PRACTICES

There are a number of patterns and best practices to consider as you structure your SOA governance organizational design. The following sections answer common questions and focus on key decisions you will face as you begin considering the optimal governance structure for your organization.

When Do You Need a Governance Board?

Governance focuses on critical aspects of your business that must receive more oversight than typical management processes. SOA governance is no different. A key SOA governance organizational design question is, when do you need a governance board versus any other policy enforcement mechanism? A governance board is appropriate when the governance concern or gap is both critical to SOA success and it impacts multiple stakeholders from multiple business domains or organizations.

Key SOA governance concerns are detailed in Chapter 3. Whether you need a governance board depends on the current criticality of the governance concern or requirements and whether it affects multiple stakeholders across more than one business domain. If the answer is yes, then you may justify establishing a governance board. The next question is: What kind of board do you need? We answer that question below.

Best Practices

- Remember: Less is more with governance. Fewer high-impact governance boards are more effective than diluted governance spread across many boards.
- The boards you are considering are candidate boards at this time. You must continually assess whether you have too many, too few, or just enough. Then you will finalize the organizational model. However, your governance model is going to evolve and change. Get it right enough for immediate success, but realize you will be changing it over time.

What Kind of Governance Board—Standing, Virtual, Working Group, or Temporary?

Another typical governance board consideration is whether to make them standing boards or temporary, virtual boards or permanent organizations, or can a series of working groups satisfy the SOA governance requirements at that time. Most SOA governance board constructs are combinations of virtual teams supported by working groups. The virtual teams are staffed with appropriate representation to meet the board's charter and goals, but they are called to action only on a scheduled basis or by governance events, triggers, exceptions, or escalations.

Early in the SOA adoption model, there will tend to be a need for many working groups to develop and define key SOA governance artifacts, policies, processes, and more. This is especially true during SOA governance ramp. During this SOA adoption phase, working groups will commonly lead efforts for defining the following governance processes or areas:

- SOA platform and overall technology stack
- SOA/Services Software Development Lifecycle (SDLC)
- Services design and interoperability standards
- SOA enterprise architecture extensions, reference models
- SOA strategy
- Preliminary SOA governance models

Once these areas are defined and policies and documentation exists, the ongoing maintenance and oversight of these process and artifacts can be accomplished by the enterprise architecture (EA) organization (assuming there is one, and also assuming it has been beefed up to support the EA demands of an SOA initiative.)

Permanent SOA governance boards with formal persistent organizations are possible, but rare. These are most likely in an organization that has very little to no formal governance over any IT disciplines (e.g., EA, the SDLC). In these scenarios, a combination of permanent boards augmented by virtual boards and working groups will be expected.

What Guidelines Are There for Board Composition?

Governance board composition is a function of the stakeholder representation required to sufficiently govern a critical SOA concern or requirement. If the governance concern is around funding and budgeting at the enterprise level, then this board should represent the business units, IT organization, EA, and IT finance. This is notional of course, but you get the picture. If the governance concern is an IT decision, yet affects business units, then the board composition may include the CIO, chief architect, relationship managers embedded in the business units, and business unit embedded architects.

Best Practices

- Keep the boards small and functional, no more than five to ten attendees. Any larger and the board ceases to be a decision board and transgresses into an information sharing board.
- Represent the stakeholders at the appropriate level (e.g., executive level, manager level etc.).
- Ensure stakeholder representatives are authorized to make decisions for the organization they are representing.
- Support SOA governance boards with working groups and supporting processes so that decisions are made in the board meetings, while analysis and recommendations have been conducted offline by working groups.

- ■ Working groups perform analysis, obtain stakeholder buy-in, and make the recommendations. Governance boards approve these decisions and implement the decision via their defined policy enforcement role.

When Would You Use a Multi-Chaired Board?

In general, multi-chaired boards are discouraged. Dual chaired and tri-chaired boards are common in federal agencies, where the demands for stakeholder representation and oversight are very complex and perhaps there is justification for multi-chaired boards. However, we feel that a single decision authority should be named, with appropriate processes for stakeholder representation, exception management and escalation procedures. Remember, our suggestion is to consider a governance board structure only when the governance concern or requirement affects multiple stakeholders across multiple business or organizational domains. By definition, all stakeholders will be represented if the board is staffed and chartered appropriately. Dual and tri-chair structures will confuse process ownership and decision authority more than they will help; thus we discourage the practice.

How Do You Allocate Voting Rights?

Voting models for governance boards should be simple. In fact, representatives for stakeholder organizations should be authorized to vote as needed for a particular governance issue. Generally, voting models can be used to make the decision, or they can be used to "take the temperature" on an issue, with the board chair being the ultimate decision maker. Both models are appropriate. However, if the decision made goes against the vote, there must be an escalation process if the decision has no concurrence from the stakeholders. If there are many instances of voting decisions being overridden by the board chair, the governance board will lose the confidence of the stakeholders, and it will fail. Be very careful about voting models and decision models, but also be clear in defining who is the final decision maker for a specific governance board.

When to Use a Decision Board versus an Informational Board?

We feel that all SOA governance boards should be decision-making boards, not information sharing boards. Information sharing and dissemination can be accomplished via other governance support mechanisms more efficiently than the governance board structures. For example, documentation of key policies, guidance, and standards can be managed via an enterprise architecture repository, a portal, an electronic newsletter, or in other meeting forums. Using valuable governance board time for information sharing is a waste of the board members' time, especially when other governance mechanisms are better for communication.

Using Overlapping Membership Strategies

An interesting mechanism to ensure alignment and continuity of governance processes and decision making is to structure board composition with overlapping memberships. For example, key business unit stakeholders who may participate on the architecture review board may also be attendees at a more senior business-IT joint review boards. This overlapping membership ensures consistency both upward and downward in the governance chain of command as well as in the communication model that supports governance.

The only risk with this approach is twofold: (1) You may end up with boards that are too large and unwieldy, which will inhibit decision-making capabilities; (2) you may demand too much time from your key governance board members, which could end up causing them to resign from the board. Again, as with anything organizational in nature, you have to find a proper balance between representation and time commitment for everyone's sake.

OTHER SOA GOVERNANCE BOARD CONSIDERATIONS

When developing a governance organizational design, you must consider other factors that are unique to your organization. How does your organization's politics affect the ability to implement appropriate SOA governance? Are there internal business champions that will better support your governance model than others?

Political Alignment Model As you establish your enterprise SOA governance organizational model, you should take into consideration the political landscape and fluidity of the power base. Reflecting on the IT structural accordion, consider who the political winners and losers are as your IT organization fluctuates between being centralized and/or distributed. The political alignment model is an important exercise to help ensure that your enterprise SOA governance organization is aligned to and can succeed given the political, social, and power structures of your enterprise.

Naming Boards and Aligning to Culture   When naming governance boards, use creativity and common sense. Do not use a name that has baggage or that will make organizations suspicious. Use words like "collaboration board" or "council" or "working group". These are more benign than names like "SOA policy board" or "governance review board."

Charters   Defining charters should be a simple exercise and you must not belabor this. If you feel you must define formal charters, make them short, simple, and concise. Publicize them and then move on. There are many other more challenging activities to focus on.

Membership   Defining membership of a governance boards is critical, as this is how you establish the stakeholder model for your SOA governance model. Depending on the governance requirements and concerns, as well as the most pressing SOA governance requirements, you will define your membership based on what organizations and representation are necessary to ensure participation, input, review and approval, and ongoing oversight for critical decisions.

Chairmanship   Assigning a chairperson to a governance board can be a delicate matter depending on the type of organization you are in. The chairperson role can be obvious, in the case of technical or IT architecture decisions. However, identifying the chairperson can be a more delicate challenge if there are organizational politics and structural discord to contend with. Remember the IT structural accordion: If there is a structural change in progress, the political and organizational dynamics must be understood to help in establishing membership and chairmanship roles.

In more politically sensitive organizational models, dual chair and multi-chair models, as well as rotating chair models, are used to ensure balance of power and decision rights. A dual chair model might represent both the IT organization and a business unit in a key decision. A multi-chair model might be appropriate for very large or complex organizations. In our experience, a multi-chair or tri-chair board can be useful but adds complexity that may fundamentally undermine the SOA governance board's decision-making ability. We would suggest a rotating chair process for these kinds of situations, although there is a downside to this model: loss of continuity for key decisions.

Be careful with chairperson models, as they tend to be more politically motivated than functionally motivated. Representation of key stakeholders is essential, so weigh the composition and chairmanship of key governance boards with complexity, decision making, and effectiveness. Find the balance, but err toward effectiveness if possible, and avoid unnecessary complexity.

Exception Management   Once your SOA governance model is online and performing, the role of governance boards will become more of an exception management process than a definition and enforcement process. In other words, as key policies are defined and disseminated, and knowledge and understanding of SOA governance expectations are more widely known, the governance boards will transition into managing exception cases. How well exceptions are managed will determine how well your governance model works.

Exceptions are opportunities to test two dimensions of SOA governance: First, they test your organization's will to enforce clear IT/SOA policies across projects and the organization. Exception management processes test your organization's commitment and credibility. If waivers are granted often and policies become just recommendations versus enforceable policies, your governance model is at risk. SOA governance requires the political will to say "No" to projects. Many ill-conceived governance models do not have the political capital or clear executive accountability to enforce policies. You may have to reconsider your governance model in this case.

Second, they test your ability to encourage innovation and new ideas, and thus your ability to adapt and evolve SOA governance by revising policies based on project or organizational input. Exception management processes are about enforcing policies, managing exceptions, and adapting governance and policies in an iterative process. Be prepared for the early exceptions, and have a prepared exception management model. Send clear and consistent messages with exception management, and make exceptions a process to be understood and not feared.

SPECIFIC GOVERNANCE ORGANIZATIONAL MODELS TO CONSIDER

There are a wide variety of organizational models that may work for your organization. In addition, the SOA governance organizational model will vary by SOA adoption phase. Some common organizational constructs are discussed in this section, but realize that you will have to create the structures and organization that makes sense for your organization.

Ad Hoc SOA Core Team

This is the initial SOA governance board in most organizations. The SOA core team is often an ad hoc team formed by virtue of a common shared interest in establishing SOA consistency across the organization. The ad hoc SOA core team is not chartered or empowered by an enterprise executive, and it is not headed by an executive representative. The ad hoc SOA core team often leads all aspects of the SOA initiative in the inception phase of SOA adoption.

As a governance entity, the ad hoc SOA core team is a limited governance organization. It can provide influence and initial direction for SOA governance efforts, primarily around initial technical standards and service design standards, but it has no authority in the enterprise.

Empowered SOA Core Team

An *empowered SOA core team* is an executive-sponsored team that has been given express authority and accountability for the initial decisions for an organization's SOA initiative under a formal charter.

An empowered SOA core team is typically small and led by a senior IT executive, e.g. chief technology officer (CTO), chief architect, or an enterprise architect. Occasionally, the empowered SOA core team is led by a business champion with some technical qualifications and IT credibility. However, the most frequent structure is an IT-led organization.

The empowered SOA core team often focuses on the following kinds of activities initially:

- Development of an initial SOA strategy, most often a simple whitepaper or short strategy document
- Definition of how SOA helps the organization
- What SOA technology and tools do we need?
- What kinds of services can we opportunistically build or expose to prove SOA value to the organization?
- What minimal SOA governance is essential to demonstrate reuse and interoperability of services?

The empowered SOA core team will get the ball rolling in your organization. Over time, the empowered SOA core team may expand or be augmented to a more formally structured SOA team with an expanded charter, more resources, and enterprise responsibility for SOA across the enterprise.

The empowered SOA core team is a focused model for achieving initial proof points for SOA and determining initial value and technical capabilities. The empowered SOA core team must be expanded and resourced better to transition SOA to an enterprise initiative.

Benevolent Dictator Organization

Open source development models offer insights into project ownership, governance, and decision-making structures.[4] Most often, open source projects are owned by the founders who then attract other developer/contributors to the project. Causes of conflict often center on four key decisions:

1. Who makes key decisions about a project?
2. Who receives credit, or conversely, who is blamed for what?
3. How to reduce or manage duplication of effort and prevent rogue versions of code from complicating defect tracking.
4. What is the overall "right thing" to do technically?

Open source project ownership models often evolve into benevolent dictator organizations and projects grow and attract developers and contributors. If the project owner remains the benevolent dictator, that person must make key governance decisions relating to allocation of credit for contributed code, avoidance of forking of the project, and key design decisions.

In an SOA context, a benevolent dictator organizational model can be useful for the informal stages of SOA in an organization as it transitions from an informal pocket of SOA interest into a broader working group structure, often involving multiple groups or organizations, yet remaining an informal working group. The key decisions will be made as a team, but with deference to the senior technical voice who would most likely be the benevolent dictator.

SOA Center of Gravity Model

SOA has become the most important IT trend of the last five years, and it is in its early adoption phase. SOA though, is a complex and challenging endeavor. Many SOA initiatives flounder early in their implementation and adoption because of ambiguities around a number of critical factors such as:

- No clearly defined SOA strategy
- Lack of SOA governance for key processes
- No clear accountability, authority, and ownership to execute SOA strategy and governance
- Lack of SOA accountability and sponsorship
- Poor balance of SOA strategy and tactical implementations across the organization.

In order to resolve these challenges, I developed an SOA Center of Gravity[TM] concept. The SOA Center of Gravity (CoG) model is simple and compelling. It concentrates organizational focus on a few critical dimensions of SOA that will ensure SOA traction and results. The SOA CoG establishes a foundation for evolving and expanding your SOA efforts. But what is a "center of gravity?" How can an organization find its center of gravity? How does a "center of gravity" fit an SOA initiative?

The following sections discuss SOA Center of Gravity[TM] and SOA Governance Center of Gravity[TM] concepts and provide a few examples of how they might be used in your organization.

What Is a Center of Gravity?

This concept is predicated on basic physics, where the center of gravity of an object describes the concentration of mass such that at that single point, no matter the object's orientation, it will be in balance. A center of gravity represents the point where the forces of gravity converge within an object, or the spot at which the object's weight is balanced in all directions. Applying force or somehow disrupting (e.g., striking, attacking) the object's center of gravity will cause it to lose its balance and fall to the ground.

Another perspective on centers of gravity is one of influence or impact. In this view, a center of gravity is the point of greatest importance, interest or activity for a given society, movement, or idea. The center of gravity concept, however, that is most applicable in our model is the military variant of Carl von Clausewitz. This center of gravity concept is taught to every officer in the military.

The center of gravity in the military sense was developed by Carl von Clausewitz, a Prussian military theorist, in his work *On War*.[5] The definition of a center of gravity according to the U.S. Department of Defense (DoD) is as follows: "Those characteristics, capabilities, or locations from which a military force derives its freedom of action, physical strength, or will to fight."

Thus, the center of gravity is usually seen as the "source of strength". Accordingly, the Army tends to look for a single center of gravity, normally in the principal capability that stands in the way of the accomplishment of its own mission. In short, the Army considers a "friendly" center of gravity as that element—a characteristic, capability, or locality—that enables one's own or allied forces to accomplish their objectives. Conversely, an opponent's center of gravity is that element that prevents friendly forces from accomplishing their objectives. American joint military doctrine suggests that, "the centers of gravity concept is useful as an analytical tool, while designing campaigns and operations, to assist commanders and staffs in analyzing friendly and enemy sources of strength as well as weaknesses and vulnerabilities."[6]

In summary, a center of gravity is a main source of power or strength which, if destroyed, causes such a debilitating effect as to terminate the war. Even if the command and control functions of an opponent are crippled, one still has to defeat the opponent's armed forces. In our construct, identifying the SOA Center of Gravity, or creating a center of gravity if one does not exist, is the centerpiece of our application of the concept.

SOA Center of Gravity Organizational Model

The concept of a center of gravity, from the previous discussion, is an appropriate model to help organize resources for the most effective planning, staffing, and execution of an SOA initiative. Therefore, we define an SOA Center of Gravity as follows:

> *An* **SOA Center of Gravity** *is an organizational construct assigned with the resources, authority and accountability for execution of an SOA strategy, implementation of SOA governance, and execution of projects and initiatives documented in the SOA strategy. An SOA Center of Gravity is large enough to manage these tasks, yet small enough to represent an agile yet adequately-staffed core team. An SOA Center of Gravity has executive sponsorship and is led by an SOA champion with credibility, budget and authority to act. An SOA Center of Gravity concentrates force on the essential aspects of SOA that will lead to SOA success: SOA strategy, SOA governance and SOA implementations.*

An SOA CoG's focus may be different for every organization. Specific projects may vary and goals detailed in the SOA strategy will most certainly vary. How SOA governance is implemented always varies by organization. However, the common theme is that the SOA Center of Gravity is empowered and accountable for development and realization of the SOA strategy, implementation of SOA governance aligned with that SOA strategy, and the initial tactics and projects that will accelerate SOA results in a given organization. This is a catalytic team whose charter will last for 9 to 12 months. After that, the Center of Gravity role must be reassigned to other members of the organization.

Exhibit 7.2 depicts a notional SOA Center of Gravity based on our definition.

Exhibit 7.2   SOA Center of Gravity Model

In this exhibit, the SOA CoG consolidates decisions and execution for SOA strategy, EA (the aspects that are SOA-specific), services design standards, data services design standards, the SOA/Services SDLC, and Enterprise SOA requirements. That is a lot of responsibility. However, as we stated above, the SOA CoG must have enough bandwidth to manage all of this, but it must be agile and nimble to provide rapid SOA execution as a model for the early SOA ramp activities.

The SOA Center of Gravity organizational model would look like the one depicted in Exhibit 7.3.

Exhibit 7.3   Sample SOA Center of Gravity Organizational Model

A Center of Excellence Is Not a Center of Gravity

Many SOA technology and software firms echo one another in pitching "centers of excellence" as a valid SOA construct. However, when you dig a little deeper, what they really represent are product-centric skills focused on application integration or enterprise service bus (ESB) middleware solutions. In other words, they are centers of excellence for one tool, not SOA or SOA governance in a broader sense. An SOA center of excellence in theory could make sense if it were comprised of enough skills to actually accelerate SOA adoption and value in a given organization. However, when a center of excellence is suggested by a software vendor, its value and composition may be compromised as a front for a product-specific SOA implementation model.

An SOA CoG, by way of differentiation, is authorized and chartered to define and execute an SOA strategy, develop and implement the initial SOA governance model, and to implement the first SOA projects in a given organization to help reach the SOA reference implementation phase of the SOA adoption lifecycle. An SOA Center of Gravity aggregates the proper personnel and skill sets to implement the SOA strategy, SOA governance, and SOA projects.

An SOA CoG should not be confused with a center of excellence. The center of excellence concept is often associated with a software tool that is new to an organization, and thus a core team is identified, trained, and becomes the focal point for all implementation activities revolving around that tool or enabling technology. In other cases, a center of excellence is narrowly focused on one activity, which may not be a software tool. A center of excellence in our opinion is too narrow a concept as compared to a center of gravity, which is broader and more strategic and has an ability to influence an entire organization in its efforts.

The following summarize the fundamental differences between a center of excellence and a CoG:

- Centers of excellence tend to be technology focused
- Centers of excellence tend to be more focused on a single activity
- Centers of gravity concentrate all necessary stakeholders to drive an SOA initiative forward
- Centers of gravity can be formed for SOA, SOA governance, or any major enterprise initiative where a concentration of key decision makers and skills can be coalesced into a center of gravity.

FEDERATED ORGANIZATIONAL MODELS

Federated IT organizations pose an interesting dilemma for SOA governance. SOA governance in itself is complex enough, and adding more complex IT management models and governance SOA in those scenarios can be challenging. In Chapter 4, we presented a simple diagnostic to help determine the current IT management structure on a continuum from centralized to distributed. Two federated IT management structures are between these two extremes: strongly federated and weakly federated. These are reviewed below:

- **Strongly Federated IT Management Structure.** Central decision authority for shared infrastructure and enterprise wide IT capabilities, while business application and business unit specific decisions are made by business unit CIOs. Business unit CIOs directly report to a corporate CIO, and report indirectly (dotted line) to the business unit executives. Business unit enterprise architects report directly or have dual reporting to a corporate enterprise architect, and directly to or indirectly to the business unit CIO.

- **Weakly Federated IT Management Structure.** In a weakly federated structure, there is central decision authority for shared infrastructure and enterprise wide IT capabilities, and like strongly federated structures, business applications and business unit specific decisions are made by business unit CIOs. However, in this case, business unit CIOs report directly to the business unit executives and indirectly to the corporate CIO. Similarly, business unit (BU) or line of business (LoB) enterprise architects report directly to BU CIOs, and have indirect reporting to corporate enterprise architecture. Corporate IT has less control over business units and decisions are more distributed.

The salient difference between these two federated governance scenarios is the reporting structure and therefore allegiance to the business unit or to the central IT organization. From an SOA governance perspective, the challenge is whether the central IT organization can or should assert control over SOA governance decisions and processes at the business unit level, or whether it should merely gain visibility to the activities at the business unit level. Or, can a more collaborative model be somehow established where the central IT organization and the business unit IT organizations can collaborate on SOA governance activities to more efficiently and quickly implement SOA governance.

SOA GOVERNANCE FOR FEDERATED IT MODELS

Federated governance structures feature one of the more popular organizational challenges in IT organizations: how to balance economies of scale and efficiency through centrally managed and delivered IT services versus enabling autonomy and innovation within individual business units in a more distributed IT management and delivery model. Federated governance structures attempt to strike the balance by centrally managing infrastructure, networks, and cross-functional IT services while allowing operating units or business units the control and decision making authority for business applications within the individual business units. Often, the relationships between the enterprise IT organization and the business unit IT organizations are, to varying degrees, strained due to the natural tension between centralized IT management and distributed IT management.

Exhibit 7.4 depicts a hypothetical federated SOA governance model. In this example, there is enterprise governance processes conducted under the management control of the enterprise IT staff, and there are also business unit-specific processes within the decision scope of business units. The enterprise governance processes include activities such as enterprise requirements and demand management, Business and IT strategic planning, new project and program submissions, enterprise architecture, portfolio management, funding and budgeting decisions, program management office (PMO), and IT acquisition processes.

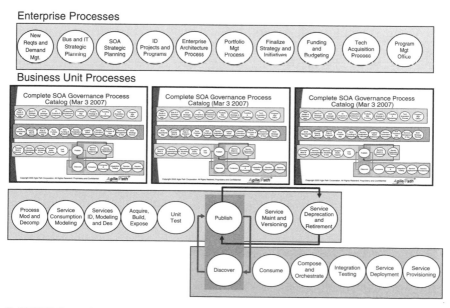

Exhibit 7.4 Federated View of SOA Governance

This view illustrates three business units, each of which has similar "enterprise" governance processes specific to the respective business units, as well as their SOA governance and SDLC governance processes. At the bottom, although this is not often the case, we show a common SDLC model shared at the enterprise level, and hopefully leveraged within each of the business units.

The hope under a federated governance structure is that SOA can be achieved through an enterprise view of governance, while driving asset leverage and consistency of services delivery across the enterprise. The strategic business units (SBU) can vary from enterprise processes and policies but are discouraged from doing so. At the same time, the enterprise can leverage innovation and learning from individual business units and propagate best practices and policies across the enterprise.

Federated governance involves trade-offs and balance of power between the enterprise and SBUs. As such, the structural accordion impacts the degree of tension between the enterprise and SBUs. There is always tension in federated governance structures, and SOA will in some respects add to this tension because there are more aspects to govern in a SOA model versus an IT model. Furthermore, there will always be variation in the maturity of various business units. Fast movers do not want to be slowed down by enterprise processes and top-down directives, while later adopters do not want to be forced into a model leveraged by an SBU whose business model is different. The enterprise wants to find the optimal model to eliminate duplicate acquisition and implementation of tools, as well as share a body of service design and interoperability policies, common enterprise architecture models, and more. Realize that there is always tension in federated structures and let the accordion affect help guide how best to structure an optimal federated governance structure for your organization.

Federated Center of Gravity

A federated center of gravity governance organizational model is an extension of federated IT management. Simply put, this approach establishes an enterprise center of gravity at the corporate level, supported by aligned yet independent centers of gravity embedded with the various divisions, SBUs or lines of business. In this manner, a federated center of gravity is not dissimilar to a typical federated governance model. However, the fundamental difference is that true SOA centers of gravity are established under clear executive sponsorship, and they are explicitly chartered to implement SOA strategy, SOA governance and the initial implementations for the enterprise (or intended scope of influence).

Federated Collaboration Models

A federated collaboration model is a governance construct particular to federated structures where a collaborative relationship between a centralized governance board and SBU, LOB, or divisional governance boards can be established. This is a more active collaboration approach than the visibility model that is described below. In a federated collaboration governance model, the governance organization is established explicitly with active joint collaboration between the corporate or enterprise governance boards and independent and often autonomous business units that may be empowered to govern themselves. In lieu of having oversight authority over the business unit governance boards, the objective is to create active participation and collaboration of business unit SOA leaders into the enterprise SOA governance process.

In this type of model, a central governance board chaired by the head of enterprise architecture or by the corporate CIO, establishes a forum for regular sharing and joint development of enterprise policies that will be adopted by the SBUs or LOBs.

One way to establish collaboration between independent SBUs or business units is to divide the SOA governance activities into multiple working groups focused on key aspects of SOA—SOA platforms, tools and technology, Service design standards (which can be further divided into the interface and the message payload), Services Development Lifecycle, or others. To create the collaboration model, assign one SBU as the lead for one of these working groups, with all others represented on that working group. By having each SBU as the lead of one board, but with all SBUs having active representation and participation on the boards, you can effectively drive cooperation and collaboration between independent business units. In this federated collaboration model, the SBUs should help establish corporate-wide governance, as well as committing to leveraging enterprise governance models and policies internally within the respective business units. This ensures consistency across the enterprise.

Federated Visibility Models

In a federated governance model, many organizations struggle with establishing a centralized body at an enterprise level and then empowering it to make decisions that affect the business units, who have enjoyed relative autonomy in making their IT, architectural, and project funding decisions among others. Thus, when implementing SOA governance in a federated model, you may not be able to establish a centralized corporate governance body that has decision authority for certain aspects of SOA governance for the enterprise. Often, the LOB or business units will not cede control for those decisions to a corporate governance body. This is a natural reaction to establishing centralized governance in a federated structure.

Rather than engaging in the normal power struggle between a corporate governance board and a business unit board, you might consider a federated visibility model instead of a federated oversight model. A federated visibility model establishes a relationship between a corporate or enterprise governance body and divisional, LOB or SBU governance bodies with the purpose of gaining visibility of governance across the enterprise. If the corporate governance model cannot obtain decision authority across the enterprise, it must minimally establish visibility of governance across the enterprise to share and disseminate best practices, lessons learned, and encourage consistent adoption of common policies and governance processes.

BEST PRACTICE SOA GOVERNANCE ORGANIZATIONAL ROADMAP

As you frame your enterprise SOA governance organizational model, consider an incremental roadmap approach that begins with focused core teams and expands over time, as necessary, and as your SOA maturity and enterprise coverage increases. You should map out a roadmap model that depicts when governance boards phase in, how long they persist, and when they can be eliminated based on the maturity of governance over time. The following represent governance organizational model best practices to consider:

- Start with an SOA core team initially, supported by one or more working groups.
- Expand the governance model to include business and IT executives, as well as an architectural review board. This will be the start of the business engagement model if the SOA initiative did not begin from a business unit or business-driven perspective.
- Expand the governance organization to accommodate key service categories and service portfolio management disciplines. Do not rush into formal and complex services portfolio management models. You will most likely need this, but not until you have enough services and SOA value generated that can be used to justify dedicated service portfolio management processes and headcount.
- Add business oversight for business architecture, business process portfolio managers, and business service portfolio managers.

■ Keep governance boards to a maximum of three supported by working groups as needed.

SOA GOVERNANCE ORGANIZATIONAL MODELING STEPS

The following basic steps will help you define an appropriate SOA Governance organization model. The key to this process is identifying critical SOA governance gaps, both process and policy gaps, and then creating a stakeholder model to help close those gaps. The stakeholder model will define the governance organizational model based on key governance processes.

■ Define governance process gaps first; do not begin with an organizational structure.
■ Define critical policy categories that support IT and SOA principles; do not get too granular with fine-grained technical policies yet.
■ Once you have defined key governance processes and key categories of SOA policies, ask the following questions:
  ■ What stakeholders should participate in those key governance decisions?
  ■ Who should have input?
  ■ Who should review and approve key governance decisions?
  ■ Who should approve?
  ■ Who has authority and accountability for the decision?
■ These answers will lead to the organizational view of SOA governance, as well as the composition and chairmanship structure for governance bodies.
■ Define a simple governance organizational structure first based on functional coverage for governance processes and key policies.
■ Once you are satisfied, begin to assign stakeholders to roles on each of the boards.
■ Last, put the political alignment dressing on the model and determine chairmanship models.
■ Finally, go back to the SOA governance assessment and confirm you have closed the key SOA governance gaps and that you have appropriate policy coverage for critical decisions.

Following these broad steps will help you make sense of governance and define an organizational model that makes sense. As we have stated, avoid establishing an SOA governance organization model first. Begin with key SOA governance process and policy gaps, and use those to structure an appropriate organizational model. Defining the functional view of a SOA governance organization will align it and help right-size it. Beginning with governance boards and then asking the question "What do they do?" will lead to overhead and governance frustration.

SOA GOVERNANCE ORGANIZATIONAL ROADMAP

You should consider developing an organizational roadmap to correspond to your SOA governance process roadmap. You will not need a large or complex governance organizational model early in your SOA adoption cycle. The SOA governance organizational roadmap will sequence your SOA governance organizational model by phases of adoption or by date milestones, whichever approach makes sense for your team. Exhibit 7.5 depicts a sample SOA governance organizational roadmap.

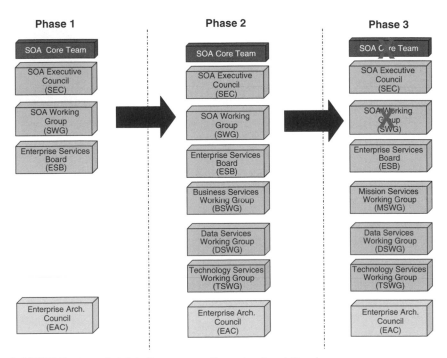

Exhibit 7.5　Sample SOA Governance Organizational Roadmap

This notional organizational roadmap shows three phases of governance boards being implemented over time. In the first phase, three boards are added to an existing enterprise architecture board. In phase two, a few additional boards are added as the scope and enterprise traction of SOA are expanded. In the third phase, a board disbands based on increased SOA maturity. Perhaps more than one board can be retired depending on the dynamics of your organization.

SOA GOVERNANCE ORGANIZATIONAL MODEL SUMMARY

This chapter has presented a variety of approaches and best practices to help you understand, define and implement your enterprise SOA governance organizational model. This is a complex subject, and how you organize governance organizations and boards will play a critical role in achieving a successful governance model.

We have emphasized that you should not begin with the organizational model as many consulting firms often do. You must first understand the governance processes and policies, then define the governance organizational model as one facet of an integrated policy enforcement model comprised of boards, processes and tools. We have presented some perspectives on various organizational designs, as well as multiple considerations to bear in mind as you approach your SOA governance organizational model. If you approach this challenge from an integrated policy enforcement perspective, you will be able to implement an appropriate governance organizational model that is right sized and with an appropriate stakeholder make up, and that will facilitate the realization of SOA governance for your organization.

SOA GOVERNANCE ORGANIZATIONAL MODEL BY SOA ADOPTION PHASE

As we have stressed throughout this book, your governance model will vary and adapt by your organization's relative maturity and current placement in the SOA adoption model we posited in Chapter 1. Exhibit 7.6 is a sample governance organizational model roadmap by SOA adoption phase. This approach may help you define what governance boards you may need and what types of boards are mapped to SOA adoption phases. In addition, we provide some descriptions of various governance boards that may also be helpful. Of course, you should adapt this to your enterprise as you see fit.

Exhibit 7.6 SOA Governance Organizations Mapped to SOA Adoption Model Phases

	SOA Inception (Ad Hoc SOA, POC, Pilots)	SOA Strategy and Planning	SOA Governance Model Dev	SOA Ramp, SOA Gov Ramp	SOA Reference Implementation	SOA Programmatic Execution	SOA Acceleration and Assimilation	SOA Steady State
SOA Core Team	X	X	X	X	X			
SOA Executive Council		X	X	X	X	X	X	
Enterprise SOA Management Council			X		X	X	X	X
SOA Strategy Working Group		X	X					
SOA Business Case Working Group		X						
EA/SOA Architecture Review Board			X		X	X	X	X
Enterprise Services Working Group		X		X				
SOA/EA Working Group	X	X		X				
SOA SDLC Working Group		X		X				
SOA Platform Working Group		X		X				

Enterprise Services Portfolio Team		X	X		X	X
Infrastructure Services Portfolio Mgt. Team			X	X	X	X
Technical Services Portfolio Mgt. Team			X	X	X	X
Data Services Portfolio Mgt. Team			X	X	X	X
Business Services Portfolio Mgt. Team			X	X	X	X
Domain-Specific Business Services Portfolio Mgt. Team				X	X	X

SOA Governance Organization Descriptions

	Description	Standing (S) Virtual (V) Working Group (WG) Temporary (T)	Comment
SOA Core Team	Core working group that plans and executes SOA strategy, initial projects, defines architecture, services and platform standards.	T	See SOA Center of Gravity, center of excellence, SOA working group

(Continued)

Exhibit 7.6 (*Continued*)

	Description	Standing (S) Virtual (V) Working Group (WG) Temporary (T)	Comment
SOA Executive Council (or Steering Team)	Cross-functional leadership team ideally comprised of business and IT executives to oversee all SOA activities, develop or delegate SOA strategy, approve funding for SOA initiatives, resolve conflicts for reuse, sharing, etc. Often, the SEC is added after an information SOA working group has begun initial pilots or POCs.	V	
Enterprise SOA Management Council	Management team comprised of key IT, business, and EA representatives to oversee SOA execution, projects and make recommendations to the SEC for approval.	V	
SOA Strategy Working Group	Working group established by the SEC or equivalent to develop the organization's SOA strategy and roadmap.	WG	
SOA Business Case Working Group	Working group established by the SOA strategy working group to develop the SOA business case, value proposition and associated metrics.	WG	
SOA Architecture Review Board	Virtual team responsible for performing enterprise architecture, SOA EA, and services design reviews across the SOA SDLC.	S	

Enterprise Services Working Group	Working group responsible for defining services design and interoperability standards, service taxonomy and domain model, initial service domains, and service implementation patterns. Responsible for execution of the enterprise services roadmap if the SOA core team does not do this.	WG
SOA Enterprise Architecture Working Group	Working group responsible for developing the SOA Enterprise Architecture extensions, e.g. SOA reference architecture, SOA reference model, SOA logical model, SOA physical model, etc. May establish additional working groups for services, SOA platform, SDLC, data and schemas.	WG
SOA SDLC Working Group	Working group responsible for defining the SOA and Services Development Lifecycle to augment the current software development and program management process. May result in a dual development process that decouples the services development from other "traditional" software delivery methodologies.	WG
Data Services Team: Governs Data, Schemas and Canonical Form Working group	Working group responsible for defining the data model, canonical data model, schemas, XSD, and other XML artifacts. Interacts with enterprise data/information architecture team if one exists within the EA or IT organization.	WG
SOA Platform Working Group	Working group responsible for defining, specifying, and acquiring the SOA platform, development, runtime and supporting tools to implement services. Responsible for execution of the SOA technology roadmap if the SOA core team does not do it.	WG

(Continued)

Exhibit 7.6 (*Continued*)

	Description	Standing (S) Virtual (V) Working Group (WG) Temporary (T)	Comment
Enterprise Services Portfolio Team	Initially, this team may be a working group supporting the SOA Core team. However, eventually it may transition into a standing team responsible for all enterprise services portfolios, with representation on it by all service portfolio management teams.	WG/S	
SOA Platform and Infrastructure Services Mgt. Team	Initially, this team may be a working group supporting the SOA core team. However, it may transition into a standing team responsible for maintaining and operating the SOA infrastructure and tools, as well as potentially managing services operations, systems monitoring, SLA monitoring, etc.	S	
Technical Services Portfolio Mgt. Team	Portfolio management team focused on enterprise technical services such security, logging, audit, publishing, XLM validation services, SSO token service, catalog service, user ID mapping service, exception handling, etc. Depending on the organization, can combine SOA infrastructure and technical services under a single portfolio management structure.	S	

Data Services Portfolio Mgt. Team	Portfolio management team focused on building and maintaining the data services layer of the SOA logical model. Initially, this can be a working group under the SOA core team, especially where there are many requirements for data services. Eventually, these may be reassigned into various business domains or portfolios.	S
Business Services Portfolio Mgt. Team	Portfolio management team focused on building and maintaining the business services layer of the SOA logical model. Initially, this can be a working group under the SOA core team, especially where there are many requirements for business, logic, and process services. Eventually, these may be reassigned into various business domains or portfolios as the quantity of services requires more formal management.	S
Domain-Specific Business Services Portfolio Mgt. Team	Portfolio management team responsible for portions of the overall business portfolio, divided into various business domains.	S
Services Management and Operations Team	Responsible for services operations and services management for in-production services. Provides oversight for services during design time and QA/testing, and has responsibility for services runtime management.	S
Business Architecture and Process Portfolio Mgt. Team	Responsible for defining and managing the enterprise business architecture, business process models and capability models, and prioritizing the portfolio of those processes and capabilities in alignment with business and IT strategy.	S

SUMMARY

This chapter described various SOA governance organizational design approaches and best practices for planning, staffing, and implementing various types of SOA governance boards in support of your enterprise SOA governance model. We strongly urge you to focus on policies and processes before you define organizational models or implement governance tools. This chapter also developed specific SOA organizational design patterns that align to various stages of SOA and governance maturity. In this chapter, we also discuss the concept of SOA centers of gravity, which we feel is a critical organizational design construct for the early phases of SOA strategy and SOA governance. Finally, we have provided a planning devise with descriptions and phasing for various types of governance organizations and boards. You may adapt this to your own purposes as you like. As we emphasize, governance organizational models should not be considered a complete governance construct. They are not. Governance organizations are essential as part of an integrated policy enforcement model, but governance boards alone are not sufficient. That said, your SOA governance organization is a critical dimension of your enterprise SOA governance model, and we hope this chapter helps with this challenging aspect of governance.

Notes

1. See Eric Marks, *Business Darwinism: Evolve or Dissolve: Adaptive Strategies for the Business Age* (John Wiley & Sons, 2002) for an interesting perspective on that.
2. This discussion is derived from Mel Conway's Web site, http://melconway.com/law/index.html
3. http://www.melconway.com/research/committees.html
4. Eric S. Raymond, *The Cathedral and the Bazaar: Musings on Linux and Open Source by an Accidental Revolutionary*, O'Reilly Media, 2001, pp. 101–102.
5. General Carl von Clausewitz, *On War, N. Trübner, London, 1873.*
6. Joint Chiefs of Staff, Joint Publication 3-0, Doctrine for Joint Operations, and Joint Publication 5-00. 1, Joint Doctrine for Campaign Planning.

CHAPTER 8

SOA and Services Lifecycle Governance

The topic of Service-Oriented Architecture (SOA) lifecycle governance is huge in scope, ranging from business prioritization decisions made at the highest levels of the enterprise down to day-to-day development and deployment activities for produced services and applications. We find it useful to consider the SOA governance landscape as a matrix incorporating the iterative process of defining, developing, deploying, and managing services, and also involving stakeholders representing portfolio, architectural, services/software development lifecycle (SDLC) and runtime perspectives within the organization.

This chapter breaks down the lifecycle governance matrix into its constituent parts, explores each part in turn, and introduces some key best practices that Information Technology (IT) organizations should adopt to maximize the effectiveness of their governance efforts.

Finally, we step back and look at the resulting "big picture" that resolves out of these details: the need to manage services as independent "products" within the IT organization.

SDLC Governance is the confluence of many governance and management disciplines in an organization. Exhibit 8.1 depicts how many of these disciplines are linked during project execution across an organization's SDLC process.

LIFECYCLE GOVERNANCE MATRIX

Central to this convergence point are the following IT and SOA disciplines:

- Enterprise Architecture (EA)
- Portfolio management/governance
- Program and Project Management
- SDLC process governance
- Runtime governance

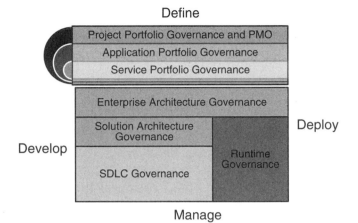

Exhibit 8.1 Enterprise Context for Lifecycle Governance

In addition to these processes, there is the identification, codification, assignment, provisioning, and enforcement of the critical policies across these processes based on the goals and objectives of the SOA initiative in a given enterprise. The relevant policies and approaches to governance have been discussed at length in Chapter 6 and will not be discussed here. However, specific examples of policies for these various processes will be discussed by way of example.

Portfolio Governance

Portfolio governance is focused on high-level business and IT decisions: what initiatives, projects, and deliverables (both services and applications consuming those services) get funded and the tracking of those projects' progress against funding and timeline objectives (project "governance" or the program management office [PMO] function in an enterprise).

Multiple portfolios must be considered and managed in an enterprise, depending on the maturity of the organization and its emphasis on portfolio management disciplines. Portfolio management is still a relatively new discipline in many organizations, and most are not yet very adept at managing and governing portfolios of any kind—program and project portfolios, application portfolios, technology portfolios, not to mention service portfolios. All of these must be considered and managed in some fashion, albeit some are managed more casually and informally than others.

SOA should force behavioral change at the portfolio governance level—breaking away at least partially from application-centric initiatives and recognizing the need to support and fund service production projects that span across applications. This hurdle can be a significant challenge for IT organizations used to funding and optimizing at the application level, but if those organizations do not make the leap to fairly evaluate and prioritize cross-application activities, they will never truly build out an SOA but rather will build old siloed applications using new Web services technology.

Enterprise Architecture Governance

EA governance within an IT organization is focused on ensuring that the services and applications developed under SOA initiatives conform to the organization's business and technical architectures and best practices. The EA discipline typically looks at the enterprise's IT needs from four distinct yet interrelated perspectives:

1. **Business Architecture.** The "how" of the business. It is represented by business processes and the resulting set of normalized business functions extracted from analysis of these processes. Business architecture can be thought of as "verbs" that describe the activities of the business.
2. **Information Architecture.** Where business architecture describes "how" things get done, an organization's information architecture describes "what" those actions affect. Information architecture describes the "nouns" of the business: customers, accounts, orders, inventory, policies, claims, and so on. Combining the "what" with the "how" allows an EA team to define the functional needs of the enterprise; it is those needs that are translated into implemented and deployed business services by development and operation teams.
3. **Application Architecture.** The preferred "style" or "styles" of application development to be encouraged, mandated, or otherwise proliferated throughout the enterprise. The term "application" is used here to encompass not only traditional end-user–facing applications but various types of "functional assembly" such as business partner integrations, internal business process automation, and so forth. SOA-based application architectures often place a premium on assembly/orchestration of services and in separating application-specific policy decisions from the underlying core business functions employed in support of those policies. Application architecture is typically delivered to the development community through a series of best practices, design patterns, and reference implementations that are then used to guide and govern application development.
4. **Technical Architecture.** The working mechanisms on which services and applications are built. Technical architectures span a wide range of technologies, including network, data/persistence, component and

service infrastructure, workflow/orchestration, and presentation capabilities. Enterprise architecture teams typically make choices of preferred technology within these areas (e.g., J2EE vs. NET component infrastructure) and also provide guidance as to appropriate/preferred use of those selected technologies.

As you have probably realized from reading the above descriptions, architectural governance at the EA level involves three key elements:

1. Making core decisions about business or technological functionality within the enterprise;
2. Sufficiently documenting those decisions so that downstream consumers (the teams responsible for developing and deploying services and applications) can quickly understand and make effective use of those decisions; and
3. Reviewing the project-specific application of those decisions. In order for an EA team to execute these tasks, it must have at its disposal an effective way to disseminate the knowledge assets it produces, to track and understand which knowledge assets are being applied to specific projects, and to document the review of those project-specific decisions.

SDLC Governance

In short, SDLC governance is the day-in day-out application of SDLC best practices (e.g., unit test before code promotion, peer review of code changes, establish a source code management (SCM) system with code promotion levels etc.) when developing services. SDLC governance focuses on the intersection of multiple critical governance and oversight processes in an enterprise:

- **Program and Project Management Processes,** as encompassed by PMO constructs to manage the project portfolio and provide project-level governance for cost, schedule and strategic alignment to business objectives
- **Enterprise Architecture Governance,** where key SDLC checkpoints ensure project compliance to the EA policies and requirements as defined by the EA team; EA governance may also include other sub-EA reviews such as security architecture, solution architecture, application architecture and data architecture. These should all be part of the EA checkpoints across an organization's SDLC.
- **Project Delivery Process Management,** which may or may not have a "natural" process owner in a given enterprise. Often, organizations assign

ownership and accountability of the SDLC processes to a functional owner for definition, documentation, training, and ultimately SDLC process oversight. This organization may often facilitate the governance reviews and checkpoints if it is separate from the PMO function. Without clear accountability and process ownership, the SDLC will often be ad hoc and not repeatable across the organization or from project to project.

- **IT Operations Management** is the recipient of projects that have successfully navigated an organization's SDLC process. However, often there are not enough opportunities for operations to review projects across the SDLC to verify their operation's readiness in production. This ambiguity becomes a point of contention early in SOA programs because of the discontinuity between service ownership, service delivery, and services management and operations.

In many ways, SDLC governance within an SOA initiative is a reflection of decisions made at the EA level. Decisions about the scope and granularity of business services to be implemented and the technical approach to be used in implementing those services must be applied to specific service production or consumption (i.e., application development) projects. However, SDLC governance extends beyond appropriate application of EA guidance to the actual analysis, design, implementation, and testing of the resulting services and/or applications required by the IT project at hand. With respect to service production, SDLC governance involves the progressive "hardening" of the service as it progresses through its requirements definition, design, implementation/unit test, and integration/system test phases to eventual deployment in the operational environment.

SDLC governance is one of the most challenged aspects of implementing SOA in most organizations. The fundamental challenge is that most organizations have not extended or adapted their "standard" SDLC processes to accommodate the requirements and processes of developing services such that they are reusable, testable, and consumable by application development teams who are essentially consumers of services on behalf of their business sponsors or the project that funded the services to begin with. The following are typical gaps we find with SDLC governance across industries as organizations begin to confront the reality of SOA:

- The SDLC is not standardized across the enterprise, with different business units, application teams, or geographies using different delivery processes, supporting artifacts and governance/review processes
- The SDLC does not recognize differences between service provider processes and service consumer processes, which are essential in an SOA initiative

- The SDLC does not acknowledge different yet interdependent work streams, such as process orchestration, composite application, and service development work streams, all of which may be related or guided under one funded project or initiative.
- The SDLC is the intersection of project management, enterprise architecture, and horizontally integrated design, quality assurance and test, and runtime processes with appropriate feedback between them.

Most people do not think of SDLC best practices as governance, but it is in fact an excellent example of fine-grained governance within IT. When defined properly, SDLC governance serves as a natural feeder to the "mid-level" architecture governance that is typically established at key SDLC checkpoints (e.g., requirements complete, design complete, preproduction). This architectural governance in turn ensures that IT projects stay connected to the objectives of their stakeholders as established by the portfolio governance activities of initiative and project prioritization (which presumably connect back to core business needs).

When applied to service consumption, SDLC governance may involve both internal project-specific reviews (e.g., have the appropriate services been selected or have requirements for new services been identified?) and external reviews from the perspective of service providers (e.g., does the use of this service within this application conform to enterprise-specific or government mandated privacy rules and does the service implementation contain open source components and if so, are the components used in a manner such that enterprise-specific intellectual property is not compromised?)

Governance at the SDLC level includes participants from the EA, line-of-business, and IT project communities, along with IT specialists such as performance and security analysts. Some aspects of SDLC governance can be automated (e.g., Web service security policy validation, unit test execution, and binary or source-level security exposure analysis). Other aspects of SDLC governance require human involvement e.g., architectural review of functional service granularity and review of service test plan completeness.

Runtime (Operational) Governance

Runtime governance (also known as operational governance) within an SOA involves enforcing appropriate business, process, technical, and security policies (e.g., who may access a particular service, what are the minimum throughput and response time requirements of a service) to deployed services during runtime service execution. Runtime governance is the portion of the policy enforcement model that we apply during runtime execution of services, as opposed to the subset of policies that pertain to design time activities and processes. Most of the policies enforced at run time are either service level agreement (SLA) policies, quality of service (QoS) policies, technical policies for connecting or binding to a service, or security policies relating to authorization and authentication, security assertions and ensuring secure end-to-end service integrity.

Runtime policy enforcement consists of a combination of business, process, technical, and security policies, which are instantiated using a variety of enabling technology solutions as part of the SOA platform (e.g., service registries, repositories, messaging platforms, web services management tools, SOA fabric or intermediaries, identity management, lightweight directory access protocol (LDAP), routers, security appliances and related security solutions). All of these enabling technology solutions become part of the overall SOA runtime policy enforcement model based on the policies that are deployed and provisioned to these various tools.

Many runtime governance policies reflect technical aspects of a service contract, which breaks down into the service interface and the SLA. The service interface is the means by which service consumers develop their client applications and actually connect or bind with the service at a technical level. In addition to the service interface, the SLA establishes many business, performance, and non-functional requirement needs of consuming a service. Examples of SLA-level technical governance elements within an SOA include:

- Pricing and access limits per the service contract
- Average throughput
- Peak throughput
- Type and description of committed SLA
- Availability
- Consuming service clients
- Hardware and software configuration
- Fault history
- Alert thresholds

These two dimensions of a service contract—the service interface and the service level agreement—have design time, quality assurance and test, and runtime implications that extend across the service and SOA lifecycle. These end-to-end governance requirements must be addressed with a comprehensive SOA lifecycle governance model.

End-to-End Governance: Why It Matters

From the design-time perspective, portfolio and SDLC governance have been around for quite some time, and a number of tools (e.g., application portfolio management, program/project portfolio management at the port-folio governance level and the traditional SCM, requirements management and defect tracking tools at the SDLC governance level) exist to support these governance activities. What SOA brings to the table due to its loosely coupled nature, is the increased importance of architecture governance—it is back to service "spaghetti" if organizations do not effectively apply architectural governance over their service production and consumption activities.

Synchronizing between the design-time and the runtime perspectives is equally important, both to reduce the manual effort (and the concomitant likelihood of errors introduced) when deploying services into production, and to improve the feedback loop from runtime governance to relevant stakeholders in the architecture, project management, and development groups back in the design-time side of the IT world. Consolidated runtime statistics such as those mentioned in the Operational Governance section above can be very useful to such teams in assessing the success of their SOA implementation and deployment approaches and fine-tuning those approaches as part of the SOA maturation process.

LIFECYCLE GOVERNANCE TOOLS AND PLATFORMS

There are a variety of tools and platforms that support lifecycle governance processes and requirements, from enterprise architecture documentation and repository tools to design-time solutions, tools for quality assurance and testing, and of course runtime governance and feedback mechanisms. (See Exhibit 8.2.)

Design-Time versus Runtime Governance

When reviewing governance tools, it is important to consider the differences in usage and performance characteristics required by these two very different perspectives. Design-time governance platforms have these key characteristics:

- They guide production and consumption of services from initial incep-tion to selection for use in end-user applications.
- They involve a broad set of asset types—components, legacy APIs, de-sign patterns, and so forth—beyond services and schemas.
- They must present information to multiple roles in their preferred views—browser, IDE integration, reports, and so forth.
- They must integrate with heterogeneous development tools—SCM sys-tems, document management systems, quality assurance and test sys-tems, defect tracking systems, and so forth.

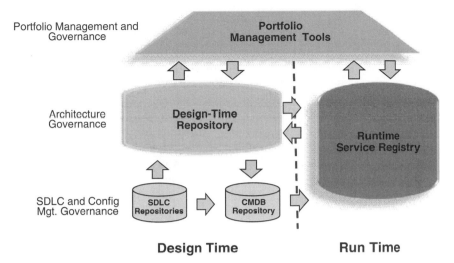

Exhibit 8.2   Lifecycle Governance Solution Landscape

Runtime governance platforms present a largely complementary set of usage characteristics:

- They deal with how a service behaves when called, how various policies (e.g., security) are enforced, how behavior is validated, and how services are replaced and retired.
- They dynamically support runtime access and behavior of deployed services—high throughput and responsiveness required.
- They are focused on service interfaces/implementations and deployment policy configurations—a limited information set when compared to the broad-based set of assets required in the design-time world.
- They require minimal end user interaction.

   Both perspectives and toolsets are valid and necessary for any organization's SOA initiative to be effective beyond a simple pilot project.

PRODUCTION VERSUS CONSUMPTION PERSPECTIVE

The reality is that every IT organization has two primary constituencies for the services it produces: production or provider-side governance stakeholders and consumption, and consumer-side service users. In addition, on the consumer side of the SDLC, there are two types of consumers: developer consumers who are primarily focused on consuming services during application development for a project often via application assembly or

composition processes, and consumers of services or service-enabled applications who are business or end-user consumers. (See Exhibit 8.3.) This dis-
tinction is important to bear in mind. Not all service consumption activity is
in reality end user or business consumption. Service is also consumed by
application assemblers who compose applications by consuming services on
behalf of their business end users. There are both consumers and providers
within an IT organization, which is a service provider to the business users.

   A design-time repository/registry must serve both sets of constituents
across the full spectrum of SOA-related Software Development Assets (SDAs),
not just the service "bits and pieces" floating above the waterline, to use the
iceberg metaphor. There are many more moving parts to a service than what
meets the consumer's eye, and these SDAs must be governed in much the same
manner as the end result they produce, the consumable service.

SERVICE REUSABILITY

As has been mentioned in previous chapters, one of the key value propositions of SOA is service reusability, both to enable business flexibility and
agility and also to reduce IT redundancy and minimize operational costs to
the enterprise. Thus, in order to fully address service lifecycle governance
we must include a discussion of SDA reusability. What makes a service (or
any other software asset for that matter) reusable? For example, does a
J2EE component become an asset simply by providing its jar file? Probably
not, unless the component's functionality is extremely simple and very obvious. While the deployable jar is a very important work product (i.e., artifact) of the software development process, it does not make the component
an asset in and of itself. In order for something to be considered an asset to
the IT organization, it must be maintainable, discoverable, and consumable.

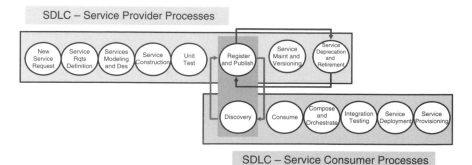

Exhibit 8.3   Provider and Consumer View of an SOA SDLC

- **Maintainability** introduces such concepts as version control (discussed in more detail below), models, and other design documentation, as well as requirements traceability (why the asset was implemented in this way from a technical and business perspective).
- **Discoverability** means potential consumers of an asset can find it in a timely fashion (e.g., via keywords, domain taxonomies, or models to which the assets are mapped).
- **Consumability** involves looking at an asset from the point of view of a future project that might use the asset: Are a user guide, a well documented application programming interface (API), sample client code, and other artifacts available to help the user rapidly understand how to apply the asset to a project? Are dependencies to other assets (and to prior versions of this asset) specified and easily navigated?

The process of building an asset creates metadata that represents the asset—describing the asset from various points of view. This metadata presents a composite view of the asset across its entire development and deployment lifecycle, with indexes (or references) into the various point tools that hold the work products associated with the asset, such as document management systems, requirements management systems, version control repositories, defect tracking systems, test automation tools, and so forth.

Let us take a deeper look at what is relevant to these constituencies. On the service provider side, your organization's objective is to ensure that produced services conform to the architectural principles, guidelines and best practices established by your EA team. In addition, they must be provided based on appropriate guidance from portfolio managers based on service requirements and demand requirements, as well as in alignment with service roadmaps.

These architectural references take the form of models, patterns, best practices, reference implementations, and so on and should be populated into your design-time SDA repository/registry for efficient delivery and regular updates to producing teams. These knowledge assets serve as a basic playbook for service producers and consumers within your organization, and collecting them in a single easily accessible location will go a long way towards improving the communication effectiveness of your key architects.

As services progress through your organization's defined production SDLC, they will reach defined architectural governance checkpoints (e.g., requirements complete, design complete, pre-deployment) at which time key design-time artifacts are validated against architectural references and guidelines. For example, as part of the requirements complete governance process, your organization may mandate that a responsible business analyst (or architectural proxy for the business analyst) must approve the functional definition of the service to be developed, ensuring that it is aligned with the organization's defined business architecture. Likewise, at the design complete stage, a technical architect may be mandated to review the proposed design to ensure it meets the specified non-functional requirements (e.g., legacy application connectivity, SLA expectations or WS-I Basic Profile compliance) established for the service. In parallel, a test lead may be reviewing the associated test plan to ensure it provides sufficient test coverage. Some of these reviews/validations may be automated (such as the WS-I Basic Profile compliance review example above) while others require human involvement. Complicating matters, the relevant artifacts supporting each of these review stakeholders are scattered across numerous file repositories, aka design-time systems of record. These point tools such as SCM systems, defect tracking systems, requirements management systems, test automation platforms, document management systems, and even network file mounts and file transfer protocol (FTP) sites, do not go away in an SOA environment; instead they need to be augmented by a design-time SDA repository/registry that presents a coherent view across all the tools in the form of a set of governed assets. The design-time repository/registry serves three primary purposes in such a scenario:

- As pointed out above, to aggregate a composite view of the relevant artifacts into a coherent whole (referred to as a software development asset or SDA);
- To coordinate, automate and document (i.e., establish audit trails) the governance/review processes specified for the asset as it proceeds through its defined SDLC; and
- To automate specific validation tasks within the governance/review processes where feasible (e.g., validate that the Web Services Description Language (WSDL) conforms to its imported schemas, validate that the WSDL conforms to the allowed options specified by your organization's use of the Web Services Interoperability (WS-I) WS-I Basic Profile, automatically invoke a service's test plan within the organization's test automation framework and post the results to the asset).

Only those artifacts (and relationships to other relevant non-service assets) that support your design-time production governance processes need to be exposed to and managed by your design-time repository/registry. Depending on the depth and degree of rigor of your governance processes, artifacts like source code, build scripts, informal design documentation etc., may not be required for production governance activities and would not be exposed as part of the service asset.

Since the likelihood of your organization implementing a service without any dependencies on existing systems is slim to none, we need to expand the scope of the design-time SDA repository/registry to manage, govern, distribute, and provide traceability over the working parts that live within a particular service implementation: the adapters, components, mainframe application APIs, data views, schemas, and other elements that allow the service to function. Each of these assets in turn has various artifacts and relationships that must be governed and exposed within the service production process. As you can imagine, only a generalized SDA repository/registry can effectively support these widely varying types of assets in a consistent and end-user–friendly manner.

On the consumption side, the WSDL (and/or any pre-generated client-side components for the service) plus supporting contextual and usage documentation are typically what is needed by the developer building an application. Typically, the supporting contextual and usage materials are mandated as part of the production SDLC and governance process and as such will be reviewed and approved as part of that process, therefore these artifacts serve dual duty in that regard. Project-related metadata (e.g., what team built the service and how much effort it took to build) may also be of interest to project and line management. Again, a design-time repository/registry plays a key role in delivering this information to the application developer, preferably via native rich UI-based integration with the developer's tool of choice, the Integrated Development Environment or IDE.

A third design-time aspect to consider when evaluating your repository needs is the topic of impact analysis. Impact analysis bridges both service production and consumption design-time activities—establishing traceability from a service to its dependencies and understanding which applications in turn consume that service—are invaluable to an organization as it maintains its SOA. As your SOA matures you will have multiple versions of any particular service flowing through your production governance process. Establishing predecessor/successor relationships between versions, understanding which underlying components, adapters, mainframe APIs, and so forth a service requires in order to function, and providing multiple ways to analyze and digest this information (e.g. graphics dynamic navigation, reports), all aids your portfolio management and architectural rationalization activities related to impact analysis. It is in this area, as well as in the ability to assemble coherent views of services and other assets across the multiple systems of record involved in design-time activities, that service-centric registries fall short of what is required at design time; to support a robust service production–distribution–consumption model with supporting governance automation.

As you have probably determined by now, a services-centric registry, either runtime-specific or one with ambitions of providing both design-time and runtime capabilities:

- Is not designed to support this broad range of asset types nor accessibility to the varied artifacts supporting those assets; and
- Does not present the information it manages in a manner that is conducive to effective review and consumption.

In particular, service-centric runtime registries have an entirely different usage profile than broad asset-based design-time repository/registries— these runtime registries exist to provide efficient real-time access to service definitions and supporting metadata (deployment endpoints, SLA policy metadata, etc.). They need to be coupled to the runtime platform (ESB, fabric, runtime management platform) to enable such efficient retrieval, and in the case of dynamic binding, need to be exposed to the runtime client code as well. In contrast, design-time SDA repository/registries must be flexible enough to support a broad range of asset types, collecting and exposing information from a variable set of systems of record and presenting that information via a rich user interface, ideally within the consumer's preferred tool of choice, the IDE. As you can see, the requirements for these two types of registries couldn't be more diametrically opposed.

GOVERNANCE GAPS IN A TYPICAL ENTERPRISE

While we have briefly defined the scope of service lifecycle governance, it is not easy to actually execute governance at a meaningful level across the combined architecture/development/deployment lifecycle. Let us take a brief look at some of the more significant issues enterprises face when attempting to execute a full lifecycle SOA governance strategy.

Bridging Business Governance to IT

Numerous examples of business-level governance have been mandated in the past few years, Sarbanes-Oxley and HIPAA being two prime examples. These mandates have had and continue to have a significant impact on the way business is done in the United States, and equivalent mandates (e.g., Basel II and III) have had a similar impact in Europe. As enterprises implement compliance models to support these mandated governance requirements, they often discover that the IT organization is the weak link in supporting this governance. Application change traceability and tracking of sensitive service usage are examples of areas where IT organizations often have difficulty in gathering the necessary information to support business governance efforts.

Making EA Actionable

EA teams are often accused of being "ivory tower" organizations divorced from the reality of day-to-day IT pressures and deadlines. While this accusation is usually unfair, it also contains more than a grain of truth for most IT organizations. EA teams are often perceived as "pronouncing from on high" without providing the necessary supporting information that allows IT project teams to act upon those pronouncements. This perception is typically triggered by one or more of the following issues:

- **Architectural decisions are delivered statically.** The once-a-year IT powwow where the EA team rolls out its vision for the next set of strategic initiatives is a highly ineffective way to deliver core IT knowledge. The 100 slide PowerPoint deck or 200 page Word document handed out at these sessions too often turns into a fine plant stand or coffee cup holder, gathering dust on the developer's desk as he or she continues to do things the "same old way."
- **Architectural documentation is inadequate and/or becomes stale.** Architects often become knowledge bottlenecks within an IT organization. While the typical architect within a large enterprise is very knowledgeable in his or her domain, that knowledge is typically bottled up within the architect's head and is transferred only through direct interaction with the architect. In such cases, the architect rapidly becomes a choke point for the organization, at best slowing development progress and at worst frustrating development teams to the point (because of inaccessibility) that they proceed without the benefit of architectural knowledge and advice. Enterprise architects need a "force multiplier" that enables them to consistently capture and automatically deliver their knowledge to the larger IT community.
- **Architectural governance is ad hoc and does not scale.** For enterprise architects to be most effective within an IT organization, they need to be actively involved in reviewing and providing advice to IT projects i.e. both the projects responsible for producing reusable services and those intending to consume those services. An enterprise architect is by nature a busy person involved in and responsible for a wide variety of activities. It is easy for an enterprise team to lose track of their governance responsibilities within the larger IT community. Since development project teams are usually under heavy pressure to deliver on time

and under budget, they are not likely to actively seek out members of the EA team if that team is not responsive to their review checkpoints and deadlines. Without some means of automating and documenting the IT project review process, enterprise architects can often be shut out of IT project activities and review cycles, greatly reducing their ability to affect and guide the IT organization.

■ **EA governance is not expressed as enforceable policies.** This is a very problematic issue for EA, as much of their guidance is just that, high-level guidance as opposed to clear policies that can be enforced across the SDLC and evaluated for compliance and tested and verified.

Coupling the SDLC to the Runtime Environment

Once services within an SOA are deployed, it can be difficult for architects, designers, and developers to gain a clear view of those services within the operational environment. Usage patterns, SLA criteria and metrics, and failure data are often lost because of the gap between operations personnel/ tools and the IT architecture/development environment and its supporting tools. This is a particularly significant issue in an SOA environment. Because of the loosely coupled nature of services within an SOA, it can often be quite challenging to understand the root cause of performance or stability issues within SOA-based applications.

Operational personnel often do not have the experience necessary to understand what information should be gathered when a failure occurs, and even when they have the necessary experience, they do not have ready means to pass that information back to the developers responsible for the failing service or application. The end result of such a disjointed environment is that operational failure and performance information, if it ever gets back to the development community, is usually stale and incomplete, making it difficult if not impossible for developers to act upon that information.

What is needed is an automated way to gather pertinent operational information, tie that information to the affected services in the development environment, and notify the affected developers of operational issues as soon as possible.

End-to-end services lifecycle management is very often a challenge for organizations that are new to SOA and services. Most of the time, organizations have not explicitly defined service ownership and support models for the complete services lifecycle, and thus the IT organization tends to be viewed as the owner of all services, despite the fact that the business should be the owner of its business services portfolio. This is an SOA maturity issue that tends to be resolved over time. However, the organizational friction from the service ownership ambiguity can be frustrating and become an obstacle to SOA ramp activities. Independent of the specific assignment of service ownership within the enterprise, the following service ownership responsibilities must be addressed as part of the organization's comprehensive service lifecycle governance efforts:

Service Ownership Responsibilities

- Define and manage service portfolio for areas of the service taxonomy assigned to your organization by business or technical domain
- Manage services as products with regular release cycles
- Manage service requirements and demand management for services within your portfolio
- Clarify services support responsibilities across the service lifecycle from requirements through development, consumption and run time, maintenance and support
- Ensure appropriate services management tools are in place to facilitate service support

The remainder of this chapter will present a series of service lifecycle governance best practices that can serve, if applied properly, to facilitate the meeting of these organizational responsibilities.

SERVICE LIFECYCLE GOVERNANCE BEST PRACTICES

The Business Domain Perspective: Meeting in the Middle

Business architecture is focused on the actions required by the enterprise in order for it to function. Often, business architectures are derived from a high-level business process analysis combined with an initial effort at normalization of the functions identified from that analysis. Where organizations can get into trouble with business architecture is when they take the up-front analysis efforts too far. In an ideal world, our business analysts would have infinite knowledge of their business domains and would have unlimited time to discuss, debate, and ultimately isolate the ideal service definitions required to flexibly support the enterprise. However, we know that the world is not ideal, and even if we had a large amount of time to fully analyze our business domain, we need to remember that the business domain itself is a moving target.

We are much better off in spending a focused amount of time laying out broad brush business architecture (aka SOA services roadmap) fleshed out by a first-pass business process modeling effort which simply attempts to identify the major functions required and assemble those functions into business ontology. What is an ontology? To quote *The Free On-line Dictionary of Computing*, an ontology is "the hierarchical structuring of knowledge about things by subcategorizing them according to their essential (or at least relevant and/or cognitive) qualities."

In simple terms, a business ontology equates to a business domain model, with domains, sub-domains, functional groups, and other sub-layers of the model identified and organized in what amounts to a tree structure. This level of domain model can be very useful in organizing the efforts of an IT organization towards developing its SOA and accompanying implementation.

Let us return to our example e-commerce domain. In our simplified example, we may derive a domain model whose top-level domain areas look something like Exhibit 8.4.

In this exhibit, we see our sample e-commerce domain model represented in both graphical and tree form. The top-level domain areas are represented by blocks within our architectural block diagram, and where sub-domains have been identified, sub-domain diagrams can be provided to establish the sub-domain breakout for that domain area. This graphical form (in combination with its underlying sub-domain layers not shown here) can be easily converted to a business domain taxonomy. Each entry in this taxonomic tree structure has an equivalent representation within our graphical domain reference model—they are simply different ways to present the same information.

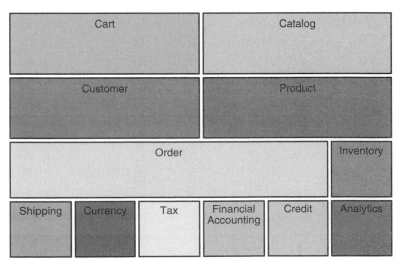

Exhibit 8.4   E-Commerce Business Domains

Top-Down Architecture: Setting the Business Context for Success

How did we get to this level of domain model definition? One approach is to apply use case modeling techniques to understand and document domain requirements. As we look at the international currency support domain, we might identify two specific use cases that are likely to expose interesting characteristics of this domain: point of sale (i.e., direct Web-based sales) and request for quote to support channel sales. If we choose to use UML[1] to document these use cases, we might end up with something like Exhibits 8.5, 8.6, and 8.7.

While these simplified use cases are clearly not exhaustive, they serve to illustrate the value of use case based evaluation in fleshing out a domain model. Our first use case relies on a simple currency conversion action using whatever exchange rates are currently in force from standard industry feeds. Our second use case points out that depending upon the customer, the exchange rate tables may vary (e.g., based on contractual agreement). In the process of working through these use cases, we have identified a currency domain with conversion and exchange rate maintenance sub-domains, and have started to identify specific functions that will ultimately be expressed as services within our SOA. Mixing a combination of upfront domain decomposition with selected "deep dive" use case development in key areas of our business domain can be an effective way to quickly get to a useful first iteration domain reference model.

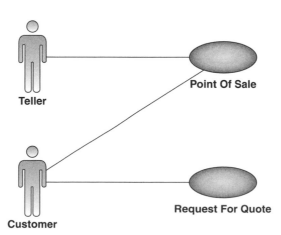

Teller

Point Of Sale

Customer

Request For Quote

Exhibit 8.5 Order-Processing Use Case 1

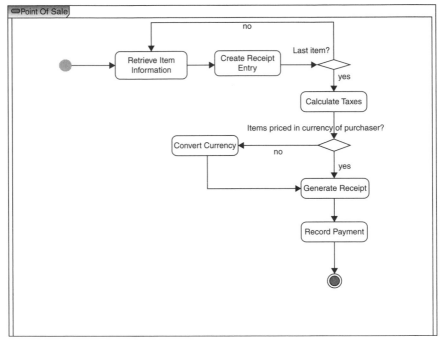

Exhibit 8.6 Order-Processing Use Case 2

Bottom-Up Service Production: Responsively Meeting Business Needs

While the promises of SOA are wonderful, we still need to deliver IT projects to the business in a timely manner. However, in doing so, we must be aware of the potential for those services under development to become solely project-focused in their functionality, not recognizing requirements from other potential consumers down the road. Keeping this in mind, an organization could consider the first iteration of a particular service to be "version 0.9" of what may become a full-fledged member of the SOA services suite over time. (By "version 0.9" we are not implying that this service is substandard from an architectural or functional standpoint, only that it does not completely support the full set of requirements envisioned by our business domain architecture.) Clearly, a service built in this manner needs to provide project-specific functionality to the team that funded its development. Once produced, this service can be considered a candidate for inclusion into the formalized SOA services suite—but not without some level of evaluation at the architectural level (meeting in the middle).

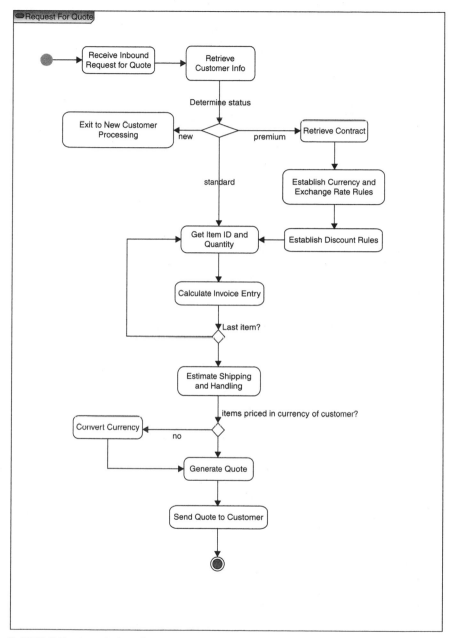

Exhibit 8.7 Detailed Order-Processing Use Case 3

Returning to our currency conversion service as an example, we may choose (or have prioritized for us) a focused implementation supporting our first use case and supporting the direct industry exchange rate feed case only. We can choose to expose this limited functionality service to the broader IT community by publishing it into a design-time repository/registry to gather both feedback on the proposed service as well as an early view into consumer-side contracts for this service. Note that since we have defined our business domain model prior to defining and implementing this service, we can map our new currency converter service into that model simply by assigning proper values to its domain classification metadata, in this case locating our service under the currency/conversion node of our domain taxonomy. Since we built our graphical domain reference model in synch with our domain taxonomy, this service has also automatically been mapped for this graphical model. It is of little worth that some design-time repositories on the market today are capable of presenting both visual and taxonomic views into a service portfolio, thus allowing a user who prefers visual navigation (e.g., a business analyst) to visually search for relevant assets as he or she assesses what is available for the next project down the road. Exhibit 8.8 shows a sample screen shot from a design-time repository that supports visual search for relevant design artifacts by a business analyst.

Since this service is now visible in our design-time SDA repository/registry, other development projects can easily discover it and determine if its capabilities meet their project needs. If so, they can initiate an acquisition and registration process (i.e., establish a consumption-side contract) for this version of the service. If not, they may choose to simply track activity surrounding this service and its subsequent versions with an eye towards establishing such a contract once the next version of the service (which presumably will extend its functionality to support contract-based exchange rate handling and the other requirements established by the request for quote use case) is published into the repository/registry. In parallel, they may choose to provide feedback on desired functionality through collaboration tools that might be integrated with SDLC governance tools or may be deployed as supporting capabilities to automate events, triggers and governance checkpoints across various governance processes.

Meeting in the Middle: Mapping Top-Down Objectives to Bottom-up Delivery

To produce services that meet both near-term project needs and support the mid- to long-term objectives of the enterprises, service production teams,

Exhibit 8.8   Artifact Search in a Design-Time Repository

and the architects and business analysts working with those teams must
consider a number of issues including:

Potential for redundant service implementations. If each service production team is focused solely on supporting the immediate project
that funded its existence, then there is considerable opportunity for
other teams to produce similar services as part of their application
development efforts. The architecture team must have cross-project
visibility over the services being produced (most likely through a
design-time service registry/repository) so that it can assess service
overlap and begin to guide those overlapping services towards a
common (and more general) single service definition.

Feedback against the SOA services roadmap and service portfolio. As part of its responsibility within the iterative top-down/bottom-up approach to service definition, the core architecture team will have produced coarse-grained services architecture or business domain model as discussed above–in effect, a roadmap defining broad groups of services which will be required by the business as the SOA matures. This roadmap should be produced through interaction with business stakeholders and should capture the enterprise's view of what is needed by the business going forward. Detailed business process analysis may contribute some aspects of the roadmap, but it is impractical to expect that all aspects of the roadmap will be derived from such analysis. Project-driven service definitions (the bottom-up half of the iterative architectural model) should be mapped to this top-down architectural roadmap to determine fit within the model. Some service definitions will fit neatly into the services roadmap, other may not. In the latter case, perhaps the roadmap needs to be modified, or perhaps the service is simply trying to do too much and should be refactored into two or more services. In any event, each project's services should incrementally augment the services suite being developed under the guidance of the organization's SOA services roadmap.

Recognition and management of service versioning impact. Services contributed from new service production teams must be guided over time towards inclusion into the services suite. Recasting such services to incorporate additional top-down functional requirements will of necessity result in new versions of those services. The core architectural team must define and manage a services maturity model that gives project teams sufficient visibility into plans for new service version rollout over time and the subsequent retirement of back-level service versions. Typically, an IT organization must concurrently maintain at least two versions of a service in production to give service consumers sufficient time to migrate their applications forward. Augmenting this approach with sufficient upfront notification of planned service versions can improve the organization's agility, both by informing service consumers early on of planned changes and by enabling those consumers to participate in the definition of those new service versions.

Completing our sample scenario, how might our updated online shopping application look from an impact analysis perspective once we have incorporated our new currency conversion capabilities? An impact analysis view into our services portfolio combined

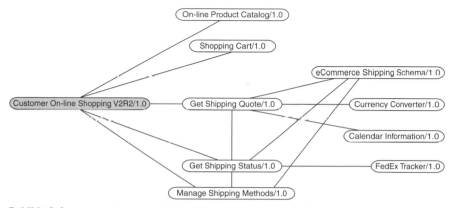

Exhibit 8.9 Dependency Analysis of Services and Related Artifacts

with the underlying SDAs (components, schemas, adapters, etc.) that make up the service implementation stack is essential to allow architects and other stakeholders to understand and evaluate impacts resulting from changes to our service portfolio and the applications leveraging that portfolio. Exhibit 8.9 shows a dependency analysis view of a service and the related software development assets of that service.

It is worth pointing out here that our application is directly consuming both services and components, and that those services in turn are in some cases consuming other services and components (see Exhibit 8.10). This is quite typical of an SOA-based application, and as you can imagine it will be necessary for our fictitious enterprise to apply appropriate governance models over their services, components, schemas and other SDAs used in application development as they progress through their multi-version obsolescence lifecycle.

The People Side: Matrixed Governance/Review Teams

Breaking down the chasm between business, EA, and IT project teams should be a major focus of any enterprise embarking upon an SOA initiative. Effective communication of business and technical architecture to the development community is crucial to the success of any SOA effort. If explicit actions are not taken to enable this communication, IT organizations too often degrade into an "us vs. them" mentality with project teams resisting all proposals from the EA team because of mistrust, poor communication, and schedule and resource pressures. Soon the "blame game" kicks in,

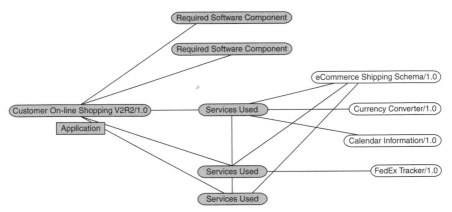

Exhibit 8.10 SOA Requires Governance of Applications, Services, and Components

with business analysts claiming, "Those IT guys never listen to our requirements" and developers complaining, "Our business analysts couldn't document themselves out of a wet paper bag"— not a pretty situation and not one that is conducive to effective SOA.

As has been mentioned in previous chapters, the boundaries between business, EA, and IT project teams can be broken down by building a *virtual/matrixed SDA architectural review team* to share the responsibility of communicating architecture decisions and applying those decisions throughout the SDLC review process.

Who should be on this review team?

- A *team leader* drawn from the enterprise architecture organization and whose dedicated responsibility is to build a successful SOA program.
- *Matrixed team members* drawn from participating business stakeholders and IT project teams—these team members should have strong communication skills on the business side and lead designer/developer skills on the IT side, and their work on this team should be recognized and allocated as a 10 to 20% job responsibility. Assignment to this team should be promoted within the organization as recognition of talent and a growth assignment for the individuals involved. A rotating membership (perhaps ranging from 6 to 12 months in duration) serves to train younger analysts in multiple business domains and younger developers in architectural principles, and then allows them to carry their newfound knowledge back to their project teams, increasing the overall breadth and skill level of those teams.

What are the responsibilities of this matrixed review/governance team? In short, promotion, guidance, and adaptation:

- **Promotion:** The team should prioritize effective communication of EA decisions and guidance throughout the IT community. Matrixed team members are in an ideal position to establish such communication to IT project teams, as they are involved directly with these teams on a day-to-day basis.
- **Guidance:** Applying EA knowledge to IT projects at key points in the SDLC will improve both the quality of project output and the ability of those projects to deliver on time. We'll discuss an example governance model with representative project checkpoints in the next section of this whitepaper.
- **Adaptation:** Architectural knowledge is never static. EA teams need to recognize this fact and be prepared to adapt project feedback on an ongoing basis. By connecting the EA team directly to projects through a matrixed team organization, feedback on EA decisions and knowledge assets is more likely to be heard and incorporated into the next generation of EA output.

The Tools Side: Automating Governance Processes and Feedback Loops

While the topics discussed in the prior sections of this chapter can be executed on a small scale through manual processes, enterprises of any size quickly realize that automation is key to enabling multi-project SDLC governance. In fact, as your SOA efforts scale and the volume of services and consumers increases, many aspects of SOA governance must be augmented with technology and tools. SDLC governance clearly is a candidate for automation and tool enablement using repositories, registries, and integrating these into a "fabric" of SDLC governance spanning design time, QA and test, and run time, as well as integrating portfolio management processes with the SDLC governance processes.

Chapter 9 discusses the tools and technologies of SOA governance in detail, as well as the technical standards that relate to policy.

SUMMARY

This chapter described the challenges of implementing SOA and services lifecycle governance. As we have stated, the SOA and Services Development Lifecycle processes in many organizations have not been revised or adapted to SOA or services, and thus the SOA process can be hamstrung with a poorly-defined and poorly-governed SDLC. Furthermore, many organizations also place emphasis on portions of the lifecycle, such as design-time governance, quality assurance and testing, or runtime governance, but rarely have they focused on the total lifecycle requirements of SOA or services. In addition, often there is no clear separation of the provider-side or consumer-side of the lifecycle either, which can be problematic for clarity of roles and responsibilities. Finally, our enterprise SOA governance model frames the SOA and services lifecycle governance processes as but one of the Four Tiers of SOA Governance. Implementing a well-governed SOA lifecycle is only a portion of an enterprise SOA governance model, and it will have connections and dependencies on higher-level governance processes we have categorized in two higher level tiers of governance—Enterprise/ Strategic Governance processes and SOA Operating Model Governance processes.

Note

1. There's nothing magic about using UML for use case development. UML can be a very effective communication and documentation tool if the group is comfortable with its nomenclature; however, other more traditional text-based approaches can be just as effective. Ultimately, you should use the approach that works for your organization.

SOA Governance Enabling Technology and Tools

Governance is defined as the policies, rules, and regulations under which an organization functions as well as the processes that are put in place to ensure compliance with those policies, rules, and regulations. Recall our definition of Service-Oriented Architecture (SOA) governance from Chapter 1:

- SOA governance is the definition, implementation, and ongoing execution of a SOA stakeholder decision model and accountability framework that ensures an organization is pursuing an appropriate SOA strategy aligned with Information Technology (IT) and business goals, and is executing that strategy in accordance with guidelines and constraints defined by a body of SOA principles and policies.
- SOA policies are enforced through various policy enforcement mechanisms such as governance boards and committees, governance processes, checkpoints and reviews, and governance enabling technology and tools.

This chapter is focused on the SOA governance enabling technology and tools that implement and enforce SOA policies across the services lifecycle, from design time, through quality assurance and test, to publishing, and discovery and consumption and the transition into run time and operations. There are many tools on the market that claim to have a role in SOA governance. You will be able to validate their claims using the concepts in this chapter.

POLICY MANAGEMENT MODEL (PMM)

In Chapter 6, we introduced the concepts of a policy management model (PMM), a policy enforcement model (PEM), and a policy provisioning model (PPM).

The PMM is the complete body of policies necessary for SOA and SOA governance to meet the business and technical objectives of the SOA initiative(s). These policies, as we have discussed, can be compliance policies, business policies, process policies, security policies, technical policies that can span design time, quality assurance and testing, publishing and registration, discovery, consumption, and runtime operations.

This is not a complete listing of potential policies. In fact, as SOA governance blossoms as a more formalized and mature discipline, you will actually be enforcing a large number of fine-grained technical policies for service design, quality assurance and testing, publishing and registration of services, and runtime governance. The sheer volume of policies will demand automated enforcement across the services/software development lifecycle (SDLC) to ensure they are enforced consistently and reliably. In addition, once a service is in production, rapid enterprise scale enforcement of policies must be accomplished at high speeds for high-volume transactions. Security policies, which are mission critical to the enterprise, must always be enforced, and this quickly, within the overall response times guaranteed by the SLA specified in a service contract. Thus, the demand for automating policy enforcement comes from the following pressures:

■ Automation is necessary to manage the high volume of policies that will eventually be defined, managed, and enforced.
■ Automation will ensure consistent and reliable enforcement of critical policies, such as security, service level agreements (SLAs), and related policies.
■ Automation will ensure performance of policy enforcement does not interfere with overall performance of services and service-based applications, such that their SLAs will not be compromised.

This body of SOA policies, or PMM, must be defined, implemented, and refined according to the goals and objectives, both business and technological, of the SOA strategy. The PMM has a direct relationship to business requirements of the organization, and serves as an essential ingredient of a complete SOA governance model.

POLICY ENFORCEMENT MODEL (PEM)

Once the PMM is completed, the PEM must be developed. A PEM determines the appropriate governance and policy enforcement mechanisms that will implement the SOA governance model by enforcing its policies. A policy enforcement model is comprised of the following elements:

■ **Governance Organizational Model.** Boards, committees, and working groups that enforce policies or make recommendations for policies that are enforced by others. The governance organizational model is responsible for policies that can only be enforced manually through review processes. Another critical role for governance organizations is to mediate conflict, manage escalations, and deal with governance exceptions.

- **Governance Processes, Checkpoints, and Triggers.** Processes and events defined through various governance processes that enforce various policies, such as design reviews across an SDLC, or architecture reviews triggered by major milestones of an SDLC. Some processes are horizontal in nature, such as the SDLC processes of an enterprise, while others are vertical and extend from enterprise processes and intersect with horizontal processes and business unit-specific processes, as in federated governance structures.
- **Governance Enabling Technology and Tools.** Various technologies and tools that can play a role in enforcing various types of policies at multiple locations or policy enforcement points (PEP) across the enterprise. Examples of common governance tools include service registries, metadata repositories, security infrastructure, XML appliances, SOA runtime fabric, Web services management platforms, and more.

Developing a PEM is a challenge, primarily due to immaturity of industry standards for policies. This challenge is addressed in Chapter 6 and will not be discussed further here. In the PEM, the objective is to allocate and assign all critical policies to the appropriate enforcement mechanisms in order to implement the governance model. How will the body of SOA and IT policies be distributed across the range of policy enforcement mechanisms and approaches—automated enforcement, manual enforcement, and technology-augmented enforcement—to provide full coverage for critical SOA governance requirements for your enterprise? The PEM defines how and where policies will be enforced and ensures a complete and comprehensive policy coverage model for your critical policies across the "governance fabric" of your enterprise.

POLICY PROVISIONING MODEL (PPM)

The next step is to actually implement the policies by provisioning them to the enforcement mechanisms across the enterprise. Once you have defined the PEM, the next step is to define the policy provisioning model and process. Once this is done, and you understand how these policies will be enforced across the complete SOA governance model using various policy enforcement mechanisms, you must provision those policies to the enforcement mechanisms and policy enforcement points. In other words, you must actually get the policies implemented in the various types of enforcement mechanisms and tools to begin enforcing them.

This is one of the fundamental challenges with policy and governance: The industry has not agreed on a vocabulary or syntax that unifies all policies in an enterprise—business, process, compliance, security, technical, performance/SLA, and more. For a governance board, the PEM is relatively straightforward: You need to assign policy enforcement roles to various governance boards, develop charters, membership and chair structures, and provide various governance artifacts to facilitate governance enforcement mechanisms.

However, for other policy enforcement mechanisms, the policy provisioning task is somewhat more difficult. This is because the process of provisioning is manual, requiring the codifying of policies in different languages using nonstandard syntax across the range of policy enforcement mechanisms and technologies across your enterprise such as Web services management tools, application routers, security appliances, identity management platforms, and more. Since these tools are not integrated and do not share a standard vocabulary and syntax for policy, the provisioning process is one of implementing, one by one, the specific policies on each device according to the particular technology and policy implementation model of that particular solution, as opposed to a more automated provisioning process where policies can be updated or revised from a centralized policy management solution and automatically provisioned to the full spectrum of policy enforcement technologies.

In Exhibit 9.1 we have identified these three policy constructs on the SOA governance reference model introduced in Chapter 2.

The fundamental message of Exhibit 9.1 is that policy enforcement, as implemented via the policy enforcement model and the policy provisioning model, applies across your enterprise at many governance enforcement points—via processes, governance boards, technology, and tools. Policy enforcement is a highly distributed and integrated process despite the lack of integration of tools, processes, and boards that most governance approaches suffer from. We offer instead an integrated governance approach that treats governance boards, processes, and tools as co-equals in creating an integrated enterprise policy enforcement "fabric".

Exhibit 9.2 further details the concepts of a policy management model, a policy enforcement model, and a policy provisioning model.

In this model, we show the flow and feedback of policies as defined in the PMM, to the enforcement (PEM) and provisioning processes (PPM) to manual, technology augmented and automated policy enforcement with quality assurance and other automated tools. This is the first published definition of an integrated governance and policy framework that can effectively establish enterprise IT and SOA governance across an enterprise.

Exhibit 9.1   Policy Management, Provisioning, and Enforcement Models

This chapter will focus on the variety of tools and enabling technologies that can actually implement a PEM and PPM. Per Exhibit 9.2, these tools will primarily focus on the activities of defining and managing policies and enforcing them using various technology solutions. How can various technology solutions be mapped into the SOA governance reference model to implement a PMM, PEM, and PPM?

It is not enough to have organizational policies that stipulate how service components and service information artifacts may be defined and used. What is needed is a way within the SOA infrastructure to define, control, and manage the governance of service components and artifacts by automating the enforcement of the organizational policies that govern them. This tooling ensures that the organizational policies are applied consistently and predictably across the SOA deployment and will result in improved quality and integrity of the services for the enterprise. The variety SOA governance tools in the marketplace can be confusing, especially with the repositioning of many vendor software tools as "SOA governance tools" to capitalize on the critical nature of governance, as well as of course the hype surrounding SOA governance.

To continue establishing context for SOA governance technology and tools, we must show where governance tooling fits into the SOA Governance Reference Model. SOA governance enabling technology fits into the bottom layer of the SOA Governance Reference Model. This positioning is not intended to diminish the importance of SOA governance technology

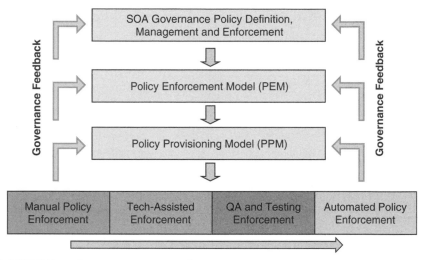

Exhibit 9.2   Policy Management, Enforcement, and Provisioning with Feedback

and tools. It is simply meant to help organizations place due emphasis on organizational, process, and policy issues first before settling on the appropriate SOA and governance enabling technology for their enterprise.

Exhibit 9.3 depicts the context for SOA governance technology and tools in the SOA Governance Reference Model.

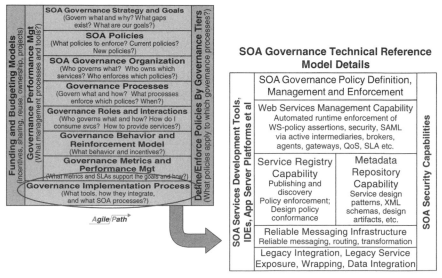

Exhibit 9.3   Governance Technology/Tools in the SOA Governance Reference Model

The bottom layer of the SOA Governance Reference Model is actually comprised of the entire suite of potential tools and enabling technologies that play a role in the definition, management, implementation, and enforcement of policies. As we will discuss below, the tools of SOA governance are still emerging and are largely immature, which explains the lack of integration and interoperability among the diverse collection of potential governance enforcement solutions. Below, we will discuss many of the governance enabling technologies and tools and place them in the context of an integrated governance fabric.

INTRODUCTION TO THE GOVERNANCE TECHNICAL REFERENCE MODEL

As discussed in previous chapters, SOA governance is multifaceted. SOA governance technology and tools span the three other governance tiers: Enterprise/Strategic Governance, SOA Operating Model Governance, and SOA/Services Development Lifecycle Governance. In Exhibit 9.4, SOA governance technology is positioned vertically to show how it can be implemented to facilitate both IT and SOA governance at every tier of the Four-Tier SOA Governance model.

Exhibit 9.4 shows how SOA governance technology and tools span all other SOA governance tiers.

Enterprise/Strategic Governance

IT/SOA Strategic Planning, Funding and Budgeting, Business and Technology Alignment, Enterprise Portfolio Mgt., Enterprise Architecture, Tech Acquisition, Reqts & Demand Mgt, PMO

SOA Operating Model Governance

SOA Opportunity Management, Service Portfolio Management, Service Realization and Utilization, Service Promotion/Demotion, Legacy Asset Retirement, Management and Process Reviews

SOA and Services Lifecycle Governance

SOA Service ID, Modeling, Design and Development, Publishing, Discovery, Consumption, Composition, Orchestration, Operations, Maintenance, Versioning, Deprecation, Retirement

Governance Enabling Technology

Design-time, Publishing/Discovery, Runtime

Repositories, Registries, Intermediaries, Policy Engines, Distributed Enforcement Points

Exhibit 9.4 Governance Enabling Technology Impacts all Governance Tiers

The governance enabling technology tier is focused on the design-time, quality assurance and testing, publishing/discovery, and runtime phases of a service. This chapter will discuss the technical implementation of SOA governance policies to include the monitoring, managing, controlling, and versioning policies.

SOA Governance Technology Reference Model

The purpose of the SOA Governance Technology Reference Model is to help explicitly define the aspects of SOA governance as a sub-architecture to a "typical" SOA reference architecture.

As governance policies are defined, they should be individually evaluated for determining the best way to monitor and manage each specific policy, how they relate to other policies, and how they can be automated through the use of technologies. While many of the tools and processes are common across the phases, each will be individually discussed as they relate to design time, publishing and discovery, and run time. As depicted in Exhibit 9.5, there are several tools and standards that are available to implement and enforce design time, discovery and publishing, and runtime polices.

The major categories of these capabilities are repositories, registries, intermediaries, policy engines, and distributed enforcement points.

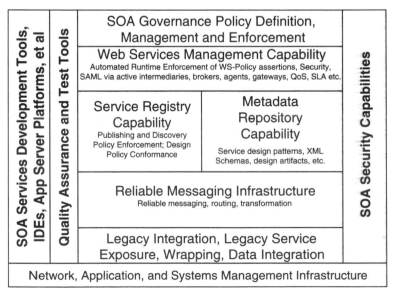

Exhibit 9.5 Governance Technical Reference Model View

In addition, these tools interact with messaging platforms, security infrastructure, and tools, as well as runtime platforms to enable a seamless and integrated governance model that spans portfolio management, enterprise architecture, design-time, quality assurance and test, publishing, discovery and runtime governance.

Many of the products produced as a result of the three governance process tiers directly impact the tooling necessary to enforce the enterprise policies. For example, from the Enterprise/Strategic Governance and SOA Operating Model tier, products will include consolidated, prioritized, and categorized business requirements to include performance and demand needs to support the business or organizational objectives. In addition, the Enterprise/Strategic Governance tier will facilitate the identification of programs or projects that are planned for delivery and therefore will need and benefit from the technical governance tooling in the enterprise to leverage design patterns and guidelines as well as potentially reusing an existing enterprise service. Likewise, these same technologies and tools can help facilitate and support the adoption of the Enterprise SOA Operating Model. Tooling can be put in place to ensure that the SOA Operating model processes are repeatable and adhered to by the service developers, deployers, monitors and maintainers for all initial SOA initiatives until the processes become optimized and ingrained.

The SOA/Services Development Lifecycle Governance tier also provides numerous artifacts that are essential to the development of governance policies that can be enforced through the use of technology and tooling. The development lifecycle (e.g., design, development/enablement, deployment, publishing, discovering, operation/run time, management, and maintenance activities) as discussed in previous chapters have differing governance needs each. This chapter will discuss the processes and tooling that can assist an enterprise in building a robust and consistent SOA environment and services.

TECHNOLOGY AND STANDARDS OF SOA GOVERNANCE AND POLICIES

SOA governance as a discipline requires technology to implement. The technology and standards of SOA governance, and in particular policy enforcement, are relatively immature but have been improving at a rapid pace over the past two years. Implementing policy-driven SOA governance relies on a body of extended Web services specifications that includes:

- WS-Policy V1.2
- WS-Security Policy

- WS-Policy Attachment V1.5
- WS-Policy Assertion V1.0
- WS-Policy Framework V1.5
- WS-Metadata Exchange
- WS-Addressing
- WS-Message Delivery

Note: While standards and revisions may have changed, the concepts in this chapter are fundamentally valid.

These emerging specifications fundamentally build on the established standards for Web services such as SOAP, WSDL, UDDI, XML, and XML Schema. However, the standards for policy management and SOA governance continue to evolve in parallel with standards and approaches to managing metadata within a SOA. Here we focus briefly on the standards relating to policies at a high level.

The primary standard for defining policies is WS-Policy. WS-Policy is related to three other specifications: WS-Policy Framework V1.5, WS-Policy Assertions V1.0, and WS-Policy Attachment V1.5. The combination of these standards and commercially available products are the underpinning required by an enterprise to create, manage, and enforce policies for their SOA implementation.

DESIGN TIME

The design-time phase includes the business service definition and the technical design of the service. During this phase, architects and software developers are in need of software design artifacts and guides to ensure that the resulting Services not only satisfy the business needs, but adhere to the enterprise architecture and SOA policies. The use of registries, repositories, and policy managers can be used to facilitate and enforce the enterprise design-time policies. Design-time governance requirements should include:

- Application of SOA policies to services development processes
- Process policies such as reuse, design reviews, code reviews, release procedures
- Technical policies such as schema usage, WS-I conformance, security policies, compliance policies
- Automation through service validation process
- Access to operational and run-time metadata

The following sections will discuss in more detail how the use of tools can support both the designer and developer of services while ensuring that enterprise policies are followed.

Design-Time Policies at the Enterprise Level

At the enterprise level, the need for the definition and enforcement of policies that are to be followed at design time is critical to the success of the enterprise SOA. Design-time enterprise policies need to be defined and placed into the appropriate repositories, registries, and policy engines to ensure that they are followed as the services are being designed and created.

Repositories

Design-time SOA governance is facilitated by discovering, identifying, and inventorying business and technology assets using metadata catalogs. Metadata catalogs are repositories for various IT assets including executables, design patterns and related knowledge assets, object libraries, software modules, and even services and related artifacts. Repositories provide support for developers who are implementing capabilities with a focus on the reuse policies and enterprise best practices. These design-time repositories integrate with developer tools and Integrated Development Environments (IDEs) for all major application development platforms. This integration enables developers to use their normal development tools and processes when they reuse Services and other software development assets.

Increasingly, these design-time metadata catalogs provide tools that support SOA governance where the specific policies intersect with the software or services development process. Service registries from Hewlett Packard (HP) (Systinet), Infravio (Software AG), and others have been increasingly crossing beyond UDDI V3 specified artifacts and are moving toward a complete SOA lifecycle repository capability that not only supports design-time governance needs, but publish/discovery and runtime needs as well.

Registries

SOA enables the building of complex service components from simpler, task-specific service components. Therefore, service discovery and reuse is an important motivation behind SOA. Registries play a significant role in the discovery of existing services that can be leveraged to support the development of new business services. Another primary function of a registry is to provide a place in the enterprise where developers will register their completed service and have it checked for compliance with the enterprise policies.

Registries fall into two primary types: UDDI and ebXML. Each of these registry types provides similar service end-point referencing capabilities and artifact stores. In many cases, these registries are coupled with the repositories discussed above to provide a robust metadata environment for the developer and consumer of the Services. The need for integration between registries and repositories are primarily based on the limited scope of the UDDI V3 specification.

Registry-Repository Integration

An integrated registry and repository capability provides a point of control and governance within the enterprise SOA environment. The integrated registry-repository with governing policies ensures that service information artifacts are stored and managed in a consistent manner and facilitates the enforcement of other organizational, business, and technical policies.

A registry-repository should provide governance capabilities that enable organizations to define and enforce organizational policies governing the content and usage of the artifacts throughout their life cycles. Since organizational policies vary, the registry-repository will enable organizations to enforce custom policies for the governance of any type of service information artifact throughout its life cycle. In particular, it should enforce conformance to such policies when a service information artifact is published or updated.

The information stored in the registry-repository is crucial to service developers during service design time. Developers can discover existing service components and the necessary metadata in order to reuse and leverage them within a new service. The typical artifacts collected are WSDLs, schemas, and any supporting documentation.

Policy Engines

Policy engines are just now in the infancy stage of development. There are several vendors attempting to tackle this topic area, but as of the publication date of this book, the policy engine vendors' capabilities are interconnected with just a few of the SOA market–leading products. This lag in capability is mostly due to the maturity of the SOA standards and the rush to the market of vendor products. This being stated, the policy engine vendors are focused on delivering a solution to meet the needs of the enterprise. The policy engine will simplify the creation, management, and validation or compliance of policies in a SOA. In addition, few of the policy engine implementations to date facilitate the definition of policies from a set of predefined assertions and rules. These policies can then be linked to other artifacts and services so that they can be validated during design time, publish/discovery, and run time.

A representation policy engine is HP-Systinet. According to HP documentation, the Systinet 2 Policy Manager product provides the following capabilities:

- **Streamline the Creation of Declarative Policies.** Transform paper-based policies into metadata that can be associated with business services and artifacts, and automatically enforced.
- **Automate and Standardize Policy Enforcement.** Allow business services and artifacts to be validated for conformance during design-time via the click of a button.
- **Seamlessly Exchange Data with Run-Time Tools.** Leverage GIF to capture run time data and to share policies with third-party tools for enforcement at runtime.
- **Ensure Existing Policies Are Accessible for Reuse.** Provide a single "system of record" for managing, accessing and reusing policies, artifacts, and compliance data.

SOA policy engines, while still emerging and maturing as governance solutions, fit into the policy definition, management, and provisioning categories of the governance frame work we are advocating. As with other technical solutions for governance, policy engines lack the industry-wide policy vocabulary and syntax, as well as the integration with the variety of tools that actually enforce policies. While we expect over time a parallel path of policy standards evolution and technology integration, and policy engines are viable solutions for centralizing aspects of policy definition and management, you must evaluate the relative maturity of the tools and your relative governance maturity, then determine the appropriate fit of policy engine solutions in your enterprise.

QA AND TESTING

An emerging and mission critical dimension of SDLC governance and governance technology is quality assurance and testing. Quality assurance and testing is the bridge from service design and development to service registration and publishing, to service consumption and eventually assembly of service-based applications. Quality assurance (QA) and testing are the gateways to runtime governance, and must be explicitly modeled into your SOA-based SDLC and factored into your SOA governance model as well.

QA and testing provide an SOA governance enforcement capability by ensuring that design-time policies have been adhered to, as well as ensuring that services will perform within the stated SLA and quality of service (QoS) requirements of the service contract. Thus, QA and testing are truly policy enforcement activities. QA and testing enforces design-time policies, and validates nonfunctional requirements related to service level agreements and quality of service.

There are many elements to SOA and services quality assurance and testing, as the following categories of testing requirements indicate:

- Service interface design (WSDL) validation
- Message and schema validation, schema version verification, and data transformation
- Version verification of services, schemas, and related metadata assets
- Security policy validation, both for technical design validation as well as compliance reporting validation
- Performance testing and load testing, again to ensure quality of service and service level agreement requirements are met when services are placed under various loads, adherence to SLA, and scalability
- End-to-end service integration across the SOA design and runtime platform, including UDDI support, pre-publishing service validation, query verification, validation, and service registry load testing
- Application integration, composite applications, and BPEL orchestration, for example integration testing for all components of a composite application, BPEL orchestration testing for process automation
- WS-I interoperability testing against the WS-I Basic Profile and Basic Security Profiles
- Testing for various protocols (e.g., SOAP 1.2 over HTTP, HTTPs and JMS, IBM MQ series, etc.)
- SOAP, PoX (Plain XML) REST, JSON, and BPEL support
- Testing for WS-* standards and related industry standards
- Testing for all services (e.g., Web services, RESTful services, JMS services, and other service implementations
- Data-driven testing through data sources
- Apply expected service-level agreement (SLA) and QoS policies and metrics to load tests for validation against expected loads

This is not a complete listing. QA and testing requirements should be directly related to the SOA governance policy model, combined with the various service requirements, both functional and nonfunctional, as defined for specific projects. From an SOA policy perspective, enforcing enterprise policies and automating them via quality assurance and testing tools will provide a foundation for policy enforcement for all services and SOA requirements, and then project- specific test cases can be added onto these.

QA and testing definitely must be explicitly considered as a dimension of SOA governance, especially as an element of the policy enforcement model. As such, quality assurance and testing tools today enable the integration and automation of testing as a continuous process across the entire SOA and SDLC.

PUBLISHING AND DISCOVERY

The second phase of the governance technology enforcement tier is focused on the publishing and discovery of services. Due to the nature of creating SOA-based systems, services will likely be developed by numerous entities. In most cases the development teams are distributed and concurrently building services for the enterprise. It is vital that each of these development groups provide common publications of their services so that they can be used by other groups within the enterprise. To facilitate the promotion of services from development through production, we recommend implementing multiple registries for development, staging, and production. See Exhibit 9.6.

By having multiple instances of the registry, the enterprise can enforce different levels of compliance at differing stages of service creation. Often, the development registry is simply used as a "sand box" where developers can place services and their artifacts in the catalog to claim names and to provide rudimentary information about the projected service.

When publishing services to a service registry for discovery, there are clear governance processes and policies to be enforced.[1] For example, the publishing process may require numerous steps to be completed satisfactorily first before the service is made available for consumption:

- Complete exposing or development of service.
- Unit test service.

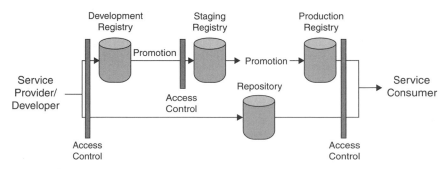

Exhibit 9.6 Service Promotion Lifecycle

- Check SOA conformance of the service to governance model and policies of your SOA.
- Receive "certification" that the service complies with our policies and is sufficient to be published.
- Store the certification into a metadata registry with an association to that service.
- Begin publishing process; verify that user has authorization to publish services to the registry.
- If user does not have publishing authorization, he or she must submit the service and conformance certification to the registry owner or librarian who has authorization to publish to the registry.
- Upon review of the service, test data and conformance certification, it will be published to the registry.

When these services are ready to be validated against the publication policies, they are promoted by the development team to the staging registry. In some instances, the development and staging registry can be one and the same and the governance or policy validation will be accomplished during the promotion to production process. Another primary reason multiple registries should be used is to restrict publication to production rights to certain individuals. A promotion process should be automated, with a man-in-the-loop approval process for promoting entities from development to staging and then on to production.

What Policies Should Be Enforced?

One of the most important questions to consider when creating the publishing policies is, "What artifacts and processes would we need to use a service?" By answering that question, you will be able to identify the core information that you will need to govern for publishing. During the publication and discovery phase, technical, metadata, and business policies should be validated. Each of the different kinds of policies should be validated through the appropriate methodology. The easiest policies to automate validation are the technical policies. Technical policies include items such as:

WS-Interoperability basic profile (WS-I)

- Namespace rules
- Organizational best practices such as WSDLs must implement a getVersion operation.

Metadata policies are a little more difficult to automate but can be, at some level. Metadata or repository policies include items such as:

- Has the service been tagged with the proper artifacts?
- Is there an architecture guide and supporting technical reference artifacts been associated to the service?

Finally, business policies should also be checked as part of the publish-and- discovery phase of the service lifecycle. Some example business policies include:

- Does the service have proper sign-off to be deployed in production?
- Does the service conform to enterprise standards?
- Does the service have established quality of service levels defined?

As described above, the types of policies vary by category, but tools can and should be in place to automate the validation of as many of the policies as possible.

Registry and Repository

While there are several registries and repository tools on the market, most of them provide similar capabilities. For the purposes of this book, we will discuss the capabilities generically.

As the services transition through the lifecycle it becomes more and more important to govern who can see or manipulate their artifacts and state. Therefore, tighter access control is required on the service artifacts. It is also critical that the people with the promotion credentials have the skills and tools necessary to ensure that the service is ready for publishing and that they have the authority to release a capability into production for discovery.

UDDI

The use of a UDDI or other registry can support the enforcement of enterprise policy. The UDDI should be configured to enforce process and procedural policies. The enforcement of process and procedural elements will enhance registry data quality, and also minimize inconsistent or incomplete data in the registry. Policy enforcement can ensure that certain data fields are mandatory and therefore must be included when submitting a service to the publishing registry. For example, the enforcement of business entity data could contain artifacts such as:

- Business Name
- Business Unit
- Organization
- Department
- System
- Program
- Project
- Contact

The actual business entities enforced should be determined by your SOA governing board and implemented as mandatory and optional per the enterprise policy. In addition, the registry should be used to enforce business entity and business services naming conventions. The naming convention should be intuitive and well understood. The need for this is based on the ability to search the registry based on these names. The enforcement of the naming convention is critical. If deviations are permitted, then the ability for consumers to find your service will be diminished.

In addition to business entities, the actual services must be published and the enterprise should determine what types of services will be published into the registry and how they will be represented in the registry. For example, the enterprise may dictate a policy that only Web services will be cataloged in the registry and the access point for each service will be a URL, and each Web service will provide an XML schema, end-user documentation, usage policies, security policies, quality of service, version, and so forth.

Taxonomies

The use and enforcement of taxonomies is also critical to the success of your registry. Taxonomies are the key to promoting the use of your services. It is the key means through which potential consumers will locate your offerings. While the UDDI specification does include some canonical taxonomies, they are general purpose and we recommend that the enterprise define, build, and enforce a custom taxonomy that supports your specific business or application to enhance the discovery of services. Common starting points for the creation of the taxonomy include: organization, business function or concept, geography, and so forth. The taxonomy should be built from the bottom up. It is very difficult to start at the enterprise level. We have found that often the first pilot SOA projects tend to create some natural categorizations of the business services. These natural breaks are often good places to start when creating your taxonomy. The following is a sample list of potential candidates:

- Organizational Structure
- Service Role
- Application Type
- Version Number
- Service Lifecycle
- Protocols
- Quality of Service
- System or Program Name
- Authentication
- Classification

You should also keep in mind that you can modify and extend your taxonomy as needed. While major overhauls may be difficult, they are rarely needed. After your taxonomy is created into the registry it is easily enforced as part of the publishing process. As services are promoted from development to staging, the registry will check to see if all mandatory fields contain valid data. If not, then the service will be rejected or the service provider contact will be notified of the shortcoming, assuming that these shortcomings are mandatory for promotion to production, and if they are not fixed during the staging process, the service will be rejected during the production publishing process. The bottom line is that the taxonomy should be enforced in the registry as part of the publishing process. The items that should be enforced are:

- Naming conventions for business entities and business services
- Service publication data structure and description
- The names and descriptions of categorization schemes for taxonomy purposes.

The registry can also enforce other publication policies. For example, it can enforce publication guidelines such as:

- All business entities must be based on organizational units within the enterprise.
- All business entities must contain a contact that includes a phone number, office symbol, and an email address.
- All business services must provide end user documentation.
- All business services must be categorized using the enterprise categorization scheme.
- All model entities that represent WSDL files must be categorized within the enterprise taxonomy.

By enforcing these taxonomy policies the potential consumers of these services will be able to easily locate, gather the published information about your services, understand the services capabilities, and use your enterprise services.

Intermediaries and Distributed Enforcement Points

For the purposes of the discussions in this book we will use the term intermediaries when referring to SOA foundational components that are considered part of the core framework (e.g., Web service management, enterprise service bus, etc.) and distributed enforcement points as components that exist on or near the edge closest to the consumer. Items that we consider distributed enforcement points are devices such as XML firewalls and load balancers.

The use of intermediaries during the publish-and-discovery phase provide some value to the enterprise during the promotion of a business service from staging to production. Web service management tools can play a role in the process and publication of Web services into the production suite of capabilities. If the enterprise is implementing Web service management as an active inline capability, then the Web service management tool is critical to the production service publishing process.

In these instances, the promotion of a service from staging into production triggers the creation of a Web service proxy for the actual service endpoint. While the actual service endpoint is placed in the production registry, its access is limited to only the proxy service and is not searchable by external users of the registry. The proxy service is a replica of the actual service and inherits all of the registry artifacts for use by the registry search engines and external consumers. In addition, the Web service management capability will expose and implement the SLA or QoS policies as part of the proxy service. The runtime governance of the proxy service will be discussed later in this chapter.

Versioning

Versioning of services can be complicated. To date, there is no one way to handle versioning and there are no industry standards to guide you. Our recommendation is to create separate end points for each version of a service and enforce an enterprise policy that stipulates that all services will support a version method on all services. Often, the difficulty lies in the deprecation of a service version. If your service has limited or no access control mechanisms in place and is not managed or monitored by a Web services management capability, it is hard to know when you can remove it from operations. However, if you are using a Web service management capability and if configured properly, you will have the necessary information to facilitate a decision. The use of a Web service management capability also provides the enterprise a way to use a later version of a service to support an older consumer. Since the Web service management tool is acting as a proxy, it can transform the payload and route requests to different endpoints if necessary.

Policy Engines

As stated before, policy engines are currently in the infancy stage of development. The use of a policy engine will simplify the creation, management, and validation or compliance of policies in an SOA to include the publish-and-discovery phase. In recent months, companies are now offering policy engines that are tightly integrated with service registries. The policy engine would contain a set of predefined assertions and rules that can be implemented and enforced in the registry. These policies can then be linked to other artifacts and services so that they can be validated during design time, publish/discovery, and run time.

According to HP documentation, the Systinet 2 policy manager product provides the following capabilities:

- **Streamline the Creation of Declarative Policies.** Transform paper-based policies into metadata that can be associated with business services and artifacts, and automatically enforced.
- **Automate and Standardize Policy Enforcement.** Allow business services and artifacts to be validated for conformance during design-time via the click of a button.
- **Seamlessly Exchange Data with Run Time Tools.** Leverage GIF to capture runtime data and to share policies with third-party tools for enforcement at runtime.
- **Ensure Existing Policies Are Accessible for Reuse.** Provide a single "system of record" for managing, accessing and reusing policies, artifacts and compliance data.

While this is a good start, the SOA community at large is still missing a policy manager capability that can span and manage the entire SOA enterprise. These policy manager capabilities are very good at providing a place to store all policies; the problem lies in the publishing of the policies on infrastructure components throughout the enterprise. Companies like HP, Software AG, SOA Software, AmberPoint and CISCO, among others, are working to provide a robust policy management, distribution, and enforcement capability.

RUN TIME

The third phase of the governance technology enforcement tier is focused on the runtime environment for the services. During this phase both internal and external entities may consume the services provided by the enterprise. For consumers to utilize these enterprise services effectively, they must be published and discoverable in a complete and consistent manner. Because of the nature of a runtime environment, runtime governance requirements include:

- Enforce policies during service consumption.
- For internal services, enforce internal policies, monitor services, feedback.
- For external services, enforce policies using minimal acceptance criteria to allow consumption of external services.
- Collect metrics and harvest best practices to influence SOA policies that apply to other phases of a service lifecycle.

Enforcing policies in an automated fashion using various technology solutions is essential for runtime SOA policy enforcement. SOA policy enforcement requires the appropriate enabling technology including tools such as service registries and repositories, intermediaries such as Web services management tools, policy validation engines, and distributed enforcement points like XML firewalls and load balancer devices, be used to efficiently enforce policies at the right place in the architecture.

In this section, we will discuss the enforcement of policies from three perspectives:

1. Providing services for both internal and external consumers,
2. Consuming internal services, and
3. Consuming services not belonging or governed by the enterprise.

Furthermore, since this book is focused on how an enterprise should govern their SOA environment, we will discuss the service provider aspects in greater detail.

Providing Services for Internal and External Consumption

One of the primary focus areas of an enterprise SOA is to make available or provide services for reuse within or external to the enterprise. To accomplish this, several architectural design and deployment decisions must be made. Enterprise architects need to look at the requirements for availability, scalability, accessibility, maintainability, and so forth for the enterprise SOA capability. The proliferation of policy enforcement mechanisms throughout this infrastructure is just another aspect of the design and implementation. Some of the governance or policy enforcement capabilities can and should be distributed throughout the infrastructure. The challenge is to have the right tool in the right location in the architecture. In this section, we will discuss a typical implementation for an efficient policy enforcement capability for the enterprise.

Repositories and Registries

Repositories and registries are an interesting topic in a runtime environment. There are people that argue that they are not needed and are only necessary for design time and publishing discovering services, while there are others that claim a significant value in having a registry-repository capability in the runtime environment. The value added from a registry-repository capability in the runtime environment occurs in the case where applications are accomplishing late-binding. This is where applications have a specific data or service need, and they introspect the registry-repository for a service that can provide the needed capability or data. For example, if an application needed a weather forecast for a particular location, the system could look to the registry-repository for a weather forecasting service, discover one, consume the WSDL, transform its request to the format needed for the discovered service, make the request, and terminate the connection. While this is possible, in most cases, applications using services are being integrated at design time and not on the fly at run time. Either way, the service must have all of the artifacts available from the registry and repository to support the calling of a service during run time.

Exhibit 9.7 depicts an example reference model for an enterprise SOA implementation. The use of the network firewalls provides a defense in-depth approach to security where different physical or logical firewalls are placed between different layers in the architecture to help protect each layer individually. The other components in the exhibit are focused directly on the SOA implementation and will be discussed in detail in subsequent sections.

Policy Engines

The use of a policy engine will simplify the creation, management, and validation or compliance of policies in a SOA to include the publication and discovery phase. In the figure above, the policy engine has the capability for

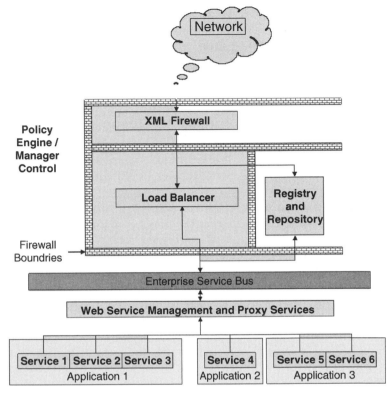

Exhibit 9.7   Sample SOA Implementation Model

an architect to create policies and identify where the policy would most appropriately be enforced, but the current state of the products do not provide a way to automatically push or publish policies to all parts of the SOA environment. There is a need for an enterprise policy repository and proliferation capability. Many of the failures of managing design-time and runtime governance occur due to a lack of a centralized policy repository and enforcement mechanism. Standards like WS-Policy and others are communicating and facilitating the creation of commercial capabilities that will eventually fulfill this need. In the meantime, having a centralized repository for policies is still a value.

Today, in some cases, each individual policy would have to be implemented on the specific device to ensure enforcement. While this may not seem like a big deal, it is when there is a change needed across the enterprise SOA implementation and the policy affects numerous platforms and differing devices, each with a different policy creation application and language. It would be nice to have a capability to express the policy in one language and have it proliferated to each targeted device in the same common language. Companies like HP, Infravio (acquired by webMethods, which was acquired by Software AG), AmberPoint, CISCO, and others are working to provide a robust policy management, distribution, and enforcement capability. We look forward to the upcoming commercial capabilities.

Intermediaries and Distributed Enforcement Points

Intermediaries and distributed enforcement points are critical to implementing a robust, secure SOA environment for the enterprise. These devices are scattered throughout the implementation (see Exhibit 9.7) and are used to enforce different policy at different layers of the infrastructure. For the purposes of this discussion, we will cover the four main types of intermediaries and distributed enforcement points which are XML firewalls, load balancers, enterprise service buses (ESBs), and Web service management tools.

XML Firewalls

XML firewalls are intermediary devices that can be used to support enterprise policy enforcement capability. These devices are often used to serve as secure sockets layer (SSL) endpoints. Implementing these devices in this manner allows for the inspection of transmitted data payloads. While they are generally focused on XML-based viruses and other vulnerabilities, they can be used to enforce certain types of runtime governance policies. For example, the XML firewall devices can be configured to examine SOAP messages to ensure that they are well formed i.e., adhere to the WS-I or enterprise policies. In addition, the data payload can be examined to accomplish XML schema validation, look at specific data for routing, transformation needs, and other business rule checking or validation. Furthermore, these devices help protect the SOA environment from denial of service attacks and are in most cases optimized for XML document parsing to ensure that the SOA transactions are processed as efficiently as possible.

Load Balancers and Other Edge Devices

Load balancers and other edge devices are used to enforce policies focused on the routing of Service requests to the appropriate destination. While many of them claim that they load balance at the application level, in most cases they really do not. By examining the routing scheme or analyzing the metrics collected by the edge device to determine routes, you can determine how and if the load balancer or edge device is routing based upon network measurements, like network bandwidth, throughput, round-robin, and so on. If the measurements do not specifically address applications or service specifics, then they are not routing by application. Either way, these devices still provide a valuable capability and are often used as policy enforcement points in the infrastructure.

Web Service Management Tools

Web service management tools can provide the same policy enforcement capabilities as XML firewalls. The main difference is that Web service management tools manage SLAs and handle exceptions for the Web services. Ideally, Web service management capabilities are implemented in an active manner where the tool can affect the performance of the Services. In an active implementation model, the Web service management tool can deploy a service proxy to create a layer of abstraction for the actual endpoint. In this configuration, the Web service management tool can provide some amount of security (e.g., access control), examine and react to data payloads. Like XML firewalls, the Web service management tools can be used to enforce certain types of runtime governance policies. Web service management tools can be configured to examine SOAP messages to ensure that they are well formed i.e., adhere to the WS-I or enterprise policies. In addition, the data payload can be examined to accomplish XML schema validation, look at specific data for routing, transformation needs, and other business rule checking or validation.

Enterprise Service Buses

In an ESB solution where end points are integrated by virtue of a highly distributed runtime container, the policy information is provided through configuration of the ESB through centralized administration of the solution. In this policy enforcement approach, care must be taken to ensure that policies are clearly abstracted or decoupled from the Services that run over the bus. In this model, the ESB acts as a distributed runtime container, therefore the policies are applied by "rules" that are defined and managed centrally for the container or ESB. However, each end point will have its own policies for services, and the ESB must be able to aggregate or know the policies for all participating end points and represent them as enforceable and decoupled policies.

Currently, the policy engines are not integrated with the ESB products and there is therefore a natural tendency to build policies that are to be enforced by the ESB within the ESB tool, and deploy the other policies in the policy engine. Several of the key vendors in this space are looking to integrate the policy engines with their ESB frameworks so that the enforcement of policies can be pushed from the policy engine or extracted from the ESB.

Consuming Internal Services

Even when consuming an internal service, the policies supported by that service should be validated against the SOA policies to verify conformance. This step is important. In some cases, there may not be a solid process for enforcing policies during the development/enablement process and subsequent publishing of the service to a registry. In fact, a service registry may not even be implemented as part of the SOA enabling technology.

Although service registries can help with the enforcement of policies prior to publishing, there is often debate as to when a service registry is needed to manage a particular volume of services. How many services drive a registry need? How many planned services will drive a requirement for a service registry? These are all decisions that must be made case by case, as there is not enough empirical data to suggest a general pattern.

Consuming External Services

Consuming a service, for example from an outside provider, requires that the service contract, or WSDL document, be validated for compliance to the consuming organization's SOA and policies, such as the security assertions contained in the SOAP message headers or the message encoding specified in the WSDL (e.g., RPC encoded versus document-literal, etc.).

In some implementations, it is expected that the external service will provide policy assertions detailing the policies associated with the specific service. In these cases, policies are simply assertions about a service that allow the consumer to find, evaluate, and invoke the services according to an agreed-upon SLA. Policy assertions "inform the requester about any additional information beyond 'plain' WSDL that may be needed to successfully invoke the provider's service." The provider's service publishes its policy information so that potential consumers can access, consume, and process it, and successfully invoke the Service. The WS-Policy standard is an XML grammar for expressing policies such that they can be consumed and evaluated using rules or algorithms to determine whether the SLA can be met and thus the service consumed.

Without digging into deep technical details, the challenge of policy-driven SOA governance is to define the specific policies that will be enforced during services consumption. The body of policies will be codified in XML using the WS-Policy specification. A potential consumer of a service requests the policy information requested as an XML document conforming to the WS-Policy specification, so the consumer can format the request for the WSDL that will be used to invoke the service. There are a few issues and challenges related to SOA governance.

First, there is no consensus about how to codify and enforce policy in an SOA. The dispute ranges from which standards should prevail to questions around the inclusion of policy assertions within the WSDL documents. Policy management is a relatively immature domain, and the number of standards combined with the widespread industry discussions about SOA governance will ensure some volatility around policy for some time to come.

Another area of discussion involves whether policy assertions should be contained in the WSDL document. There has been recent discussion of the need to decouple policies from service descriptions because it is likely that an organization may apply different policies to the same service depending on who is consuming it (internal or external consumer), how it is being consumed, and by what process. Given this reality, decoupling policies from the service contract makes sense, so an organization can centrally manage, modify, and update policies in an abstract fashion separate from the WSDL descriptions.

As with the other standards of SOA and Web services, the policy management standards will eventually be resolved. In the meantime, workarounds for SOA governance are quite straightforward: Use manual policy enforcement for design-time governance and automate policy enforcement of basic mandatory policies within the WSDL document. When the standards mature and the clear winner emerges, then the notion of decoupling policies from WSDL will most likely be realized. Decoupling policies from services will allow the central definition, management, and enforcement of policies in a holistic SOA governance and policy enforcement model.

BATTLE FOR CONTROL OF SOA TECHNOLOGY GOVERNANCE

In light of the amount of vendor activity focused on governance, SOA governance is still overly complicated and requires sharp systems engineering skills. Most if not all SOA product vendors claim to deliver or manage some aspect of SOA governance. While their statements are usually true, the lack of an integrated language and enforcement capability continues to exist. We are sure that the various SOA vendors have a role to play in the implementation of policy-driven SOA governance fabric. However, the real question is one of control. Where should SOA governance be controlled, and by what solutions? We believe that there is a need for the creation of a centralized policy management engine where all policies can be defined and then pushed or automatically implemented throughout the infrastructure as determined by the SOA enterprise architects or governance body. These same policy engines must not only have integration points into the runtime environment, but must be integrated into the design-time and publish-and-discovery phases of the Service lifecycle. This approach, which is fundamentally the right one, creates two further SOA governance requirements:

1. SOA policies must be decoupled from the services and not embedded in the implementation of the service.
2. SOA governance must be implemented across multiple technology solutions that maintain control of those SOA life-cycle processes (e.g., services design, publishing/discovery, and runtime).

Service registries, based on the UDDI standard, are trying to assert control of SOA governance by being the primary solution for defining and managing policies in addition to being the registry service for publishing and discovery of services. This seems somewhat reactive since UDDI has not lived up to its original role in an SOA technology stack. Furthermore, service registries do not maintain control of the design process or the runtime process. Thus a distributed model with a centrally defined and managed body of policies must be used to implement SOA governance.

SOA governance promises to be an interesting domain. Although there is much more to SOA governance than technology and integration, these challenges certainly will be very real over the next few years as automated enforcement of policies becomes mainstream for achieving the goals of SOA initiatives across widely distributed IT organizations and business enterprises.

SUMMARY

SOA governance and policy enforcement is an essential ingredient for SOA success. We have shown what governance is comprised of, how policies implement an SOA governance model, and how these policies can be implemented using technology solutions for the major phases of SOA and service delivery (design-time, quality assurance and testing, publish-and-discovery, and runtime). We also provided several policy best practices and how and where in the infrastructure they should be implemented. Despite the relative immaturity of governance, policies and policy enforcement, governance tools, and SOA in general, we feel that the model we have developed will serve to guide the overall industry adoption of SOA governance and policy. SOA governance enabling technology and tools are essential to your governance model and policy enforcement process. As you define and implement your SOA platform, you must then consider its support for SOA governance and policy enforcement. As we have discussed, policies are enforced using a combination of mechanisms, including governance boards, governance processes, and governance enabling technology solutions. A complete SOA governance model will require all of these policy enforcement mechanisms, working together to create an integrated fabric of SOA governance. Automated SOA policy enforcement is critical to SOA success, but only as an element of a total governance model.

Note

1. Eric Marks and Michael Bell, *Service-Oriented Architecture: A Planning and Implementation Guide for Business and Technology*, John Wiley & Sons, 2006.

CHAPTER 10

SOA Governance and Beyond

This chapter will explore the future of governance in all forms corporate, enterprise, Information Technology (IT), and Service-Oriented Architecture (SOA) governance. We have by now painted a fairly comprehensive picture of how to plan, model, and implement enterprise SOA governance. We have explored general concepts of governance, developed various tools and mechanisms available to you to help implement governance, and suggested many best practices and approaches we hope will help your organization realize SOA value through effective SOA governance. We feel that governance in general, and IT and SOA governance specifically, are immature yet emerging disciplines. There are many dimensions of governance that must be better understood and defined in order to ensure stakeholder input and oversight over critical aspects of enterprise IT and SOA initiatives.

For example, we always find a clear and direct relationship between the organizational structure of a firm, how its IT organization is structured, and the resultant SOA governance organizational model. The factors of organizational size and structure, as well as the industry they compete in and the relative strategic impact of IT operations on their corporate performance, all add up in the establishment of a viable and effective governance model. It is no surprise that the IT organization is a reflection of the corporate structure. The governance of IT then will be directly impacted by the corporate structure and distribution of decisions across the enterprise. What is less clear, however, is how directly existing IT governance structures and processes shape and constrain SOA governance. While IT governance can be a relatively static and stable process, SOA governance not only has more moving parts, but must clearly change and evolve as SOA maturity and organizational learning increases. How does the structure of SOA governance inhibit or support the inevitable changes that will be necessary to evolve and adapt SOA governance?

Governance and management are two interrelated yet different functions in an organization, and there is not clear agreement as to what constitutes a governance process versus what constitutes a management process. We offered a perspective that is slightly different from one advocated by

Weill and Ross.[1] We believe that governance is the process of ensuring appropriate stakeholder representation in decision-making processes for critical issues, while management is the execution of those decisions by those who are held accountable for the outcomes. IT portfolio management is a process of managing IT investments across a portfolio of IT assets. Governance of the IT portfolio management process ensures all stakeholders of the IT portfolio have input and voting representation in portfolio investment decisions. Execution of the IT portfolio management decisions is a management process, but governance ensures the stakeholders are represented throughout all phases of the process. Of course, the determination whether there must be stakeholder representation is the key difference between governance and management. Governance is essential where multiple stakeholders must be represented, while management is execution, either after stakeholders are informed or involved in the decisions, or where they are not necessarily involved.

Determining who the stakeholders are and whether they should be involved in a particular decision domain is also subjective depending on the type of organization and style of management that exists. SOA governance has many stakeholders, and thus demands a governance process where appropriate stakeholders are involved at the appropriate points. Again, part of the art of designing governance models is determining what decisions or processes are sufficiently critical such that governance, or stakeholder representation, is necessary.

Often, governance is directly associated with allocation of corporate resources—most notably, funding and budgeting. IT governance blossomed in the wake of the reckless exuberance of the later 1990s to reign in spending on IT that was not directly delivering organizational value and was not aligned with business unit demands. However, SOA governance adds more governance requirements to the IT governance burden, and therefore creates more complexity. SOA governance requires more technical oversight for the SOA and services extensions to the enterprise architecture governance process. While SOA governance and enterprise architecture governance are related to funding and budgeting processes, they are as much related to technical conformance to design policies and principles. There are many more governance "policies" that must be enforced technically in a SOA context, and this is where SOA governance can potentially become a very complex endeavor. Complexity often engenders more boards and more process in governance, and this is not necessarily a positive development. Complexity can be managed without adding structural overhead to your organization.

To prevent SOA governance from becoming an organizationally burdensome activity, we urge organizations to explore adding nontraditional governance organizational models into their formally defined existing corporate and IT governance processes. Below, we will briefly discuss alternative models of governance that can be used to augment or support more formal governance constructs necessary for corporate governance and IT governance. SOA governance cannot be entirely successful with informal governance constructs, and in fact we have made the case that it demands as much and perhaps more discipline than generic IT governance by virtue of its sheer complexity.

However, it is this complexity that we feel augurs for the exploration of alternative organizational models for SOA governance not only to help deal with the complexity, but allow the organization to achieve agile governance and rapid SOA innovation through these organizational models. While SOA is justifiably heralded as a potential IT and business innovation and transformational force, we also feel that the SOA governance imperative offers the opportunity to create new organizational models for IT delivery and IT decision making that may well be the best SOA outcome of all: an ability to create stakeholder collaboration and joint decision making using emergent self-organizing concepts and alternative governance approaches. The unintended side effects of this may perhaps be better agility and rapid decision making at the lower and middle management tiers of the organization, where often times corporate initiatives fail precisely because of middle management inertia.

GOVERNANCE AS A STRATEGIC COMPETENCY

A clear objective of this book is to set the stage for the evolution of governance into more than a compliance driven requirement, as well as to suggest ways in which all governance, whether it is IT, SOA governance, data governance, or corporate governance, can and must become more of a scientific endeavor. We feel that governance will become a fundamental competitive advantage-enabling core competency that ensures shareholder value, appropriate leverage of all corporate resources, and transparency and oversight for critical decisions in an enterprise, from the corporate board of directors to specific aspects of SOA governance. Governance in all its shapes and forms is an essential tool in the corporate executive's toolbox.

GOVERNANCE BEYOND POLICIES AND EDICTS

Another idea we want to leave you with is that governance does not have to be a checks and balances mechanism or an enterprise policing process. Governance can be implemented in ways that make it more of a value-added and collaborative process. In this model, governance is far more than a policing function. Governance must be an educational and behavioral guidance process as well. Prescriptive SOA governance can only get the governance transformation started, but prescriptive policy enforcement does not scale well. Top-down policy enforcement in a command hierarchy environment can work for narrowly-scoped mission critical requirements, but for larger organizations with the wide-ranging governance requirements demanded by SOA, command hierarchy governance must be augmented by collaborative, community and related bottom-up and middle-out governance engagement mechanisms. Culture and behavior guided by community norms rather than top-down edicts scale extremely well. Thus, SOA governance must transition as quickly as possible to a normative behavioral model from the prescriptive policy model we espouse initially. These governance styles are not mutually exclusive either.

EVOLVING GOVERNANCE: POLICIES TO NORMS TO CULTURE

As governance processes and capabilities mature, and especially as SOA gains more momentum across large enterprises, the scalability of governance models will be challenged. Scaling governance will be a mid- to long-term requirement, and planning for enterprise-scale implementations of governance policies and policy enforcement mechanisms—organizations, processes and technologies—is going to be essential. This calls into question how an organization can scale governance for an enterprise.

The answer is simple and profound. In order to scale governance, governance must become the culture and normative model of enterprise behavior. Culture scales very well, based on norms and expectations and community models of governance. Explicit policy enforcement is more difficult to scale, particularly for an enterprise. The goal is to establish a body of policies that can become norms through community adoption via educational and awareness activities.

The following characteristics define the ultimate evolution of governance into a normative model:

- Policies transform into behavioral norms.
- Governance boards evolve into exception management teams; their policy definition role becomes a community process.
- Rigid policy engines and repositories are augmented and then ultimately replaced by dynamic collaboration governance tools, chat rooms, virtual boards, and community policy oversight models.

- Penalties and nonconformance are replaced by encouragement and education.
- Governance becomes, in effect, an exception management tool as enterprise behavioral expectations are the cultural fabric of the enterprise.

These are not simple ideals and idle SOA governance aspirations. These are essential models for planning a future for governance that is both effective and scalable.

COMMUNITY MODELS FOR GOVERNANCE: OPEN SOURCE AS A GUIDE

As SOA governance models become more pervasive, most organizations will wrestle with the challenges of adding new governance processes and oversight models into their enterprise. For many organizations, implementing any new governance or formalizing what was previously informal governance will come with a price. Governance does mean reallocation of long-held decision rights for key resources and responsibilities, and these are often accompanied by funding and budgeting responsibility.

Anytime there is funding on the line, organizations and individuals will respond in ways that will preserve their current authority, budgetary control and decision scope. There is a natural tendency to "preserve the silo" in any organization, while SOA encourages the dissolution and federation of silos. SOA governance will most times redistribute decision rights in a far different fashion than they are currently allocated. The transition from informal governance to explicit policy enforcement will always be challenging for most organizations.

In that case, there are perhaps other models of governance that are effective and can be leveraged for SOA governance. We believe that one such example is the community governance process embodied by the open source movement. As open source development models proliferate by targeting key segments of enterprise and desktop software for new open source projects, the communities that form around these projects become self-organizing, self-governing, and self-perpetuating. They have very effective governance models, informal yet very effective policies, and they are astonishingly effective at producing high quality software for enterprise as well as individual consumption. In the sections below, we explore aspects of open source development models to identify community governance processes that may be appropriate for use inside the walls of global corporations.

GOVERNANCE OPEN SOURCE STYLE

An interesting feature of the open source community is that the collective and individual behaviors are shaped by the community through a body of largely undocumented norms and expected behaviors. These "governance" rules are very stable, and consistently understood and enforced by the community. For example, the following are governing principles of the open source community:[2]

- No forking projects
- Distributing changes without the moderator approval is not done
- Removing a person's name from the project history, credits, or maintainer list is not done without that person's explicit permission

Open source governance customs and norms have evolved over time in a consistent direction that emphasizes the following:

- Public accountability
- More public notice
- More preservation of credits and change histories in ways that establish the legitimacy of current project owners.

In fact, the rarity of governance violations of the open source governance model is astonishing! Raymond notes that over 20 years and hundreds of open source projects, he can count the number of significant violations using his fingers.[3]

Community governance and self-governance models are absolutely critical as supporting models to top-down, policy-driven governance models. A policy-driven approach is essential, but we feel that the sharpness and intrusiveness of policies can be eased by introducing collaboration models and community-based approaches in parallel, or shortly after implementing policy-driven governance.

This discussion introduces a potential enterprise SOA governance misconception that we must dispel immediately. *Policy-driven governance does not mean top-down governance*. Policy-driven governance is a style or approach to governing, and how those policies are enforced can vary through the use of multiple enforcement mechanisms. But we emphasize that policy-driven governance can be realized top-down, bottom-up, or middle-out, or in combination. There is a certain efficiency and effectiveness to be gained from having executive leadership supporting enterprise policies and a top-down approach, but absent leadership support, collaborative and community approaches to policy-driven governance can be very successful.

Now, consider Wikipedia as a self-governing model. Can we establish community-based governance that self-governs much as Wikipedia and similar models? We believe that it is possible. SOA governance must implement aspects of top-down command hierarchy governance blended with market exchange, competition-based models, and supported by communities and collaboration, which ensure engagement by the adopting and consuming community, or those being governed. They, as stakeholders, have a voice and input from the consumption side of governance.

GOVERNANCE OF THE INTERNET: THE MAC DADDY OF COMMUNITIES

A useful read is the online work "Why the Internet is Good: Community Governance that Works Well" by Joseph Reagle.[4] This work describes the self-governance model that has been arguably the most successful technology and social governance model ever. The Internet self-governance model recognized that social norms, perceptions, and expectations regulate behavior. When one thinks of the Internet, one thinks of a decentralized, far flung, heterogeneous, and unregulated space. However, there are strongly held social norms that regulate (affect) the behavior of Net users.

As pointed out by Lessig in "The Laws of Cyberspace,"[5] there are four "laws" that regulate or govern cyberspace:

1. Laws (by government sanction and force),
2. Social norms (by expectation, encouragement, or embarrassment),
3. Markets (by price and availability), and
4. Architecture (what the technology permits, favors, dissuades, or prohibits).

The factors of cyberspace governance are eerily similar to those we have discussed in SOA governance. Laws are the equivalent of policies. We emphasize norms as replacements for policies over time. We discussed the layers of governance based on command hierarchies, built on top of market exchange models, which are supported by community models based on collaboration, self-governance principles, and stakeholder engagement mechanisms.

I encourage you to read "Why the Internet is Good"[6] as a reference prior to finalizing your SOA governance model.

INTEGRATING GOVERNANCE PARADIGMS

Our discussion above suggests that there are many organizational and economic models that can be implemented in a society or organization depending on relative resource constraints it faces. Resource-constrained environments produce command hierarchies where resources are controlled, while resource-rich environments manifest gift cultures, where status and power are realized by giving wealth away. Of course, in the middle are market exchange models, where wealth and status are achieved through trade, and community models, where status and power are ascribed to those who share and collaborate.

A total governance model, given no constraints, might be best conceived by blending all of these approaches into a cohesive fabric of governance. Every governance model requires a command hierarchy, where command and control decisions are imposed by empowered leadership over those subordinate to them in an organization. Command hierarchies are almost always successfully installed in conjunction with exchange-based models where market economies are successful.

A market exchange model is based on open exchange of goods that have trade value for the community. Interactions are voluntary based on satisfying needs through exchange of trade goods using market pricing dynamics, supply and demand, and exchange principles.

We feel that a combination of command hierarchy supported by a market exchange model and both built on a community-based collaborative foundation, offers the best approach to an enterprise governance construct. What will vary is the relative "thickness" of each layer of governance.

Early on in the SOA governance transition, a command hierarchy with explicit policy enforcement will dominate the governance model as mission critical policies are implemented and enforced. Consider as an example corporate security policies, which are absolutely managed using top-down command hierarchy approaches. Corporate security is mission critical, often has corporate compliance requirements associated with it, as well as tremendous corporate risk. Thus, policies pertaining to security will be very amenable to enforcement using command hierarchy, top-down policy enforcement styles.

Eventually, a market exchange governance "layer" will become more dominant, with trade and market economy dynamics driving the governance model, as opposed to command-hierarchy approaches. Perhaps over time the market exchange model will thin out (not as much as the command hierarchy layer) and give way to a more preeminent community and collaborative model. At this point of governance maturity, self, community, and collaborative governance will take hold. Policies will become norms, and policy enforcement will become normative behavior.

Again, from this discussion, we want to emphasize that policy-driven governance is not necessarily a top-down capability. Policies can be enforced through a multitude of enforcement mechanisms (boards, processes, and tools) and supported by various governance "styles," such as command hierarchies, market exchange models, and collaborative community approaches. Blending these enforcement mechanisms and governance styles will be very much an art based on the cultural dynamics and relative governance maturity of your enterprise. The evolution of governance styles and the "layering" of these styles based on governance maturity is very much an emerging concept. More research is essential to evaluate and understand the patterns of governance adoption and the relative emphasis or weighting of these governance styles based on the types of policies to be enforced.

GOVERNANCE PERFORMANCE MANAGEMENT: A NECESSARY DISCIPLINE

As SOA governance places increased pressure on IT governance processes and capabilities, and as corporate compliance continues to be a mandate for publicly traded organizations, we feel that the seeds have been sown for a new discipline of governance.

Governance performance management is our phrase describing the process of implementing a sustained governance capability in an organization and managing its performance and effectiveness through time. The following activities are dimensions of governance performance management:

- Governance process ownership and accountability
- Governance process execution and facilitation
- Governance management, metrics, and performance management
- Ongoing governance principle and policy management

We feel that SOA governance will be a catalyst for the realization that governance is an ongoing and strategic capability for an organization. Governance must become elevated into a standing management and operational capability, and managed as a permanent process focused on execution of strategy and achievement of corporate or organizational goals. Governance performance management is what I call the ongoing process of governance in an enterprise. SOA may be the reason for the renewed focus on governance, but the elevated interest and understanding of governance concepts will help raise the profile of governance into the formalized discipline that it should be.

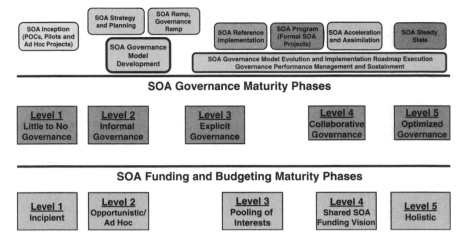

SOA Governance Maturity Phases

SOA Funding and Budgeting Maturity Phases

Exhibit 10.1   SOA Governance Across the SOA Adoption Lifecycle

Exhibit 10.1 depicts the SOA adoption model we discussed earlier in the book. This time, we have shown how governance must be a sustained process that begins early and extends in an ongoing fashion.

Governance must be established as a continuing discipline. We call it governance performance management here. Whatever the name, it must encompass the roles and responsibilities we have articulated above, with sustainment of the governance discipline being a fundamental requirement.

CREATION OF AN ENTERPRISE GOVERNANCE EXECUTIVE

An interesting recent trend in IT organizations is the appointment of a governance executive and supporting organization with a direct reporting relationship to the chief information officer (CIO). While not widespread at this time, we believe this is an increasing trend, certainly for publicly traded firms where Sarbanes-Oxley compliance and other regulatory compliance issues justify such a role. These enterprise governance organizations are established to provide a single point of process ownership for all IT governance activities and extensions to IT governance relating to funding oversight and budget management. In some cases, IT security may fall under this organization. In public firms, this structure provides a focal point for IT governance activities that relate to and support compliance requirements.

With the increased interest in SOA and SOA governance, we feel that linkage of corporate, IT, and SOA governance is essential to foster alignment of all governance and oversight under one executive; either reporting directly to the CIO for IT and SOA governance, or to the chief executive officer (CEO) for corporate governance.

SEPARATION OF ENTERPRISE AND IT GOVERNANCE FROM THE PMO

Another recent trend we have seen in the field is the separation of IT governance from the program management office (PMO) function within the IT organization and its establishment as a separate dedicated governance function directly reporting to the CIO. This organizational positioning of IT governance clearly signals the strategic importance of governance and positions it as an authoritative function within the enterprise. This recent trend in no way diminishes the importance of the PMO process in an enterprise. Rather, we feel it enables the PMO to be more focused on its core mission of providing program and project oversight for key enterprise initiatives without being distracted by the additional requirements of SOA governance.

When governance is an outgrowth of the PMO process, its charter can become overly focused on project and program governance with the emphasis being program execution—cost and schedule and scope management issues—as opposed to SOA governance issues. While the PMO function has IT governance roots with its funding oversight role for key enterprise projects, the PMO process is fundamentally different from SOA governance because as we have stated before, SOA governance is a series of cross-cutting oversight processes that govern technical, process and funding and other decisions. The PMO process is inappropriate for this, not because of lack of capabilities, but because its charter is different. So, while the PMO seemed like a natural home for certain IT and SOA governance processes, we have seen the realization that IT governance and even SOA governance are in many respects bigger than the PMO oversight. While they all must work together, we applaud the separation of IT and SOA governance from the PMO organization and the PMO process. It will allow the PMO function to become more focused on its mission and for SOA governance to focus on its core mission.

PLAN FOR THE STRUCTURAL ACCORDION: CENTRALIZED TO DECENTRALIZED TO CENTRALIZED AGAIN

There are two things that are certain: death and taxes. Add a third item to this list: IT organizations inevitably transition from centralized to decentralized back to centralized structures over time. As these accordion-like

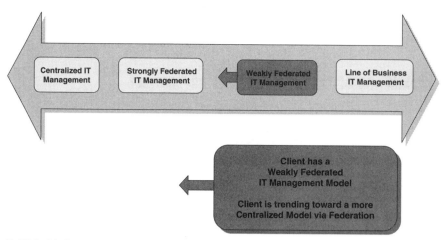

Exhibit 10.2 Central to Distributed IT Continuum

structural shifts take place, you must understand the dynamics and organizational tensions that accompany these transitions. Exhibit 10.2 depicts the structural continuum from a centralized to a distributed IT organizational model. See Chapters 4 and 7 for detailed discussions of this concept.

If your organization is decentralized and the IT organization is also decentralized, there will be political tension from centralizing funding and decision authority for aspects of IT that used to be under decentralized control. Another aspect of this transition tends to be the implementation of chargeback schemes, which add to the organizational angst about transitioning from decentralized to centralized IT structures. Similarly, the transition from centralized to decentralized IT structures is fraught with similar political organizational dynamics.

As you implement your governance model, consider a long-term view of how you might adjust certain governance and management processes to accommodate either a more centralized or more decentralized organizational model. Determine how the governance organizational model might be adapted to these inevitable transitions.

GOVERNANCE GOING FORWARD: THE WAY AHEAD

We have tried to describe in this book a pragmatic systematic model for assessing, designing, and implementing SOA governance using a generalized governance model design framework. We also pointed out in Chapter 6 the flaws and immaturity in current policy approaches in the industry. The way ahead for enterprise governance demands attention by the end-user and vendor community on the following concepts.

DEVELOP A UNIFIED MODEL OF POLICIES

One of the most critical efforts required of standards bodies is to develop a unified model for SOA policies that integrates business policies with process, technology, design, and runtime policies. The following research areas should be considered:

- Establish a broad policy model that integrates and maps policies vertically and horizontally in the enterprise based on policy enforcement requirements.
- Develop industry standards for enterprise governance policies for compliance, business, process, and technical policies.
- Develop a unified policy model that establishes an ontology and taxonomy of policies, as well as the relationships of policies to one another by category, such that enforcement can be accomplished using an integrated policy enforcement model.
- Develop technical standards and a policy syntax that support the realization of a universal policy model. While Web services standards are evolving for Web services policy enforcement, there are different approaches and vendor proprietary models for network policy enforcement, security policy enforcement, service level agreement (SLA), and quality of service (QoS) policy enforcement and more.
- Encourage the integration of tools that support an integrated policy enforcement model. While a governance interoperability framework was proposed at one time by a vendor consortium, little progress has been made to add non-Web services standards into the picture, much less integrating policy enforcement using manual and process-based enforcement concepts.

In many respects, the unified policy model is a root cause for the challenges that face the SOA and IT governance industry today. Addressing some of these challenges will go a long way toward resolving the current policy shortcomings.

INTEGRATED POLICY ENFORCEMENT MODELS

Along with the unified model of policies, we need to develop an integrated concept of policy enforcement. We identified the barriers to an integrated policy enforcement model in Chapter 6. Here are the actions to be taken going forward in addressing this governance gap:

- Encourage the horizontal integration of tools supporting end-to-end SOA and service lifecycle processes.
- Establish a mapping of designtime policies to quality assurance and testing and runtime policies, and a consistent syntax and enforcement model to support it.
- Establish integration standards for designtime tools with governance tools supporting design, quality assurance (QA)/test and runtime policy enforcement.
- Establish industry standards for the vertical integration of enterprise, corporate, business and process policies with technical policies enforced across a corporate SDLC or project delivery processes.
- Demand the development of integration between key governance processes and tools with project execution tools (e.g., portfolio management tools integrated with Integrated Development Environment (IDE) and software development tools, which may integrate with policy engines and policy repositories).

These are only partial solutions, but taken together, they may help in the creation of widely adopted industry standards for policies and policy enforcement models. Even a partial improvement will take us miles down the governance highway!

DEVELOPMENT OF GOVERNANCE COLLABORATION TOOLS

One area of development is establishing appropriate governance collaboration tools and platforms to facilitate enterprise governance for large organizations with very distributed operations, yet which want to establish a consistent and effective governance model. Such tools would create virtual organizational models, establish governance process workflows, and manage events and policy enforcement triggers as defined by a governance process owner.

Without overspecifying what a governance collaboration tool might do, we envision the following high-level capabilities:

- Allow definition of governance organizational models based on various corporate, IT, and governance organizational templates (e.g., functional structure, federated governance, autonomous business units, geographic structures, product line organizations, etc.).
- Support a library of governance process models for major categories of IT and enterprise governance, including portfolio management, enterprise architecture, funding and budgeting, project and program

management/PMO, and even SDLC governance. These process models should be customizable to support tailoring them to your organization's requirements. Furthermore, such process modules would allow the linking or threading of governance processes into extended processes based on multi-level policies such as reuse and security, which can be enforced at multiple levels and across multiple processes in an enterprise.

■ Provide a policy management module for the creation, validation, management, versioning, and provisioning of policies to a policy enforcement fabric for design and runtime enforcement of key SOA policies. The policy management module should consist of a repository of base policies and policy categories to facilitate creating organization-specific policies, using pre-design policy templates, and following a policy model that treats business and technical policies in a consistent manner. This policy management module would provide the following capabilities:

  ■ Collaboration module to allow for feedback, bidirectional model for policy generation, refinement and affectivity dates, as well as solicitation for comments from the broad SOA community.

  ■ Unified Policy Model: A policy management module must address a unified view of policies that integrates business, process, technology, architecture, services design and runtime policies. This tool might offer a policy modeling grammar or vocabulary to help standardize the modeling and provisioning of enterprise policies.

  ■ Integration with policy provisioning and policy enforcement tools.

  ■ Policy deployment, versioning, and management across a wide range of runtime tools, such as SOA messaging platforms, Web services management platforms, security appliances, network infrastructure, application routing infrastructure, and more.

"THAT GOVERNANCE IS BEST THAT GOVERNS BEST WITH LEAST"

The bottom line with any governance is to make sure it is right sized and targeted at a particular problem domain. Governance of any form can get heavy handed and over burdensome with time commitments imposed on those whose roles and responsibilities involve the implementation, management and enforcement of governance. To that end, the following quote is instructive: "That governance is best that governs best with least."

This quote is adapted from Henry Davis Thoreau's famous quote from the essay entitled "Resistance to Civil Government," also known as "Civil Disobedience," in 1849: "That government is best which governs least."

While this quote reflects Thoreau's displeasure with the federal government, his treatise more broadly reflected his thoughts on the role and rights of individuals in relation to civil government.

The following guidelines will help you implement this governance tenet as you design an effective SOA governance model for your organization. My version, "That governance is best that governs best with least," is a simple call to action to be careful of how you structure your SOA governance models in light of the fact that governance will be doomed to failure if it is too heavy handed or cumbersome.

- **Focus.** The best governance is appropriately focused on mission-critical problems rather than being all-encompassing and confusing. Maintain focus for your initial SOA governance efforts. Stay within the maturity and capabilities of your organization.
- **Close critical governance gaps.** As with any new discipline, governance requires focus and attention on identifying and closing critical SOA governance gaps in your enterprise. As you begin your SOA governance journey, continually ask how you can make your governance model more focused and critical-capability aligned. Do not close every gap now, even though there may be many. Prioritize your efforts and focus on key inhibitors to your SOA governance success now. You can and will iterate and learn, and therefore you will have many opportunities to add additional governance process coverage as well as tune and refine your current SOA governance processes.
- **Think small, focused, and effective.** Do not try to govern everything in your enterprise all at once. Close critical gaps with necessary polices. Plan to scale governance over time in sensible increments.
- **Never begin with a governance organizational model.** As we have maintained throughout this book, never begin a governance model with the organizational model and boards. That is a sure way to create overhead and dismay with governance. Focus on key processes and policies first, then determine the integrated governance model that best enforces those polices using boards, processes and tools. If you begin with boards, they may be difficult to eliminate. Remember the PP/OT rule: Define policies and processes first, then define the organization and implement the supporting tools. Define policies and processes first, then add the governance boards, and lastly determine the governance tools you need to shore up and support the model.

- **Do not buy governance tools before developing a governance model.** This is a very common trend now, and it must be reversed. Establish the requirements for governance, the policies and processes, and the policy enforcement model that you need. Then determine the tools and technologies that will support your governance model.
- **Enterprise SOA governance is always more effective when there is a solid enterprise architecture or IT governance process in place.** If you have a solid governance process of any kind in place, implementing SOA governance will be easier. However, if you have a strong Enterprise Architecture (EA) governance process, SOA governance will be even easier to implement. However, do not fool yourself. Governance of any kind is challenging and difficult. Be prepared and plan for the bumps in the road.
- **Implement governance in bite-sized chunks.** Plan a phased implementation of governance capabilities versus big bang. We suggest using implementation roadmaps of at least three increments or phases, with the first phase being 6 to 12 months. You should determine the implementation phases based on your organization and culture.
- **Never start with portfolio management.** Portfolio management, as compelling as it sounds, is usually too challenging for most organizations to implement for services under a SOA initiative. If you have not implemented and had success with portfolio management processes previously, do not begin it with services portfolio management. We suggest you hold off on that and focus on other lower hanging fruit of governance.
- **Begin with SOA governance basics.** For example, SOA EA, services governance, SOA/Services SDLC, and evolve to more sophisticated governance processes such as portfolio management, funding and budgeting models, and other more advanced governance dimensions.
- **Total SOA governance necessitates the policies, processes, organization and tools be integrated vertically and horizontally.** Consider how your SOA policy model will be integrated from higher levels of your enterprise based on business and enterprise policies, to lower levels of the enterprise via fine-grained technical polices, which intersect with horizontally integrated policies across your SDLC.
- **Good governance will be subtractive over time, yet ubiquitous via community-based self-governance.** We feel that if you design a governance model well, it will be subtractive over time. This means that boards will be retired, processes will simplify, and policies will transform into norms, and policy enforcement will be replaced with normative behavior. Your governance model will evolve into community-based, self governance with high degrees of collaboration. It will be

subtractive, but it will be more ubiquitous as policies become norms.

■ **A little governance is more than people want.** Any governance is "over-governance" when you have not formalized any governance processes, policies or enforcement mechanisms. This is why we emphasize to be pragmatic, and right-size your governance model in accordance with critical SOA governance requirements balanced against the tolerance of your culture for governance.

■ **Accelerate the transition from policy-driven governance to norms, normative behavior and culture.** Emphasize education, collaboration, engagement with stakeholders and participants via collaboration models, two-way channels for feedback, and broad engagement with the community of stakeholders.

■ **Learn from community governance processes exemplified by the internet, open source, wikipedia, and social networking movements.** Self governance and community processes are effective governance mechanisms, but they still need command hierarchies and market exchange models as well.

SUMMARY

This is an imperfect book. We have tried to make the art of governance more scientific. We challenged the industry to address gaps in standards and integration based on policies and policy enforcement models. I hope we have at least helped organize your SOA governance pursuits into a repeatable framework that makes sense and helps you get governance right. For feedback and comments on this book, please email me at emarks@agile-path.com.

Notes

1. Peter Weill and Jeanne Ross, *IT Governance: How Top Performers Manage IT Decisions for Superior Results*, Harvard Business School Press, 2004.
2. Eric S. Raymond, *The Cathedral and the Bazaar: Musings on Linux and Open Source by an Accidental Revolutionary,* O'Reilly Media, 2001, p. 73.
3. Ibid., p. 76.
4. Joseph Reagle. "Why the Internet is Good: Community Governance that Works Well." Working draft, Berkman Center for Internet and Society, Harvard Law School, March 1999c. http://cyber.law.harvard.edu/people/reagle/regulation-19990326.html.

5. Lawrence Lessig, "The Laws of Cyberspace," Draft 3, ©Lessig 1998: This essay was presented at the Taiwan Net '98 conference, in Taipei, March, 1998.
6. Joseph Reagle. "Why the Internet is Good: Community Governance that Works Well." Working draft, Berkman Center for Internet and Society, Harvard Law School, March 1999c. http://cyber.law.harvard.edu/people/reagle/regulation- 19990326.html